SAILING TO WIN!

*A Complete Introduction
to Model Yacht Racing*

N I C K   W E A L L

ARGUS BOOKS

Argus Books
Argus House
Boundary Way
Hemel Hempstead
Herts HP2 7ST
England

First published by Argus Books 1991

© Nick Weall 1991

All rights reserved. No part of this publication
may be reproduced in any form, by print,
photography, microfilm or any other means
without written permission from the publisher.

ISBN 1 85486 077 1

Phototypesetting by The Works, Exeter.
Printed and bound in Great Britain by
Clays Ltd, St. Ives plc, Bungay

Contents

Dedication

This book is dedicated to all those skippers who have got the better of me in the protest room, thus helping to teach me the rules.

To Roy Gardener of Gosport, who, besides contributing so much to model yachting over the years, was my early sparring partner. His arguments on the water encouraged me to invest in many rule books and started my love affair with the rules.

To Graham Bantock for being the man to aim at, setting all of us within the sport a fine target to try and topple from his pinnacle of achievement.

To Colin Hayes and his supporting letters.

Finally, to Lindsey with whom I have a love affair of the heart.

Acknowledgements

My grateful thanks are extended to the IYRU for allowing me to reproduce parts of the International Yacht Racing Rules 1989–92 Edition.

I would also like to extend my thanks to all those people who have previously taken their time to write on the subject of yacht racing and the weather. Many authors have contributed to my acquired knowledge besides my experience gained on the water — I thank them all. More special thanks must be extended to Mary Pera and Bryan Willis for their well written books expanding upon the rules. Their books listed in Appendix 1 originally taught me most about the rules.

Introduction

This book sets out to introduce the skills required to begin successfully to race radio controlled model yachts. It is addressed to the complete newcomer to the sport and also to the club skipper who is struggling around at the back of the fleet.

The book covers all of the basics required to get the model yacht up and running, how to get the yacht moving in the right direction with speed and, more importantly, how then to begin to race and get used to the yacht racing rules. The structure is such that in order to get the best out of the book it is necessary to read it all from cover to cover.

After having set out all of the basics, the main body of the book takes an imaginary novice skipper and follows that skipper's progress around an Olympic style of yacht racing course, drawing attention to the various basic tactics that are employed to try and gain positions and also to defend positions already gained. Naturally, as this race progresses, the reader is introduced to the basic rules that are required to be known in order to be able to survive a race safely. By the end of the book all novice skippers should be well equipped to more than hold their own in club races.

One of the first questions that has to be answered is why race radio controlled model yachts when you have the choice of racing full-sized dinghies or windsurfers for very little extra initial investment? I used to do a lot of windsurfing — mostly, as I progressed, just high wind stuff, because that was where the greatest challenge was. I've also done some dinghy racing, cat racing and playing around on bigger stuff. There is no getting away from the fact that sailing around on British waters is distinctly cold even in the summer. I like to keep warm, however, I also like to race. When I came across radio controlled model yacht racing some years ago I was immediately hooked. Someone lent me their model and I tried a couple of races. The following Sunday I went back and again for a couple of races I borrowed a model. That week I bought a secondhand radio controlled Marblehead yacht for £100.00. That included three sets of sails, radio transmitter, receiver, servo and winch. Plus two sets of rechargeable batteries for the boat and one set for the transmitter and finally, a battery charger capable of charging six sets of batteries at once.

Why was I hooked? Well you can pack a lot of races into one-day radio controlled racing. For example, at club level at Gosport it is not unusual to get eighteen to twenty races into one day. You could never get that sort of concentrated full-size racing in one day — you'd be very lucky to get three races and at most clubs you're more likely just to get one! Just imagine if you blow your start in the one full-sized club race, you've got all week to think about it! Whereas in model yacht racing if you blow one start — so what — in fifteen minutes' time you can have another go. Radio controlled model yacht racing really is an excellent way of perfecting your tactics and learning the rules. I recommend anyone languishing in the lower half of the full-sized club league table to devote a season to radio controlled yacht racing — I am sure you would notice a big improvement in your performance if you ever go back to full-sized racing.

Another major advantage is that radio controlled model yacht racing is open to all ages. For those skippers of dinghies who are finding it increasingly hard to hang out over the side for hours on end, forget it — come and potter around on the pond side and use your experience to give everyone else some grief. I know of people well into their seventies very able to race competitively. Eyesight is the biggest handicap — if you have to wear glasses and it is raining it can be hard to judge your yacht's position on the water relative to other yachts and, more importantly, buoys.

It is also, of course, an environment which is much safer to try out tactics such as slam dunking. The risk of serious damage is much less with models than with their full-sized counterparts, although on rare occasions it is quite possible to sink another yacht.

Naturally enough the running costs of racing a radio controlled model yacht are a lot less than the full-sized alternative, even if you are racing at National or International level. Talking of National and International levels of competition, I would like to make it quite clear that radio controlled model yacht racing is taken extremely seriously and most racing is conducted under the current IYRU Racing Rules amended by Appendix 16. These amendments are minor amendments which take into account the fact that the skipper of the racing yacht is not actually aboard the boat.

Protests are heard after each race as a rule, so that the next race is held with amended positions being awarded. This is important because in the bigger race meeting each race may be split up into sections called fleets, the reason being that it is unusual to have more than twenty boats on the water racing at the same time since too many boats can obscure each skipper's view of his boat. That is the main disadvantage for bankside skippers, however, the biggest advantage is that you can easily see the whole fleet and choose your tactics accordingly. Although of course your position in the fleet will, to some degree, determine your initial tactics anyway.

Maintenance costs will also be dramatically lower — no mooring charges, sailing club berths etc to worry about. Simply de-rig the model, put it in the car and take it home.

Finally, radio controlled model yacht racing is an excellent way of introducing young people to the many skills involved in boat handling and racing, without risking their lives. There is also the added bonus of having experienced skippers right alongside the learner, to give instant advice if required.

So, if the thought of entering a sport that can give you continuing challenges at levels starting from club racing, to open events, to district events, ranking races, National and International events, in an environment that offers everchanging conditions and courses, governed by a set of rules that have been evolved over many years, structured to be as fair as possible with safety as a prime consideration, look no further. Find out where the nearest radio controlled model yacht racing club is and get in touch with them.

1. Harnessing the Power of the Wind

The driving force of your yacht — the wind

I suspect that ever since man first put a craft on the water and used paddles, hands or oars to propel it, he was dreaming up ways to save himself the effort needed. I can certainly remember that the first toy boats I made as a child had a mast with a crude square rigged sail.

So it was with larger craft — the first wind-powered or wind-assisted craft had simple square rigged types of mast, boom and sail where the boom was affixed to the mast somewhere near its mid point, supporting the upper edge of the sail. There are many variations of this theme and dhows may still use one such variation. The main disadvantage of all these sails was that their ability to propel the vessel to windward was nil. Running before the wind and reaching was, and is, all they are good for. This could be the reason behind winds being called trade winds because literally you waited until the trade winds were favourable before sailing from Africa to India for example. You might then wait several months before the trade winds reversed the direction of their steady flow before sailing back home again.

This was the case for thousands of years until not so very long ago, when someone somewhere discovered the Bermudan type of rigs commonly used today. The distinctive triangular shape of the sails mounted fore and aft of a near vertical mast with a boom at the bottom of the sail aft of the mast, allowed a vessel to sail much closer to the wind. Sailing to within forty-five degrees of the direction of the wind was now possible.

It was not just the shape and design of the sails

however — improvements were made to the hull design and, more importantly, to the keels that resist the lateral forces the wind imposes on a vessel as it attempts to sail above ninety degrees or so to the wind. Keels used to run the length of the hull and not hang too deep relative to the depth of the hull. These types of keels provided very steady control of direction to windward and were often considered to be the best sort of keel to keep a yacht out of trouble when sailing near a leeshore.

However, for a racing yacht they have the distinct disadvantage of not allowing a yacht to turn quickly. As you can imagine, if you have not already tried it, when you are racing a yacht there are other yachts involved in the same race it is an advantage to be able to turn your yacht to a new direction quickly to avoid collisions and to get round marks of the course quickly. Towards this end, it was found that shortening the keel in length from bow to stern helped enormously. Later it was found that shortening the keel even further from bow to stern, and lengthening it to act as a counter balance to the heeling forces put on the sails by the wind, enabled a yacht to sail even closer to the wind. Separating the rudder from the keel and putting it nearer the stern of the yacht gave even better manoeuvrability and further assisted the resistance to lateral forces.

Developments such as these finally produced the sort of shape you'll see on a modern racing model yacht — a narrow deep keel fin of efficient aquadynamic shape with a bulbous lump of lead on the bottom of it, so as to get the counter balancing weight as low as possible. There will be a separate rudder usually hung under the stern of the yacht, but on rare occasions it might be under the bow of the yacht instead. The sails will be of a Bermudan style and the whole effect will be to allow a properly trimmed yacht to sail at around thirty-five degrees to the wind in a reasonable wind. Diagram 1.1 shows the various points of sailing as usually described by old salts, nautical people the world over and most model yachtsmen too.

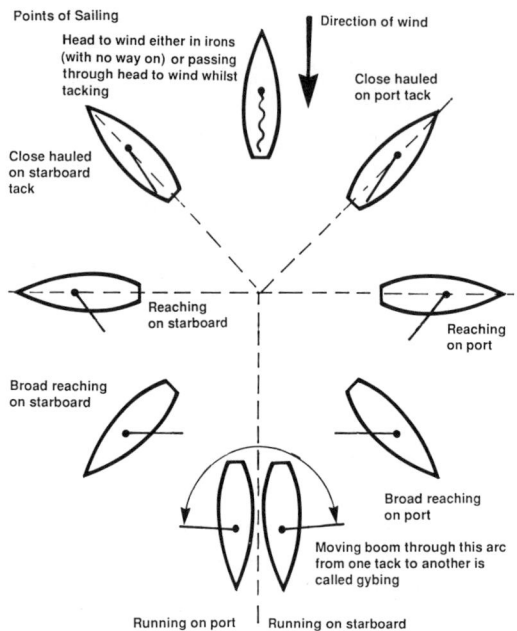

Diagram 1.1

Setting your sails to the same sort of angle as shown in the diagram relative to the boat's hull and the wind will enable you to get your new craft moving through the water.

One of the constant questions the new yacht skipper will be asking is 'How do I tune my boat?'. He may express the same question as 'How do I set my sails?'. Now the big danger is that everyone has a different opinion as to what is required to achieve optimum performance from a yacht. This might be a slight exaggeration but the big problem is who do you listen to? The easy answer is no one who does not consistently win races. After all, if they are such an expert, how come they are not winning races? Personally I do not claim to be an expert. I know what I want, I know how to get it, but even so sometimes the very fine tuning takes trial and error.

The first thing is to get the yacht moving. Set up the mainsail's boom so that, when the winch has it hauled in tight for close-hauled work, the boom is five degrees off the centreline of the yacht (bow to stern). Now get the jib boom set to around ten to fifteen degrees off the same centreline. Now let's put a bit of belly or curve into the sail section of both the mainsail and the jib — a little less in the jib than the main. The diagram will give you some idea of the sort of shape that will do to start with. It looks a bit like the sort of section you might have seen on the upper surface of a glider's wing. The method of introducing or reducing the amount of curve in the sail is by means of the clew mounting point backwards or forwards along the boom, or by increasing or decreasing tension in the outhaul.

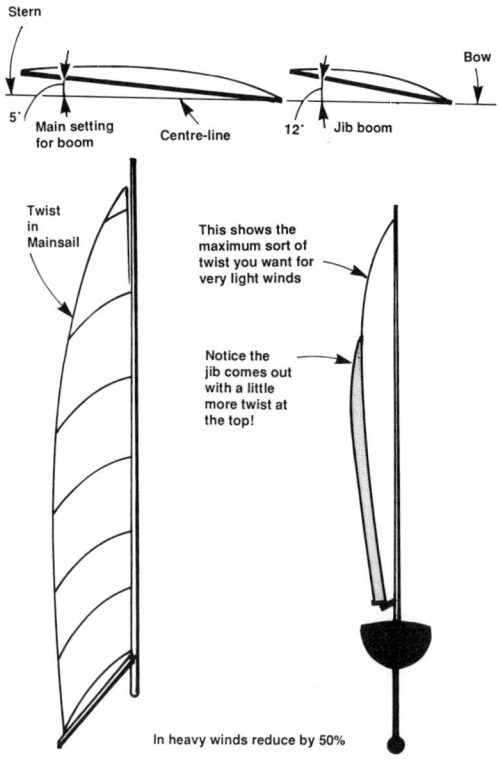

Diagram 1.2

Now we want to introduce some twist in the leech of the sails. Twist is the amount the sail bends away from the vertical line formed at the luff of the sail either by the main mast or the jib stay. On a Marblehead tall suit main we are looking for around an inch or two at the top of the

8

mast. The diagram hopefully shows this better than my description — it is rather hard to describe accurately. Try to imagine the wind as a fluid and realise that we are trying to divert the direction of this fluid in as smooth a way as possible, so as to gain some motion in the object that is diverting the fluid. Think of the sort of shape propellers have, smooth complex curves that generate thrust if they are spun or generate energy if mounted on a shaft and fluid passed over them. Those are the sort of shapes we are trying to introduce into our sails. We don't want crinkles or flat spots — we want regular smooth complex curves that can gently divert the course of the wind, avoiding as many rough bits as possible that can generate back eddies and worse. Once we have got something close to these objectives, check that the sails are sheeting in and out at the same rate, or with the jib going out slightly faster than the main, and put the yacht on the water. Gently sheet in the sails until the wind is caught in them a little and watch the yacht start to move smoothly through the water. As you gain forward motion sheet in the sails more and more and find your closest course towards the wind. You already know that it is going to be between forty-five and thirty-five degrees to the wind's direction. Now, with the yacht sailing on its close-hauled course, touch nothing on your transmitter and see what happens. The yacht can either luff up into wind, stay on a steady course or fall off away from the wind. Make a mental note of the result and tack across to the other tack and try again. Now if it does the opposite on the opposite tack you need to check the rudder setting, because it is highly likely that it is not quite centralised. The easiest way to check is to sail the yacht straight downwind with little wind in the sails and see in what direction the yacht wanders off. Otherwise bring the yacht ashore and stand it up on its bulb. Squat at the rear of the yacht and line up the rudder with the keel fin. Now centre the rudder using the fine trim adjuster on your transmitter. Then move the rudder to the left and release the transmitter lever and then move the rudder to the right and release the transmitter lever. Does the rudder return to centre from each side? Sometimes you can get a dodgy servo that will not

return quite to centre from one side. If you have such a servo you will either have to compromise your rudder setting or accept that you will always have to move the rudder through to the good side before releasing the lever to centralise the rudder! (That is very fiddly!)

Having sorted out the rudder, fling the yacht back on the water and repeat the earlier exercise. Now if the yacht heads up into the wind by itself on both tacks the centre of effort is too far back. The easy solution is to move the mast forward at its foot or sometimes just moving the jib slightly forward will be enough. The opposite result of the yacht falling off on each tack (bearing away) requires the centre of effort to be moved back. So move the jib slightly back or move the mastfoot back a touch. Such actions may well require you to reset the shape of the sails and to alter the lengths of fore and aft stays. Try again and keep playing around until the yacht can sail itself to windward. Different people have different objectives. I like to set up my yacht so it sails itself to windward and will lift up into wind to respond to any increase in the wind's speed. You most definitely do not want to be holding the yacht's rudder off the centreline to keep the yacht sailing to windward. You are slowing the yacht down by doing so! Get it balanced correctly and save yourself heartache. If you find after checking the rudder settings that your yacht is still behaving in different ways on opposite tacks, you will need to investigate further. It might be that the keel fin is not mounted in a straight line along its length from front to back in line with the centreline of the yacht from bow to stern. It might be that the yacht's hull has a different shape on each side of the centreline. It might be that the mast is not vertical to the beam of the yacht. It could be that the rudder is not mounted vertical to the beam. It could be that the rudder is in a sloppy mounting that allows movement. It could be that the method of connecting the rudder to the servo is unsatisfactory in that it allows the rudder to move from side to side under load! (It is most important that you ensure that you have a method of connecting your rudder servo to the rudder that does not allow this to happen. I use a thin carbon fibre tube as a connecting rod that is rigid enough not to flex under load.) It might be that the keel fin is loose within its mounting or that the fin is not stiff enough and flexes too easily.

These are all things that will need checking out if you have such a problem. As to how big a problem it is will depend on how drastic the results of the problem are! Let me assure you however, that having depressed you with the number of things that might be wrong, it is rare to find more than one of them being the cause. If you are planning to build your own boat, these are the points to be very careful about. A well balanced boat should be easy to sail. For example, Graham Bantock's yachts are a piece of cake to sail provided that they have been carefully built following Graham's instructions. One or two people who thought they knew better have simply built themselves expensive logs!

An aside on building yachts is that spirit levels and plumb lines make the job easy and accurate. (I'll cover this again later in the chapter.) A well-built yacht is going to provide you with endless pleasure. A yacht that is thrown together might very well disappoint its owners through its sorry life.

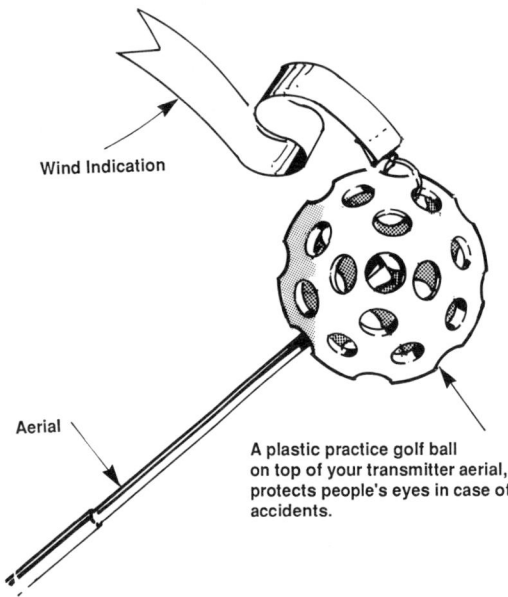

Wind Indication

Aerial

A plastic practice golf ball on top of your transmitter aerial, protects people's eyes in case of accidents.

Tuning! This is much the same as the way you used to have to be constantly twiddling the dial to get Radio Luxembourg to get any sort of decent reception! Boat tuning needs constant attention according to the conditions. High and low pressure weather systems most certainly effect the strength of the wind more than radio waves! The set of your sails in light winds needs to be different to the set in heavy or medium winds. So does the size of sail! Most of us, when we get drawn into this magnificent sport, tend to have far too few sets of sails. There is nothing wrong with that while you are getting a feel for the sport, but once you are hooked you ought to consider getting a full range of sail sizes to suit your yacht. Some classes only allow you three sets of sails or so. Others, like the Marblehead class, allow you many more. If you have bought a secondhand boat then my priorities for getting that boat up to maximum potential would be:

1) Get it waterproof.
2) Ensure that the electrics are waterproofed and reliable.
3) Get the motor going right, tune it up and beef it up!

"Hm, I thought yacht racing was all about fair racing, sailing using only the wind and water to increase, maintain or decrease her speed etc!" questions a reader. "Absolutely" says I, "but your sails are your motor, they alone snatch a teeny weeny bit of the wind's energy to produce the drive required to move your intrepid yacht through the water!". Right, back to the ordinary script, I hope you get the point — nothing else is going to move your yacht through the water in the direction you want to go, with the help of fin and rudder, better than the wind. Tide, currents, jellyfish and string all have their limitations. In my humble opinion nothing else is likely to have the dramatic effect of influencing the potential speed of your yacht (discounting plastic bags, weed, jellyfish etc) than the set of your sails and the quality of the actual sail.

Let's look at the quality of sails. I am not going into all the different types of material available for making sails and what is best for what. If you want to race, and to race competitively, you need decent sails. Where do you get decent sails? From a sail maker! Where do you find decent sail makers? The MYA Year Book tells you where, price £1.50 from David Hackwood, 10 Grange-wood, Coulby, Newham, Middlesboro', Cleveland TS8 0RT (price correct at time of going to press). There are, over the length and breadth of the country, a handful of model yacht sail makers. I think the best test of a good sail maker is can he or she sail their own sails to success and here are the names of three who can do just that: Graham Bantock of Sails etc., Peter Wiles of P.J. Sails and Martin Roberts of House Martin Sails. All of these gentlemen can talk to you most knowledge-ably about the type of sail that would be best and the type of material that would most suit the size of sail required. Mr Bantock will even go so far as to give you written tuning instructions too, if you ask. I rely totally upon my sail maker to make the best choice of material, sail ratio etc for the type of yacht for which I require it. All I will tell him is the overall size of sail area I require and the type of rig I am going to use. I might specify the colour required and I most certainly will remember to ask for a set of sail numbers and jib numbers together with any class insignia required. Who do I use? — I would be happy to use any of the three mentioned but I use the one nearest to me, since that is the most con-venient should I wish to visit and discuss matters. Some people make their own, it is not easy and takes time — probably a lot of time since you are quite likely to make several suits of sails just trying to get it right. I'm sure there is a lot of satisfaction to be had once you have mastered the art. I have one friend who just dived into it that way and in the end produced some quite nice com-petitive sails. He was very good with his hands and well into boats, full-sized as well as models.

Having made the effort to get a decent suit of sails you might as well make sure that the things you hang them on are going to allow you to set the sails to the shape you require. Now I know that I am repeating myself here to some degree, but hopefully it will help some of you grasp the basics. It is important that your mast is truly vertical on the port/starboard axis. On the bow/stern axis it may need to be vertical or have a slight rake aft. The mast itself should either be completely straight or have a regular gentle curve on the bow/stern axis with the belly pointing forwards. Your main sail should be cut either with a straight luff or a curved luff to suit. The things that initially control the mast's position and aspect are the stays on a conventionally rigged yacht together with a mast foot plate or tube, and solely the mast tube on a swing rig. You can check the set of mast tubes by firstly setting up the hull so that it is supported on its waterline level fore and aft, with the keel vertical. (A plumb line taped to the centreline of the hull just in front of the keel will help you to establish this.) A spirit level across the beam of the hull aft of midships will tell you if the deck is level or not (it does not matter if it is slightly out, but you ought to know). The spirit level will also show you from above if the hull moves from its set-up position. Next get a straight piece of dowel or something similar that fits snugly into the mast tube and that is around the same length as your mast. Suspend a plumb line from the top of the mast and hey presto, you have all the feedback you require for checking. If the tubes are not in the right position or are not set at the correct angle, rip them out and start again!

Having actually got a mast that has the correct rake and position we need to consider all the various things there ought to be on the yacht to enable us to alter the set of the sails. Diagram 1.3 will help to explain. I have chosen to illustrate a stayless conventional rig, since that removes the necessity to show the side stays and forestays that hold the mast in a vertical position on an ordinary deck-stepped conventional rig. Obviously if your boat is conventionally rigged with stays, you use the stays to get the mast perfectly set before you start to mess about with the sails. Then the first thing to do is put the sails on. There are various different methods of doing this, especially fixing the main to the mast — luff cord going into groovy mast, rings around the mast, vertical wire and hooks etc. I'm not going into the relative merits of different types of rigging here other than to mention that I always use the ring method. I feel that it presents the best section to the wind other than a rotating airfoil mast. The trouble with rotating airfoil masts is all the pivot points required which add to the friction resisting the turning motion.

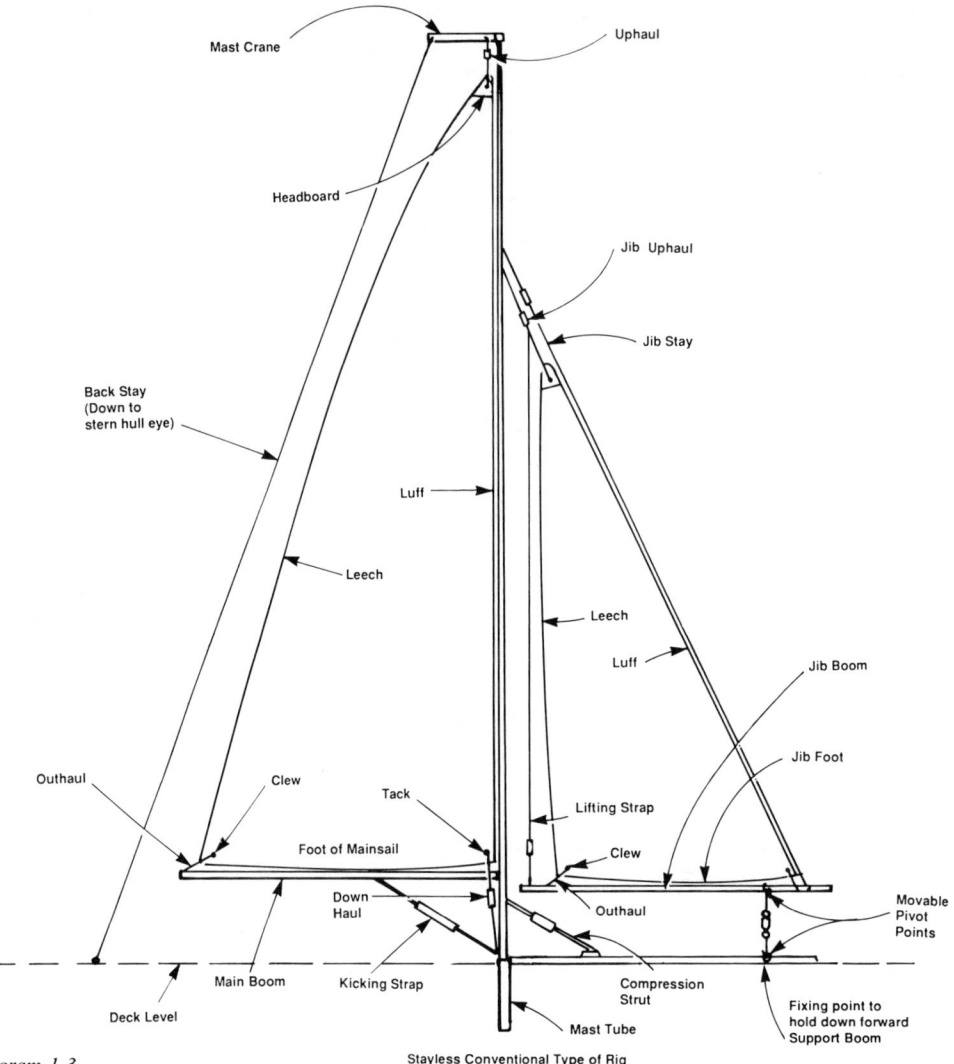

Diagram 1.3

Stayless Conventional Type of Rig

Labels in the diagram:
Mast Crane, Uphaul, Headboard, Jib Uphaul, Jib Stay, Back Stay (Down to stern hull eye), Luff, Leech, Leech, Luff, Jib Boom, Jib Foot, Outhaul, Clew, Tack, Lifting Strap, Clew, Foot of Mainsail, Outhaul, Movable Pivot Points, Down Haul, Deck Level, Main Boom, Kicking Strap, Compression Strut, Mast Tube, Fixing point to hold down forward Support Boom

On the main the downhaul attached to the tack of the sail and the uphaul attached to the head-board are the two adjustable lines that can put tension in the luff of the main and alter its position up and down the mast (within the measurement bands on Marbleheads!). The uphaul will also take or put some twist in the main.

On the jib the jib stay produces the mounting point for the luff of the jib, usually by means of a luff tube/pocket or tabs on the luff of the jib. Tension is introduced by means of a bowsie up by the mast. The head of the jib is also attached by a separate line and bowsie at the mast. The jib tack is usually fixed to the boom by means of a

line or hook. The curve or belly introduced into both sails is by means of the outhaul attached to the clew. There are, again, various types of adjust-able outhaul — sliding or screw in and out hooks, grommets that are a tight fit to the boom but that can be slid up and down, movable eyes and lines etc. Just make sure that whatever type you use stays in the position you want and does not distort the sail. I prefer to use line to attach my clews to my outhaul adjusters rather than hooks because I think it allows the sail to move through to a proper shape more easily on both tacks than a metal hook type of attachment. Twist in the sail is introduced by means of the kicking strap (also

12

called vang) on the main and the lifting strap on the jib. The back stay should simply hold the mast in position and prevent the mast from bending forward when on the run. It can also be used to introduce the appropriate amount of bend required for the main to fit nicely all the way up the mast. The compression strut shown forward of the mast is really there only to stop the support boom lifting. It can also be used to help control the shape of the lower mast. It is not essential, so don't worry if your boat does not have one. It is not seen on swing rigs either. All the other twiddly bits mentioned are, in my opinion, necessary if you really want to control completely the shape of your sails (provided that they have been correctly made).

The movable pivot points from the jib support boom (or deck on a proper conventional rig) to the jib boom allow you to get the jib back as close as possible to the mast, and also to adjust the pivot point upon the jib boom so that the jib swings out easily as you sheet out for the reach and run. Finally, you will have on each boom an attaching point for the sheets that go to the winch. It is important on conventional types of rig that the jib sheets out no slower than the main and should ideally be slightly faster. This is achieved by having the radius of the attachment points slightly different if you want to have the jib sheeting out faster — the jib radius should be smaller than the main's radius of attachment point.

To set your sails up have the main sheeted right in to the close-hauled position, say five degrees off the centreline of the hull fore to aft. The jib should *always* be further off the fore to aft line than the main. Opinion varies but it should be somewhere between ten and fifteen degrees off the fore to aft centreline when the main is five degrees off. Once you have done that you want to check to see that you have a nice curve or belly in both sails, perhaps a little less in the jib than the main. Try to get the sort of shape you might see in the cross section of an aircraft's main wing. Next pick up the yacht by the keel and look at the main and the shape of its leech from the stern of the model. If possible get the wind to fill the sails at the same time. What you want is for the leech of the sail to twist away gently from the

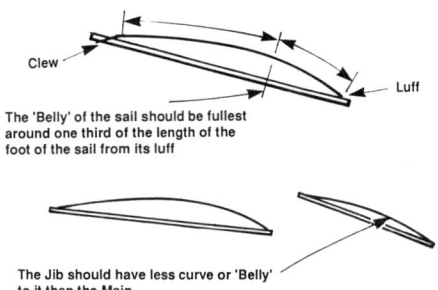

The 'Belly' of the sail should be fullest around one third of the length of the foot of the sail from its luff

The Jib should have less curve or 'Belly' to it than the Main

Diagram 1.4

mast to leeward as you progress up towards the mast top. You then want the jib to copy this twist parallel to the mains twist for the first two thirds up and then to have slightly more twist at the top. The amount of twist required varies according to conditions and sails. For a Marblehead in light to medium winds a couple of inches from top to bottom in the main would be a rough guide. The important thing in tuning is do not be afraid to experiment — find out for yourself what makes your yacht go best. To do this effectively you need other boats to pace yourself against and you should only adjust one thing at a time otherwise you will not really know what caused the difference in performance. The other thing to watch out for is that most pondside skippers love to offer their opinions as to what constitutes good tuning. This advice is often confusing however well meant. Be selective in receiving advice, make sure that it is coming from someone who is in the habit of winning races not losing them. When there is an open meeting in your locality go along and look carefully at how some of the visiting competitive skippers have their sails set, make a few notes and go back and experiment on your own yacht again. The last point I want to cover on tuning is do check that your mast is mounted in the right position fore and aft so that you can sail close-hauled to windward, hands-off on both tacks, without the boat falling off or luffing badly into wind. If you want to have it deviating at all from a steady course then a very slight tendency to luff up is to be preferred. I prefer my yacht simply to sail straight up the course by itself, responding to any increase in wind strength by pointing higher.

Final thoughts on trimming

Sails in tight, yacht pointing in a close-hauled direction, but yacht simply moving sideways. This is what we call making leeway in its extreme. The wind is simply pushing on the sails and thrusting the yacht sideways through the water. Cure: let the yacht's sails out a bit and turn away (bear off) from the wind a little. As your yacht gains forward motion again, gently pull the sails back in for a close-hauled setting and head up to a heading of between forty-five and thirty-five degrees to wind. This problem usually shows itself immediately after doing a bad tack, or after you have got into irons.

Although the sails seem to be set much the same as other boats, you just don't seem to get the same sort of speed at all. Check the amount of twist in the sails and the slot setting. Only alter one thing at a time, unless you know what you are doing, so you can see the result of your one alteration. Remember that the wind has to be able to flow over your sails, producing drive as it does. You are not trying to hook all of the wind's power into your sail, unless you are on a dead run!

If you have the slot too tight, it can kill the speed of the yacht quite a bit, and there may also be a tendency for the boat to want to bear off all the time. The wind passing through what little slot you have may be backing the main a little near the mast. Backing the main means that the sail is being pushed towards the opposite side to that which the wind ought to be filling. This is caused by the wind flowing through too tight a slot. Too loose a slot will result in the jib flapping around a little as you are on a close-hauled beat.

I don't confess to know everything there is to know about trimming up and tuning yachts. Although I seem to be able to get mine going pretty well I suspect I could get it to go that little bit better if I spent more time on it. One trick for roughly establishing a slot setting is having set your main around five degrees off the centreline, set the sort of slot suggested earlier of around ten degrees more than the main off the centreline. Now hold your yacht into the wind on a close-hauled setting so that the wind fills the sails. Is

the main backing? No, good. Is the jib flapping a bit? No, also good. Now keeping the wind in the sails, turn the yacht in your hands fairly slowly up into wind. Do both the sails break from the wind close together? If not alter the slot until they do, perhaps with the jib losing the wind a millisec before the main. Now put the yacht on the water and give it a try. Hopefully it will be better. Try it on both tacks and then, if successful, try sailing close to another close-hauled boat to compare speeds.

Another reason that can cause the jib to flap about a little on a close-hauled beat is that you have insufficient tension in the jib's luff line, otherwise known as the jibstay. Remember that as you increase the tension on the jibstay, you will have to check the shape of the mast and the amount of twist now in the main and jib, because you are likely to have reduced the amount of twist in both. That is why we have a lifting strap for the jib, so that you can reintroduce some twist into the jib, while still enjoying good tension on the jibstay.

If, as you are beating up to wind, the top of either sail is fluttering in the wind, it is because you have got too much twist in the sails. Cure: take some out, check the mast shape first — if that is OK use the kicking strap for the main or compression strap. Use the lifting strap for the jib. If, as you come off the wind and onto a reach, the jib does not go out as far as the main, you are going to have a problem. Because once again only one sail is going to be doing the majority of the work. You need the jib to either move out at exactly the same rate as the main or a little faster. The way to alter this is to alter the radius of the point where the winch sheet is attached to the jib boom, in relation to the radius of the point where the winch line is attached to the main boom. You want the radius of the jib boom to match that of the main boom or, as I prefer it, have the jib's radius slightly smaller than the main's so that the jib moves out a tiny bit more than the main as you sheet out. Remember that you do not want the jib and main to go out further than 90 degrees from the centreline, unless you know what you are doing. While learning, it is a good idea to alter your winch's travel so that when the control stick is fully pulled down, your yacht is fully sheeted in to the close-hauled position and when the control stick is fully up, the sails are fully out in the dead run position.

In fact I like my sails to be able to go beyond that point. That way I can depower the yacht on the run if I want to when a sudden squall approaches. I can also continue to sail on a starboard tack on a wider range of direction, by sailing by the lee slightly beyond the normal point at which you would gybe across to the other tack. This can be an advantage when approaching a mark which you will be rounding and then hardening up on the same tack. It can also be useful when attempting to overhaul yachts clear ahead that are running on the port tack. As a starboard tack approaching yacht they have to take some regard of your course. They certainly cannot luff you up and once you have given them room and opportunity to keep clear, they have to keep out of your way!

If your yacht is almost uncontrollable, burying its bows in the water while on the run and heeling well over while beating, then it is odds-on that you have too much sail up. Cure: change down sails. If you do not have any other sails, try putting more twist in your existing sails to let some of the wind's power out of them and try not sheeting in quite so far when beating. The tops of your sails will now flog in the wind, but you may now have more control and still be able to race.

If you have a conventional rig and you are finding it difficult to get the jib to come out on the opposite side to the main on the run, consider moving the pivot point of the jib further forward on the jib boom. This has the effect of putting more of the jib's area behind the pivot point and thus giving more leverage for the wind to move and hold the jib out. Remember to alter the attachment point for the winchline though or you will be increasing the radius of the attachment point, which means that the jib will sheet out slower than the main!

If, when you have got your yacht moving at the same sort of speed as other club members, you find that you still seem to get left behind, concentrate for a while on improving your tacks, trying to retain boat speed right through the tack. Try to round marks smoothly, holding the wind in your yacht's sails throughout the rounding. Resist the temptation to twitch your rudder all of the time. Try and make all rudder movements very gentle, except when taking emergency avoiding action.

One last little tip on tuning is that once you have got your sails and rig set up and driving well, mark the lines with waterproof marker at the point they pass through the bowsies. You will then have a good reference point for all future trimming and will be able easily to get back to a basic good trim after derigging etc.

2. The Start of the Race

Racing your model yacht is the most natural progression from just sailing it around on a lake. After all, if you have ever sailed a model yacht or a full-sized yacht idly around, as soon as you have it near to another yacht it is likely that you have started to pace it — to see which is faster. If you want to find out if you have trimmed your sails to optimum performance you need a similar yacht, with similar sails, to sail against to be able accurately to evaluate what differences changes in sail trim make to your yacht's speed relative to the other boat. In model boats we have to do this more than in full-size boats perhaps, since we have very little means of accurately recording a boat's speed through the water for a given wind strength. Since the wind strength constantly varies from minute to minute anyway, it is far better to be pacing another yacht.

Racing model yachts is not just about winning races. It is marvellous how model yacht racing provides endless challenges and pleasure. Within each race of a fleet of model yachts, there will be little private races going on of yachts near to each other within the race trying to outdo one another. The results of these, as they battle to the finish line, are just as exciting to the participants as the win is to the whole race winner. You just won't be able to wait until the next race to have another go. The great advantage of model yacht racing is that you will not have to wait many minutes before you can achieve this aim! As opposed to full-sized racing where it is most unlikely that you would get more than two races in a day, in

model racing you may get up to twenty races in one day and usually will get around twelve, except at very large meetings where there are several fleets racing within each overall race. That is because it is most unusual to have more than eighteen boats racing each other on the water at any one time, mainly because it can get very confusing trying to follow your boat at the start and around the first buoy or two if you have any more. The sails of the yachts can effectively blanket from view the yachts behind. Even with eighteen yachts this can be a problem, and you need to develop pretty good judgement of how to sail your yacht for a few seconds when you have lost sight of it! So say, for example, that you have a total race entry of sixty yachts for a weekend's racing. What would happen is that the total entry of sixty yachts would be divided up into four fleets of fifteen boats. For the first three races those four fleets would go on the water one fleet at a time and race each other. After the first three races you would have four sets of results, each of the four fleet's three races. Everyone's best two results from the three races they have raced are taken and points awarded. The results from all four separate fleets are now lumped together and a pecking order for the entire race of sixty boats is established. A point of interest is that in yacht racing it is the person with the *lowest* number of points who is the winner!

We will now have a set of results that lists the entire race meeting in order of success, although of course at this stage there are quite likely to be several people with matching results. Now the entire race is divided into four fleets according to those results. The top fifteen results become A fleet and so on, down to the last fifteen results which become D fleet.

Racing now carries on using these fleets for the remainder of the meeting. You might well ask how does anyone who is not in the A fleet after the first three seeding races have any chance of winning the regatta? The answer is there is a chance because in every subsequent race the top four yachts in B, C, & D fleets get promoted up a fleet. So the winning four boats of B fleet move up into the next round A fleet race. The opposite also happens! The bottom four boats of A, B & C fleets all get put down a fleet. So the bottom four boats of A fleet for example find themselves in the next round racing in B fleet. By this means movement is guaranteed through the fleet, until each yacht finds its natural position for the conditions in force at the time of the regatta and the potential of the skipper at that time.

Of course it would be better to have all sixty boats racing on the water at once, but I can assure you that it would end in tears! We have to recognise the restraints of remote controlled yachts and the need to be in a position to see your yacht for most of the time is most certainly the biggest restraint to large fleet racing. I can also assure you that fleet racing is a lot of fun and it is useful to have a little time between each of your own races to watch how other people do it — you can learn a lot.

Also, as I said earlier, racing is not just about winning the regatta outright. In a regatta of sixty boats there might well be thirty or more individual races going on between couples or triplets vying for their own objective of finishing in a certain position within the overall results. At the end of the regatta, even the man who came last will go home remembering the race when he got up to C fleet and managed to stay in the fleet for two races! He may well also remember some new racing tactic that was used successfully against him in one race and try it out the following weekend against other members of his local club, hopefully with some success.

So do try to remember that, whether you are at the back of the fleet, as most novices will be to start with, or up near the front of the fleet, there is plenty of satisfaction to be gained. Plus, of course, there is the simple enjoyment of being near the water, watching yachts glide through the water while feeling the sun on your back — hopefully!

However, the first few times you try your hand at racing models are likely to be fairly nerve-wracking occasions. This is something most of us have to go through. You simply have to get used to all the new strange tasks of keeping your model yacht moving through the water in the direction you want it to go, while avoiding all the other yachts that are in close proximity to yours. You will soon get used to it but you are bound to make mistakes to start with. Making mistakes is the usual way of learning a new skill; gradually you will learn to overcome such mistakes and to be able to concentrate on the next challenge. You certainly will not learn overnight to become a successful yacht racer, even with the gift of natural talent, if there is such a thing. Surely at the end of it all we have our natural levels of ability, but even that with practice can be significantly improved upon.

The knee-knocking, teeth-rattling jitters that you might experience in your first few races will go away as you become more familiar with your surroundings and the action upon the race course. From club race to open race to open district race, to ranking race to National Championship race to International race to World Championship race — each step presents new challenges. Pre-race nerves may never completely go away and, in fact, I think they are good for you and may well help you concentrate and sharpen yourself up a bit.

The thing that deters most potential yacht racers is, having built or purchased a yacht and indulged in a little friendly racing against another yacht or two, they would like a bash at some more serious racing, but . . . the thought of all those rules!!

The 1989–92 International Yacht Racing Rules run from **Rule 1** to **Rule 78.7**. Before you faint or decide that you will take up tiddlywinks instead, relax! The main body of rules that you need to know for racing on the water are known as **Part Four, Rules 31** to **46** inclusive. You'll need to read the other rules sometime — they are there for many reasons — but you do not need to remember them.

People often try to race without using the rules or to use a simplified set of rules. However, they usually find in the end that the IYRR are as simple a set of rules as you can get and that they cover all of the many situations that can develop while racing yachts.

The racing rules really are quite simple if you approach them correctly — one step at a time, gradually acquiring the knowledge over a period of time as you actually race. The main purpose of this book is to help to introduce you to the basic rules that you need to know and, much more importantly than that, help you understand how to use the rules in a tactical sense. Being the fastest yacht on the water is not enough. Without the knowledge that this book will give you, the fastest yacht will not necessarily win! Why? Because such a yacht will inevitably be caught up in incidents as it tries to pass other yachts which will result in protests being called upon the water. A yachtsman who does not know the rules has three choices:

1) Accept that he was in the wrong and retire.
2) Accept that he was in the wrong and do the alternative penalty turns.
3) Let the protest go to a protest hearing after the race, where he'll very likely find himself disqualified. (Assuming that the protesting yacht knew the rules enough to know that the protested yacht was in the wrong.)

The obvious choice for the yachtsman who does not know the rules is choice 2, because that at least keeps him in the race, free to carry on and win, if possible, after doing the alternative penalty of one or two 360-degree turns.

There are four fundamental rules in all to be found right at the start of the Rule Book.

A) Rendering Assistance
Every yacht shall render all possible assistance to any vessel or person in peril, when in a position to do so.

This rule obviously applies far more to full-sized racing skippers than model yacht skippers. However, there may be times when, for example, a radio controlled yacht skipper has lost control of his yacht and the out-of-control yacht is either sailing away into the distance or, worse, sailing at good speed straight towards some object such as a concrete bank that will undoubtedly cause damage to the yacht should it sail into it. Under such circumstances, if your yacht was near enough to the out-of-control yacht to divert it without causing damage to your own yacht, you could break clear of the racing fleet calling out loudly and clearly your intentions, asking for your current position within the race to be noted. After the race, you would then be able under **Rule 69** to appeal for redress. Without doubt you would be awarded the position you were holding on the water at the time of breaking away to render assistance.

B) Responsibility of a Yacht
It shall be the sole responsibility of each yacht to decide whether or not to start or to continue to race.

Again, this rule is far more applicable to full-sized yachts where the dangers of high winds, for example, can put human life at risk, besides risking the safety of the yacht. In model terms, while you may certainly risk sinking your model yacht, you are highly unlikely to be putting human life at risk. However, the point is that it is no good complaining to the race organisers if your yacht sinks in high wind conditions. It is entirely up to you whether or not you take part in any race. The only penalty to you is that you get awarded one point more than the number of yachts entered into that race as a result. If you seriously believe the conditions to be too bad to race your model yacht safely, that is a far better alternative than the risk of seriously damaging your boat and perhaps even sinking it. If a yacht sinks in three or four feet of water, it is not such a problem. In deep water however it most certainly is. Model yachts do not sink very often — I see or hear about one or two a year. The ones I know about have always been recovered, albeit in one case by a diver a week or two later! So remember, the onus is always upon you and no one else as to whether or not it is safe to race or to continue to race.

Now the next two Fundamental Rules are fairly new additions and apply just as much to model yacht skippers as they do to full-sized skippers!

C) Fair Sailing

A yacht, her owner and crew shall compete only by sailing, using their speed and skill, and, except in team racing, by individual effort, in compliance with the RULES and in accordance with recognised principles of fair play and sportsmanship. A yacht may be penalised under this rule only in the case of a clear-cut violation of the above principles and only when no other rule applies, except Rule 75, Gross Infringement of Rules or Misconduct.

This Fundamental Rule sums up the whole approach to yacht racing — it is a sport where honour plays a large part. You have to be honest with yourself and with your fellow competitors. A win achieved by cheating is a hollow victory indeed. Please read and reread this rule. If you cannot feel comfortable about this rule, you will not enjoy yacht racing. Should it ever be suggested to you that you reread this rule, take the suggestion seriously and carefully think it through. Was the suggestion justified or not? If you ever get disqualified under this rule, which is extremely rare, then you ought very carefully to consider whether or not you wish to change your approach to the sport or simply take up some other pastime.

Yacht racing is a sport and we expect participants to behave in true sporting fashion.

D) Accepting Penalties

A yacht that realises she has infringed a rule shall either retire promptly or accept an alternative penalty when so prescribed in the sailing instructions.

This final Fundamental Rule takes us back to the options I wrote of earlier for a yacht involved in an incident upon the water. If you are involved in an incident upon the water and realise that the fault is most likely yours, you must break away from the racing yachts into clear water either to execute your penalty turn/s or to sail clear away to retire, without further interfering with the yachts

still racing. Obviously, you would be allowed enough time, say a minute or so, to think the whole incident out in your mind but, as soon as you have the incident clear in your mind, you must accept, if applicable, a penalty or retire. In model yacht racing you will most often have an observer call out the incident, although the observer is not meant to call out who was right and who was wrong. That is for the skippers involved to sort out, or to risk taking it to a protest hearing after the race. Skippers may talk about the incident at the time, but a running argument should not develop.

Now this Fundamental Rule is again really all about honour. A lot of the time we rely upon the honesty of racing skippers to police the race. If a skipper touches a mark, for example, and realises it, he ought to do his penalty turn/s whether or not anyone else saw the incident. In the same way, if two yachts touch each other in an incident, one of the yachts is clearly in the wrong and ought to do her penalty turn/s whether or not an observer calls the contact.

These may seem like heavyweight rules but in reality they are not. They simply set out the standards of sportsmanship and safety we expect in our sport. I hope they will give you an understanding that all of the Rules are about fairness and above all else safety. In fact, I hope the Fundamental Rules go some of the way towards answering the very basic question that is often asked — why have rules?

Racing rules have evolved from the basic rules of the road at sea. Those rules in turn evolved to make sailing at sea safer and to make the actions of a sailing vessel predictable according to its relative position to another sailing vessel nearby. These rules were established by putting the obligation to take avoiding action upon the sailing vessel less inconvenienced by taking such avoiding action. Thus, a ship sailing off the wind would give way to a ship beating to windward. Obviously, as regards port tack giving way to starboard tack, it was necessary to nominate one or the other of the two tacks and starboard won the toss.

Thus in any situation where ships were close to each other, they knew not only what action to take themselves to avoid a possible collision, they knew what action the other ship would also be taking, if any. During the nineteenth century, when yacht racing began to develop upon modern lines, clubs formed their own rules based upon the rules of the road at sea. By the late nineteenth century, the Yacht Racing Association had been formed and all of the separate clubs' rules unified into one set of rules. The early twentieth century saw the beginnings of International racing and by 1959 the International Rules became the world's authority.

The International Yacht Racing Rules are revised every four years after the Olympic Games. In addition to the International Yacht Racing Rules, the IYRU publishes interpretations, i.e. decisions that have been made by appeal hearings of the member nations. New cases are published each year and all new cases are updated to the latest version of the Rules every four years. Therefore we have evolved a finely tuned set of racing rules that, above all else, are concerned with safety and fairness, covering all known situations or potential incidents.

It is not necessary to know the rules 'parrot fashion'; indeed, as we show, it is only necessary to have a very basic knowledge of a few of the rules to start racing in safety. As your racing continues, your knowledge of the rules will develop slowly by experience and, hopefully, by reading this book not just once, but by referring to it again and again. That is the sensible way to learn the rules and the complex skills of racing.

Another important point is that there is little point in knowing the rules if you cannot appreciate the tactical advantages that they offer, both for defensive and attacking sailing. This is quite legitimate use of the rules and as I said before, anyone who thinks that they can continually win races with just good boat speed is quite wrong. Boat speed has an important part to play, but tactics using the rules more so.

When sailing at a club, or entering any radio controlled model yacht race, you must check with the race organisers before turning on your transmitter as to which frequencies are available or which frequency you have been already allocated. If you use a 27MHz set, you should have three solid colours and three split coloured frequencies

as a minimum available (although, of course, at club level for the newcomer every effort is made to help those with less frequencies available). If you have a 40MHz set, then only three different sets of crystal numbers are at present required as a minimum. Race organisers will do their best to try to keep everybody on the same allocated crystal all day long but, in the larger events, especially if there are two or more fleets racing, you may well have to change crystals from race to race. It is very important, therefore, that you continually check to ensure that you are still on the same crystal in such circumstances. Also, if not actually racing, do not turn your transmitter on — someone else who is racing at that moment might have the same crystal allocated as you are on. The standard rule is: as you come off the water turn your transmitter off as quickly as possible. If you have been allocated a coloured crystal peg, return it as soon as possible to the peg board, so that the next user of that colour can in turn collect the peg and know that he is then safe to turn on his transmitter. (A peg board is an easy foolproof system of controlling crystal allocation and allows the organisers to see at a glance which frequencies, if any, are free at any time.)

It is most frustrating to be doing well in a race only to have your yacht malfunction for some reason or other. Common reasons are battery failure, rigging failures and electrical problems involving water usually in the boat. It is strongly recommended that you keep your receiver and battery pack in a plastic pot having a screw down sealing lid, fitted through the deck in such a way so as to have access to the screw top lid above deck level and the remainder of the pot below deck. Wires going out of the pot to the servo and winch can be sealed at their exit point from the pot with a rubber grommet and some Dow Corning Silicon Sealer. The aerial should be fed through a short length of PTFE tubing glued into the pot side wall and passed up through the deck, at which point it should also be glued. The aerial should be laid along the deck and well covered from exit point to beyond its end with insulation tape.

Winch failure or servo failure happens to us all

at some time or other. However, if you use either Tony Abel's or Dave Andrews' excellent winches, your problems ought to be at a minimum, provided you look after them carefully in between racing by ensuring that all water within the hull is well drained out and that air can circulate freely through the hull. All screw heads and wire exit points on servos and winches should be additionally sealed using dabs of Evostick glue, which has the advantage of being fairly easy to remove at a later stage if required.

Ni-Cad batteries do have a life after which they will not hold a charge for so long. This seems to occur some time between two and five years after purchase. All wiring has a tendency to deteriorate to the dreaded black wire state and thus ought to be checked and probably renewed each year. Vaseline on the plugs seems to help prevent corrosion at that point. While salt water is more corrosive than fresh water, provided you keep a careful eye on everything it is not that bad. It most certainly should not be avoided at the cost of not racing. The club I belong to has one of the best lakes in the country filled with salt water, which has never given me any problems.

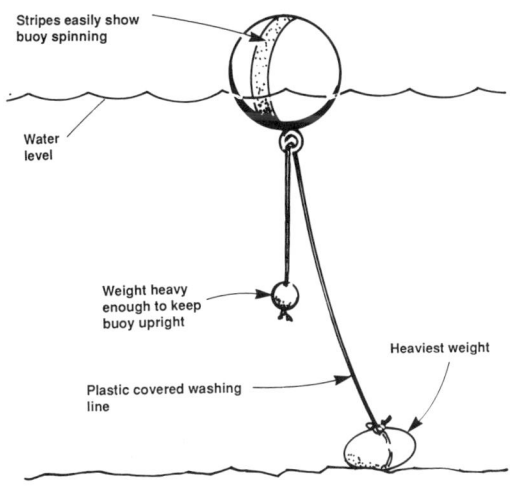

Stripes easily show buoy spinning

Water level

Weight heavy enough to keep buoy upright

Heaviest weight

Plastic covered washing line

Diagram 2.1

Before racing, the first thing a club or group of keen model yachtsmen have to do is set a course to be raced around. This is usually done by putting buoys (also called marks) in the water, held in position by weights attached to the end of a line. If you have two weights, one slightly heavier than the other, attached to each end of a line, having passed the line through the attachment eye on the underside of the buoy, it is possible to get the buoy to adjust itself the length of its anchor line to cater for rises and falls in the water level while keeping the buoy sitting in a totally upright position. You may think that this is unnecessary in a lake where the level of the water is more or less static, but I can assure you that it is necessary. Once the water builds up a chop in a wind, there is enough variation going on in the level of the water to lift up a buoy attached to a fixed length anchor line that is set tight, and move the buoy! It is very important to have the buoy sitting upright in the water for two reasons. One, so there is little chance of the keel of yachts rounding the buoy catching on the anchor line. Two, so the only thing that is going to make the buoy spin is a yacht scraping the side of the buoy. If a buoy is lying to one side in the water instead of upright, the wind can push the buoy around in the water as can the wake of yachts rounding the buoy. This makes it very difficult to see whether or not the yacht has touched the buoy. The yacht has to do penalty turns or retire if it touches the buoy, hence the care needed in laying them correctly.

Buoys should be easily visible, but not so large as to obscure the controlling skipper's view of his yacht as it passes behind a buoy. The buoy should have strips of contrasting colour vertically upon it to easily show up the buoy when it rotates. This gives a clear sign of being scraped by a passing yacht! The actual length of line used and the weight of the anchor weights will need a bit of experimenting with to suit the depth of water and the buoyancy of the buoys used.

The usual type of course used by radio controlled model yacht racers is one called an 'Olympic' type of course. First you establish the direction the wind is coming from, and place the windward mark near the end of the water nearest to the direction the wind is coming from (the upwind end of the lake). Then, following the wind's direction, you place another buoy directly downwind as far as possible from the windward mark. This then becomes the leeward mark. Around halfway between these two marks you lay two smaller buoys, making a line between them at right angles to the line between the windward and leeward marks. The length of this line should be the total of the lengths of the number of yachts starting at any one time in a race. For example, twelve radio controlled Marblehead class yachts starting in each race would mean a line twelve time the length of a Marblehead, which is 48 odd inches long. So four feet by twelve feet gives you a start line somewhere near forty-eight feet long. That in turn means that there should be twenty-four feet of start line each side of the line running from the windward mark to the leeward mark. (See Diagram 2.2.) The wing mark or gybe mark should be laid so as to make a triangle with the windward and leeward marks. The ideal sort of triangle to try and make is one where the angle between the base line of the triangle (the line between the windward and leeward marks) and the apex of the triangle is forty-five degrees. (Look at the diagram again.) Of course this is very much an ideal and in practice many waters preclude such a precise course being set, but it is the sort of course you should be aiming to get as close as possible to.

The most important objective in setting a course is ensuring that the line from the windward mark to the leeward mark remains directly in line with the wind, or in the middle of the sector of the wind's shifting pattern. If this means re-laying the course as the day progresses and the wind moves to a new direction, then so be it. It is most important to present a course with good windward beating, especially to the first mark after the start of the race. You will find that in major races we tend to want as long a distance as possible from the start of the race to the first mark to be rounded (the windward mark). To do this, the start line is moved right downwind of the course adjacent to, or even behind, the leeward mark. To make the windward beating sections of the course even longer the finish line of the race course will be another line laid right up by the windward mark.

The usual course sailed around the courses set out above is what we call a triangle followed by a sausage! The yachts will all start from the downwind side of the starting line, crossing the line once the starting gun has been fired to beat up to windward and towards the first mark — the windward mark. This mark they will sail round

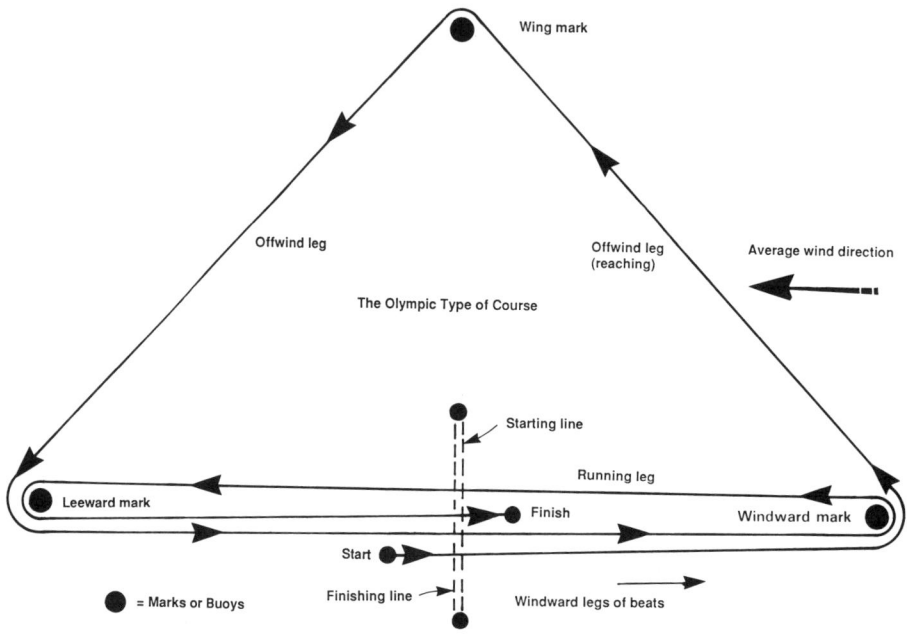

Diagram 2.2

leaving it to their port (left). They will bear off and sail towards the gybe mark on a broad reach. They will again leave the gybe mark to their port and gybe to the opposite tack and sail on a broad reach towards the leeward mark. They once again leave that mark to their port and round it, hardening up to a close-hauled course beating up close to wind towards the windward mark again. They once again leave the windward mark to port but this time swing right around to run directly before the wind towards the leeward mark. They finally round the leeward mark, leaving it again to port before hardening up for the final windward beat to the finish line.

Whenever possible in serious racing, the course is laid so that the marks are left to port. This is because you tend to get less incidents occurring around the marks in port roundings than you do in starboard roundings. The reason being that in starboard roundings a lot of yachts will be approaching the buoy on starboard, but tacking to port to round the mark directly in the path of boats coming up astern still on starboard, and since port tack boats give way to starboard tack boats this can be tricky. Whereas on port roundings, a starboard approaching yacht simply bears off to round the mark which is much safer.

Going back to the problem of the wind changing direction through the course of the day and ideally having to re-lay the course. Some clubs will lay extra buoys in the water at the start of the day and then simply nominate for each race which particular buoys make up the course for that individual race. Obviously, you then need different coloured or different shaped buoys for ease of identification.

Just before the start of each race the yachts participating are called to the water. Remember to collect your crystal peg if applicable. Remember to switch on your transmitter first and then the receiver. If you do it the other way around, there is a good chance that your receiver will simply pick up the signal from other nearby transmitters on frequencies near to your own and start moving the winch and rudder, sometimes with annoying results. Check that the rudder servo is working and centring properly from both left and right positions. Check that the winch is sheeting fully out and when sheeting in that the boom settings are correct for close-hauled work, and that the winch is not straining to pull the booms in further than they can go. Lastly check that the drain bung is in, the pot lid firmly screwed down and all deck patches well stuck down. Launch your yacht and sail her to the area around the start line.

When all of the yachts are on the water and under control, the Race Officer or Officer of the Day (O.O.D.) will start an audible countdown, the last minute of which is usually counted down in ten second intervals from sixty seconds down to ten seconds. The final ten seconds is counted down second by second to one. One is called, and one second later the 'gun fired' usually expressed by a short sharp word such as 'Go'. All of this countdown is done by means of a tape cassette being played in a tape recorder. There are no visual signals used similar to the flags used in full-sized racing — it is all down to the audible countdown. I'm afraid if you have hearing problems you are most definitely going to have problems racing model yachts, because all communications on the water are verbal.

At the start the objective is to be approaching the start line with speed so as to cross the line just after the gun. The start line is the imaginary line to be found between the two start marks on the side of the marks nearest to the first mark of the course — the windward mark. If any part of a yacht or its rigging is over the line as the gun goes off, you will be called by your jib number as an early starter. The call will most likely be "99 over the line!" You, as jib number 99, then have the responsibility of returning back across the line and restarting once your yacht is completely back over the leeward side of the start line. During the time you are returning to the line you must *not* get in the way of any yacht that has started correctly. (**Rule 44**). You lose your right of way while returning to restart. If you find yourself in this situation with yachts both sides of your yacht hemming you in, simply sheet out the sails — this will slow you down allowing the other yachts to draw ahead and you can then safely turn about back towards the start line. Don't worry too much about this at present, though, because if you follow my basic starting plan it will not happen to you. However, you need to be aware of what happens because other boats near your yacht might be early starters and you do not want to waste time giving way to them as they try to return. It most definitely does not pay to start early unless you enjoy an enormous challenge! To be able to achieve a start you must know the following:

The difference between port and starboard tack. The rule definition is 'A yacht is on a tack except when she is tacking or gybing. A yacht is on the tack (starboard or port) corresponding to her windward side.' Other ways of working out which tack you are on are:

a) Your main boom will always be on the opposite side of the yacht to the tack you are on.

b) If you were actually sitting in the yacht on the windward side facing the sails, then your right hand would be nearest the bow while on starboard tack and vice versa.

c) As a visual aid, stick a green bit of tape on the starboard bow above the water line and a red bit of tape on the port bow.

Green = starboard = righthand side.
Red = port = lefthand side.

The reason you need to know what tack you are on is because one of the most important basic rules of sailing, whether racing or not, is that port tack gives way to starboard in most situations. This is known as **Rule 36**.

It is not necessary for you to remember rule numbers or the exact wording of any rule, they can always be looked up in the book of rules later. It is necessary to have a good grasp of what the rules mean and certainly to be able to have a good working knowledge of the rules covered in this book. Don't worry, it will be quite painless — by the end of this book you will know all of the basics to be able to survive very well the demands of club racing. So let's look again at **Rule 36 Opposite Tacks — Basic Rule**:

A port tack yacht shall keep clear of a starboard tack yacht.

This rule is so simple, yet it probably causes more arguments than any other rule. It shouldn't, it is very simple — port gives way to starboard! As a beginner that is all you need to know! Yachts on

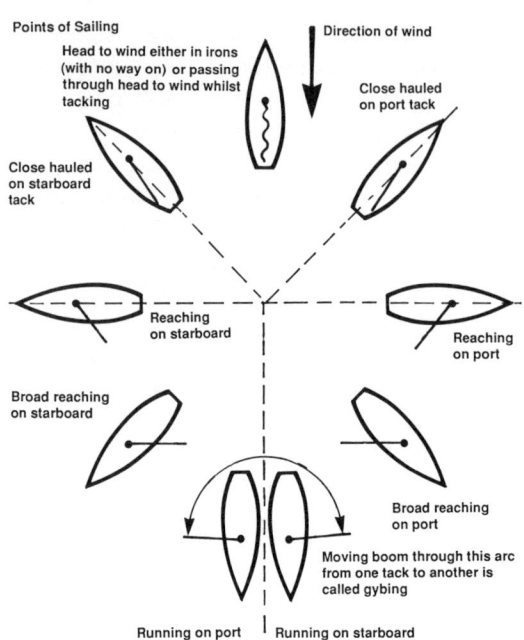

Diagram 2.3

starboard approaching a yacht on port will usually yell ''starboard'' at port boats that seem to be on a collision course. They do not have to hail, but it helps their case should any incident occur that goes to protest. It also warns the other boat and most likely gets the attention of a race observer too. If you are in any doubt, get out of the way! How? Either by tacking to starboard yourself immediately provided that does not put you directly in the way of the hailing starboard yacht or alter your course while remaining on port to take the stern of the starboard yacht. To take the stern of a yacht means to sail past the yacht near to its stern rather than crossing in front of a yacht near its bow! The other basic rule you need to know is that a windward yacht keeps clear of a leeward yacht on the same tack. Windward is the yacht nearest to the direction the wind is coming from.

Now back to the start. If you think about the start and **Rule 36**, you may realise that it is going to make it a lot easier and safer to approach the start line sailing on a starboard tack. That way you are not going to have to give way to any port tack boats and will be one less thing to worry about. Windward and leeward will still need to be considered, but not port and starboard. If the start

24

has been laid correctly, there should be absolutely no advantage from starting either from the starboard or port ends of the line, or on either tack other than the fact that starboard tack yachts have right of way over port tack yachts. Because of this, as you can imagine, starboard approaches to the start line tend to be much more popular than port tack approaches. It ought to be pointed out that it is the hardest thing in the world to get a start line laid absolutely square to the wind's direction, because the wind has the annoying habit of continually changing its direction most of the time around its mean direction. This tends to favour first one end of the line and then the other. For beginners it hardly matters, you need to be able to perfect your starts on starboard first, before having to worry about more detailed plans of attack at starting. Good starboard starting technique will gain you more positions than it will lose you in any event! At your present level of racing starboard starting is by far the best plan of action.

The next problem is: how are you going to get to the line on starboard on time just as the gun goes off? The easy answer is that you are not! I want you there just one second after the starting signal! This is just as difficult to achieve, but slightly safer since it allows you a slight margin for error! Without doubt it takes a lot of practice, but this is how you can set out to achieve your objective. Once your yacht is put onto the water and you have sailed out to the starting area, sail up to the starboard mark and sail away from the starboard starting mark downwind on a broad reach on port. (This should be the reciprocal course to the course you will be sailing to approach the starting line on starboard!) Around twenty seconds from the line, note your position in the water, by using some landmarks to set transit lines, i.e. your yacht's relative position to such landmarks will give you a very good idea of where you want to be twenty seconds before the gun.

You ought now to have time to try a couple of trial approaches to the line to check out the time it does actually take. Also time how long it takes to turn your yacht through 180 degrees. Once the countdown tape starts you can simply sail to and

from your twenty second spot adjusting your position so as to be pointing in the right direction in the right position at twenty seconds. Of course, it is terribly easy for me to write this; however it is a little harder to achieve in practice because there will be a few other yachts doing much the same sort of thing. As time goes by, and you have done a few races, you will find ways of altering this basic plan a little bit to cater for such handicaps though. As a very basic emergency plan, if you aim to start on starboard at the starboard end of the line right by the starting mark just behind all the other yachts you still will not be in a bad position! If you can manage to achieve that and cross the line with good speed, I very much doubt that you will be the last yacht round the windward mark for the first time! The reasons for my thinking this will be explained in the next chapter which covers the windward beat, but for the moment take my word for it!

The sort of angle of approach you want to be sailing your yacht towards the starboard mark of the starting line should be at around forty-five degrees to the wind or more. This angle should be a higher number than your best angle of attack to the wind, so as to allow you room for manoeuvres. (See Diagram 2.4.)

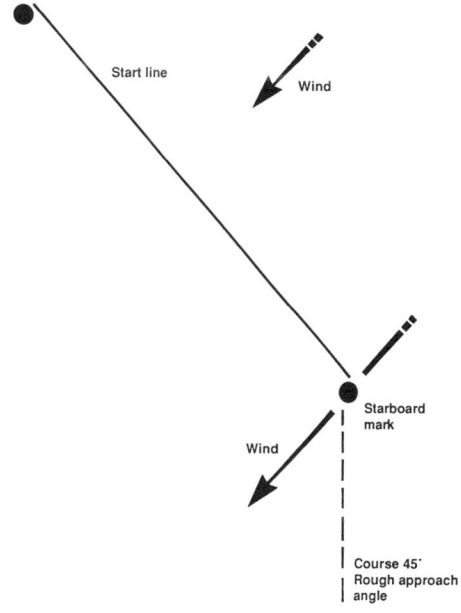

Start line

Wind

Starboard mark

Wind

Course 45° Rough approach angle

Diagram 2.4

25

Now let us have a look at Diagram 2.5. This diagram shows the position of five yachts one second before the starting gun goes off to allow them to cross the line and start the race. Yacht A has mistimed its approach and arrived at the line too soon, thus having to bear off and reach down the line. This is a dangerous position to put itself in, since any boat to leeward of it, sailing on a closer course to the wind such as yacht X, will oblige A either to harden up and risk going over the line early, or to bear off behind yacht X losing more ground and increasing the chance of it crossing the line late. In the situation as shown in Diagram 2.5, at one second before the gun, yacht A will be able immediately to harden up its course to its best close-hauled course and miss X. If there had been more than just one second to go to the gun, though, A would have had to try and bear off to miss X, which would have been impossible to do. All A could do in such circumstances is to sheet out rapidly to try to lose drive, so as to slow down or go over the line early, and then bear off once past X's bow to get back behind the line again in order to be the right side of the line for starting again before getting to yacht D. If the same situation had arisen, at say, ten seconds or so before the starting gun, a better alternative might have been for A to have immediately hardened up, gaining speed by doing so, crossed the line, and then immediately tacked to port and wheeled back around the starboard mark to come in again behind yacht C.

Going back to the position shown in Diagram 2.5. Yacht D is well placed for a port end start, although immediately after starting it is highly likely that it will have to tack to starboard to give way to X who, of course, is already on starboard (**Rule 36**). If D had approached the line at full speed, and all the other yachts starting on starboard were travelling at a speed well below their best speed, it might well be possible for D to cross the bows of the starboard yachts safely. If it can be done, it should be, since that would be by far the best thing for D to do. The reasons for this will become clear after you have read the next chapter — D will be able to tack back to starboard, having crossed all of the starboard yachts' bows and then be to windward of them all controlling the fleet.

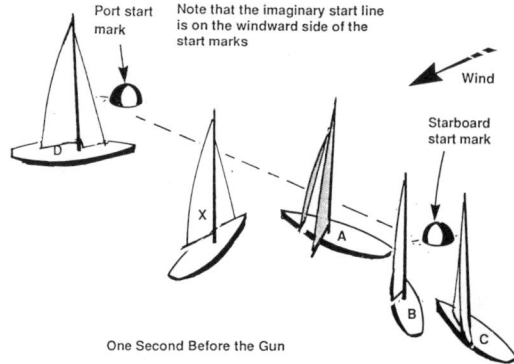

Diagram 2.5

Back to Diagram 2.5 again, yacht B is in the perfect position — approaching the line at speed on starboard at the starboard end of the line with no yacht close to leeward to cause trouble. Yacht B is also in command of C's destiny for the next few seconds. Yacht B is not obliged to give any room to C at the start to pass between C and the starboard starting mark! (**Rule 42.14**). So yacht B can shut yacht C out! Yacht C is your yacht for this book. As a novice, you have done very well to get your yacht in the position it now finds itself. All you need to do is to keep your nerve and let your sails out a little so as to slow down just a touch relative to the speed of yacht B. This will let B draw ahead and you can pull your sails back in (sheet in) getting your yacht back up to full speed, crossing the line behind B and getting as close to the starboard starting mark as you dare. You are then exactly where I want you to be to start your first windward beat.

Before we can get on to the next chapter and the windward beat I'm afraid there are still more basics to be learned. A word of warning, first; if you are trying to cut close to any mark when heeled over, do remember that your keel will be sticking out under water to windward and it is more than possible to hook up on the mooring tackle of the mark. While it is not against the rules to touch the mooring tackle, it has the rather terminal effect of often drawing the mark up onto your yacht's hull and trapping the yacht on the mark for a considerable length of time! This is why it is so important to get the mooring lines of race marks as near to vertical as possible. It is not fair to expose racing yachts to this sort of hazard.

While we are on the subject of rounding marks, the other danger to watch out for is, when the mark is on the leeward side of the rounding yacht, a sudden puff of wind may lay the yacht further over causing the yacht's sails to brush onto the mark. The trick is to keep your eyes on your yacht, and if you see it starting to heel over further than planned let your sails out a little (sheet out) in order to keep the yacht more upright until past the mark.

Back now to **Rule 36**, which, as you will remember, gives the starboard tack yacht right of way over a port tack yacht. This rule does not give the starboard tack yacht the right to chop the port tack yacht in half if it gets in the way of the starboard tack yacht! The starboard tack yacht has an obligation to try to avoid serious damage (**Rule 32.1**). Let us look at this a little more carefully. You are sailing along on a starboard tack when you notice a port tack yacht approaching on what appears to be a converging course with every chance that you are going to hit it. You immediately hail the other yacht with a simple call of "Starboard!". Usually the other yacht will respond by tacking to starboard itself to get out of your way or will bear off or change course in such a way as to miss your yacht. (It gives way to you.) However, if there is no response either by action or word, repeat your hail once more. If there is still no response, the situation should have developed to immediate action being required to avoid a collision. Call "starboard yacht tacking to avoid collision with port tack yacht" and tack. If there is no room to tack to port because of nearby yachts also on starboard to windward of your yacht, then consider bearing off instead behind the port tack boat to avoid the collision. If there are boats leeward to your yacht, also on starboard, then call for room to miss an obstruction (the port tack yacht that is failing to respond to your hails). If all else fails just try to minimise the impact of collision as best you can. Once the danger is over, register immediately your protest against the other yacht, by calling twice your jib number protesting the jib number of the offending yacht. You need to keep an eye on the other yacht to ensure that it does its penalty turn/s because, if it doesn't, you will

need to fill in a protest form after the race has finished.

Rule 36 does not give the starboard tack yacht the right to chase port tack yachts all over the water. Once a starboard tack yacht is sailing near to port tack yachts on converging courses, the starboard tack yacht has a duty to maintain a steady predictable course. There is a rule that covers this — **Rule 35 Limitations on Altering Course:**

When one yacht is required to keep clear of another, the right of way yacht shall not alter course so as to prevent the other yacht from keeping clear, or so as to obstruct her while she is keeping clear, except:

(a) to the extent permitted by Rule 38.1, Luffing Rights, and

(b) when assuming a proper course:
either

>*(i) to start, unless subject to Rule 40, Same Tack, luffing before clearing the starting line, or to the second part of Rule 44.1(b), Returning to Start.*
>*or*

>*(ii) when rounding a mark.*

Bits of this rule will not make any sense to you at present — don't worry, we will be covering those bits that you need to know at the relevant time in the book.

For now it is simply important to realise that, as a starboard yacht, you have a duty to maintain the predictable straight line steady course required as a port tack yacht is manoeuvring to keep clear of you. After all this is basic common sense. How on earth can a port tack yacht keep clear of you if he cannot predict accurately your course? He suffers penalty enough giving way to you, without running the risk of getting confused by your unpredictable behaviour on the water.

When a starboard tack yacht hails a port tack yacht "starboard" it may well receive the reply "hold your course". This means that the port tack yacht is well aware of the presence of the starboard tack yacht, and is of the opinion that it can either cut across the bows with inches to spare or that it can bear off and cut tight to the stern of the starboard yacht. Woe betide the port tack yacht that makes such a call to a starboard tack yacht which then gets hit by the starboard tack yacht and damaged! Unless it can prove that the starboard tack yacht altered course so as to prevent the port tack yacht keeping clear, the port tack yacht will have to accept the alternative penalty turn/s and just grin and bear any damage!

Now let's suppose the worst has happened and a collision has occurred. The collision may be only the slightest touching of the booms or masts, a brushing of the sails or the merest kissing together of the two hulls — any contact invokes a penalty! Also, any manoeuvre by a port tack yacht that forces a starboard tack yacht to have to take avoiding action also invokes a penalty! What happens? Immediately at the time of the incident occurring, one or both of the yachts involved will yell ''Protest'' to be quickly followed by a more reasoned call ''Yacht 88'' (your jib number) ''protests Yacht 99'' (the other yacht's jib number). If you cannot see the other yacht's jib number identify the yacht by some other call such as the black hull with the pink strip. You will have to repeat the call one more time, by which time, hopefully, the jib number will be visible. By now one of the skippers will have had time to think the incident through and realise that he was at fault. He'll now shout ''doing my turns!'' and break free of the racing fleet to do just that. As the other yacht involved you will have kept any eye out for the other yacht to do penalty turns and can now relax. If neither yacht accepts responsibility on the water for the incident and thus does turn/s, the incident will go to the protest committee after the race has finished. Each penalty turn consists of doing one tack and one gybe thereby completing a *complete* circle in the water. It may be a clockwise or an anti-clockwise circle but, if there are two turns to be done, they must be done consecutively and in the same direction!

If you started off your penalty turn on the starboard tack, your penalty turn is not complete until you are back on the starboard tack again, after having tacked to port, borne off and gybed back around to starboard and hardened up to a close-hauled course again. That is a 360-degree turn — naturally enough two consecutive turns is called a 720-degree turn. The 720-degree turn is the alternative penalty listed in the rule book under Appendix 3, 1.1. If you touch a mark, the alternative penalty is still a 720-degree turn under **Rule 52.2** (a). Both of these rules are often amended by the sailing instructions to one turn — a 360-degree turn. We will come across sailing instructions again later on, for the moment just understand that they are a variable set of rules for each individual race meeting that can modify some of the standard racing rules. They thus have the full status of rules and should always be read carefully.

As a novice, it is inevitable that you will be doing lots of turns as you learn how to control your boat accurately in congested conditions. Until you know the rules fairly well, there will be many occasions where you will simply have to assume you are in the wrong and accept penalty turns. For this reason it is well worth spending lots of time practising doing turns as fast as you can *without losing boat speed*! The trick is to keep the wind in your sails right through the turn. In order successfully to achieve this, you need to develop good co-ordination between your right thumb controlling the rudder of the yacht and your left thumb which is controlling the sheeting out and in of the sails. Once you can do this well, you ought to be able to minimise the effect of doing penalty turns.

Sooner or later, however, you are going to end up in the protest room. I will cover this in more depth later in the book, but for the moment here are the bare bones. Firstly as per **Rule 68.5**, a protest shall be made in writing and be signed by the protesting skipper and include the following particulars:

(a) the identity of the yacht being protested.
(b) the date, time and whereabouts of the incident.
(c) the particular rule or rules alleged to have been infringed.
(d) a description of the incident.
(e) unless irrelevant, a diagram of the incident.

At minor club meetings, the protest might actually be allowed to be submitted verbally in the mistaken belief that a verbal protest will be resolved quicker than waiting the two minutes it takes to jot everything down on paper. The problems of allowing a protest to be submitted verbally are that it allows the party who sees the protest going against him to start to vary the basis of his version of events. You can thus end up with an argument going round in circles instead of having a well structured hearing with the starting points down in black and white. A verbal hearing is also unsatisfactory for the participants because they are now relying on the protest committee to remember all of the relevant facts. The final drawback is that, if any of the parties concerned wish to appeal against the findings of the protest committee, they will not be able to, because the protest committee have not conducted the hearing correctly documenting everything down. **Rules 71** to **74.6** lay down how a protest committee will act and Appendix 7 offers further guidance! It is worth reading these rules once to give yourself more of an idea as to what to expect. However, as a novice, 99.9 per cent of the sort of incidents you are likely to be involved in will be fairly obvious to experienced skippers, so we'll just run through what an informal bankside verbal protest hearing ought to sound like.

The skippers involved will be allowed a short time to scuttle away to dig out their battered or pristine copies of the IYRR. Frantic questions will be asked of skippers around as to what number rule applies. With any luck, someone might have an idea and that rule is quickly read and re-read and possibly others in turn referred to from it. By this time, someone will have been nominated as the protest committee chairman and in small race meetings that is all there will be — the one person. That one person should have a reasonable working knowledge of the rules. He will call the offending parties together and ask the protester to present his version of the incident. Little models of the yachts are often used to show the relative positions of the yachts involved, before, during and immediately after the incident. A little model representing a mark is also useful and an arrow to show the direction of the wind. The protester should also state which rule he/she is protesting under — although it does not have to be the correct rule it obviously helps if it is!

After the protester has offered up his version of events, the protestee is offered the opportunity to ask any questions of the protester. Then it is the turn of the protestee to offer up his version of the

incident, again using the models to demonstrate. After this, the chairman will call up any race observers who saw the incident, one at a time, to present their evidence. Next the protester will be allowed to call up any witnesses he wishes to call and then, of course, so will the protestee. After all that, the chairman will either come immediately to a decision or may wish to retire for a minute or two to consult his own rule book. If that is the case, both will then be called back once he has reached a decision and they should be told the facts found, the rule/s broken and the decision of the committee, which is usually to disqualify one of the skippers involved. Sometimes both get disqualified and sometimes the protest just gets thrown out. Without anything in writing it is rough justice, but to be fair the decisions found are more often right than wrong and the emphasis is very much 'let's get on with the next race', rather than having everyone hanging around listening to a protest hearing. However, protest meetings are very instructive — they do force people to study their rules books and actually get to know a bit more about the racing rules.

I love them and, while I was learning the rules, I most certainly found them the best way of learning the finer points of the rules a little at a time. I certainly learnt a lot of rules the hard way in the protest room getting disqualified. Eventually it sinks in that the best place to win races is on the water, not in the protest room! I have even been disqualified when in the right because I failed to protest the other boat involved at the time! This leads us on to **Rule 33 Contact between Yachts Racing:**

When there is contact that is not both minor and unavoidable between the hulls, equipment or crew of two yachts, both shall be penalised unless: either
(a) one of the yachts retires in acknowledgement of the infringement, or exonerates herself by accepting an alternative penalty when so prescribed in the sailing instructions,
or,
(b) one of both of these yachts lodges a valid protest.

So be warned that it is very much in your own

interests to make absolutely certain that, if your yacht is involved in a contact with another yacht, you either immediately protest that yacht or break away to do turn/s. Do not reach out in hope towards the words 'not both minor and unavoidable' in the aforementioned rule. For that to apply, the conditions must be almost drifting conditions whereby yachts no longer have enough way on to control their direction. Then, and only then, might the words 'minor and unavoidable' apply!

Don't be frightened of the protest procedures — no one knows all of the rules. The worst result of a protest hearing is a disqualification, or DSQ as it is known, but people still speak to you! We have all been disqualified at some time or other — no one likes it but you shake the other party's hand and look forward to the next race. At the end of this book, Appendix 1 lists useful publications. I strongly recommend that you invest in a copy of the IYRR if you have not already done so. This book certainly provides you with enough extracts from the IYRR to turn you into a competitive racing skipper, but it is not the purpose of this book to replace or to try and improve upon the several excellent books already in print that dig into the rules in great depth.

3. The First Windward Beat

Do you remember that I wrote in the last chapter that the yacht that followed my instructions and started on starboard at the starboard end of the starting line, right up by the starboard starting mark, would have a very good chance of not being last at the first windward mark? You may also recall that your yacht that I have lent you for this book made just such a start exactly in the right position but starting just a little bit behind everyone else. Diagram 3.1 shows the position of the five racing yachts a few seconds after the start. Yachts X, A, B, and C had all started on starboard, with X, A and B having reasonable speed. Your yacht C had to slow down a little bit because B did not leave you any space between itself and the starboard starting mark — so you eased your sails out a bit and headed slightly up into wind, so as to slow down that little bit. You then almost immediately sheeted in again gaining speed and, just missing the mark, you hardened up onto a close-hauled course covering B's starboard stern quarter.

Yacht D had started with good boat speed on the port tack right down by the port start mark. She then had to tack to starboard to miss X, since port tack yachts must give way to starboard tack yachts (**Rule 36**). She might have chosen to bear off under the rest of the fleet's sterns — but she was a little too near to X to be able to do that without having to lose too much speed. This sets up the scene for our first windward beat. Now the windward beat should, if the windward mark has been laid correctly and there has not been a sudden wind shift, consist of a series of close-hauled tacks beating up to windward in a zig-zag

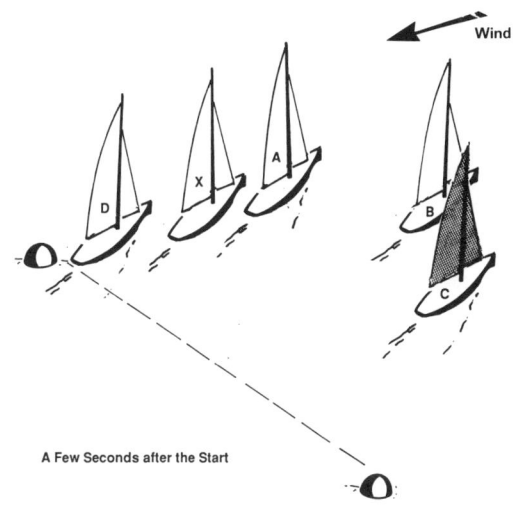

A Few Seconds after the Start

Diagram 3.1

course until the windward mark is reached.

In Diagram 3.2, accepting that the wind is being very kind and blowing at a steady strength and from a steady direction, then sailing along any of the courses shown will bring you to the windward mark having covered approximately the same distance. Since we are sailing on a lake, we do not have to worry about different tidal strengths or river currents. You will notice that the outer lines radiating from the windward mark are called laylines so-called because when you arrive at a point intersecting those lines it is time to tack, because you can then 'lay' the mark i.e. you can reach it on a close-hauled course without having to tack again, except actually to round the mark if you are approaching the mark on a port tack.

So, the basic conclusion to be gained after carefully studying Diagram 3.2 is that from a distance point of view, you are likely to cover the same distance however many times you tack going up the windward beat. Why then, you might well ask, do yachts tend to get separated out to some extent going up the windward beat? Well they will not all enjoy the same boat speed for one thing, not only because they will all be tuned slightly differently, but because not all of the yachts will be sailing in clean air or water. Supposing for a moment that they were all to enjoy the same boat speed, there are still a number of factors that will make some courses better than others. The most obvious factor is tacking. Usually tacking will reduce boat speed — models cannot produce the drive you can get when executing a roll tack in a dinghy, which in light airs can produce more drive in the sails than the wind alone would do. The amount of speed lost depends very much upon the skills of the skipper sailing the yacht and the design of the yacht.

Methods of tacking vary from boat to boat and the strength of the wind at the time of tacking. In light airs one should be very very gentle with the amount of rudder used. The objective has to be to maintain momentum at all costs right through the tack and onto the new course. You will quite likely have to tack through more than ninety degrees, letting the sails out a touch to gain maximum boat speed on the new tack before sheeting in and hardening up on your new course. In medium winds, you might well still turn gently for the first half of your tack, but as you pass through the head to wind position, you will speed up the turn a bit until upon your new course. In heavy wind you may need to bear off a little from your close-hauled course to gain yet more speed and then slam the yacht around to the new tack, sheeting in and away on the new close-hauled course. In such heavy wind conditions you need to also consider the waves and any gusts of wind moving across the water. It is a waste of time trying to tack into a wave, it will usually push you straight back onto the tack you were trying to tack away from! Wait until the bow is over the wave before starting to tack — tack down a wave

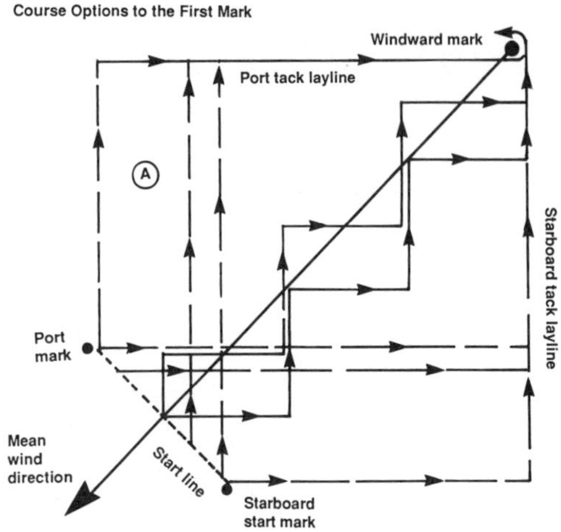

Course Options to the First Mark

Windward mark
Port tack layline
(A)
Starboard tack layline
Port mark
Mean wind direction
Start line
Starboard start mark

Whichever course is chosen, overall lengths are the same

Diagram 3.2

not up a wave! Tacking in a gust is making the whole job of tacking harder than it need be. So if possible wait until the gust has passed before tacking or put a tack in before the gust comes! Remember that you can see a gust coming by the darker water underneath it as it passes over the water. The water is darkened by more ripples being formed. The point is that the most experienced skipper should lose the least amount of speed when tacking and know how to regain lost speed the quickest too. Thus it is up to you as a novice to get out there on the water, sometimes by yourself, and just practise your tacking. Take some time out to study how other skippers are tacking and never forget that the rudder acts just like a brake! The more you turn it the more you'll slow the yacht down!

The other most important factor on the windward beat is that you are not alone! The other yachts around your yacht do not allow you to do exactly what you might wish to do in any event. Therefore you might get carried way beyond the point at which you would have chosen to tack if sailing your yacht all by yourself. A yacht sailing behind your yacht, but to windward, effectively stops you from tacking your yacht into the path of the windward yacht. Why? Well there is a little rule, number 41 to be exact, that goes like this: **Rule 41 Changing Tacks — Tacking and Gybing**

41.1 Basic Rule

A yacht that is either tacking or gybing shall keep clear of a yacht on a tack.

41.2 Transitional

A yacht shall neither tack nor gybe into a position that will give her right of way unless she does so far enough from a yacht on a tack to enable this yacht to keep clear without having to begin to alter course until after the tack or gybe has been completed.

41.3 Onus

A yacht that tacks or gybes has the onus of satisfying the protest committee that she completed her tack or gybe in accordance with Rule 41.2.

41.4 When Simultaneous

When two yachts are both tacking or both gybing at the same time, the one on the other's port side shall keep clear.

We will be looking at this rule in some depth as the book progresses — for the moment you ought to be able to realise now why, if you have a yacht to windward of your yacht but slightly behind, you cannot tack across into its path even if you are going from port to starboard. All you can do is wait until the other yacht tacks and then tack to follow it. Of course if you are both on port tack and a starboard tack yacht sails into view on a collision course, you are both going to have to tack to starboard to give way to it. You must ask permission of the yacht to windward to tack to starboard first. You would need to call "Water to tack to avoid a starboard boat please!". As soon as the other yacht replied, either by tacking or shouting "you tack", *you must* immediately tack to starboard. The alternative might be to bear off under the starboard yacht's stern. In that case the yacht to windward might call for "Water to bear off under the stern of starboard yacht please!". You in turn would then need to bear off a little more to give that yacht room to miss the starboard yacht's stern.

So yachts on starboard can also force port tack yachts back to starboard as we are all beating up to wind. Thus it really does pay to look well ahead and to be planning what you want to do to get to the windward mark with the least hassle.

Other points that will vary boats' performance are: the ability to point high into the wind; some boats will be able to sail a course closer to the direction of the wind than others, which will enable them to sail a shorter overall distance to the windward mark — although they might be sailing that shorter course at a slightly slower speed; concentration will differ from skipper to skipper; some boats will overlay the mark thereby sailing farther than they have to; some boats will get involved in incidents and the resultant penalty turns, others might pick up a piece of weed or rubbish to slow them unfairly down etc etc. Also once we get into the real world instead of basic theory we will soon discover that the wind is anything but predictable. It is very annoying to discover that the wind seldom blows from a steady single direction for any length of time. It will very often come from a general direction but be swinging from that mean direction from side to side. Therefore the actual direction of the wind can shift about from within a few degrees to a major shift of up to ninety degrees! The usual sort of shift pattern is more likely to be a few degrees rather than the major shifts. The strength of the wind does not remain constant for long either! It tends to wander up and down around its mean average. The direction the wind is coming from tends to effect the characteristics of that particular wind. Winds that travel a long distance over land tend to have larger shifts associated with them than winds that have had a clear passage over sea. For the moment all you need to know is that the wind does alter direction and strength over the day. It can also vary in direction and strength on different parts of the course you are racing on. You need to keep an eye out for this sort of thing!

Let's now look a little more closely at one or two basic things about the wind in relationship to the windward beat in particular. How do we know when the wind shifts? The easiest way for the novice to notice is by keeping a close eye on the behaviour of the other yachts racing, especially those yachts closest to his own. For example, if you notice that all the yachts on the same tack as your yacht have started to head up into the wind more than your boat then you should try gently altering the course of your yacht to the same new heading. If you have balanced up your yacht correctly, as covered in the previous chapter, you ought not to have to do this as the boat should do it automatically. If you are beating up to windward on a close-hauled tack and the wind shifts to a new direction that allows you to sail your yacht on a course more directly towards the windward mark, it is called a 'lift'. It should follow that, if your yacht is enjoying this sudden generosity from the wind, anyone on the opposite tack will be put on a new course that is taking him farther away from the windward mark than he was previously sailing. This is called being 'headed'. Thus the sensible thing to do for a yacht being headed is to tack to the other tack so as to enjoy the lift!

If you study Diagram 3.4 you can see the extremes of effect that a minor 10-degree shift of wind can have, favouring on this occasion the boat on Course A. If you have no idea what the wind is going to do next, then it would be wise to sail a course that is not too far away from the rhumb line — that is the imaginary line going straight from the starting line to the first mark (or from any mark to the next mark for that matter). In other words, it is the shortest distance between two marks. However wind shifts can develop into a regular pattern and experienced yachtsmen will, if they have the time before the start of a race, make a note of the wind's direction and of the timing and direction of any shifts that come through. This should take them between ten and thirty minutes or so to establish and, by doing this, they have a chance of predicting the side of the course that will best serve them to sail up and position their yacht where they want to be on the starting line. It is not a thing for a complete novice to worry about at this stage in his racing career, but it is nice to know all of the tricks for later.

However, reacting to a wind shift that has occurred most certainly is something for the novice to consider, especially if all the other yachts already have! This is a good moment to give you a little warning — there is always the person that wants to do the opposite of the rest of the fleet. If all of the fleet sails towards the port side of the windward beat, this fellow sails towards the star-

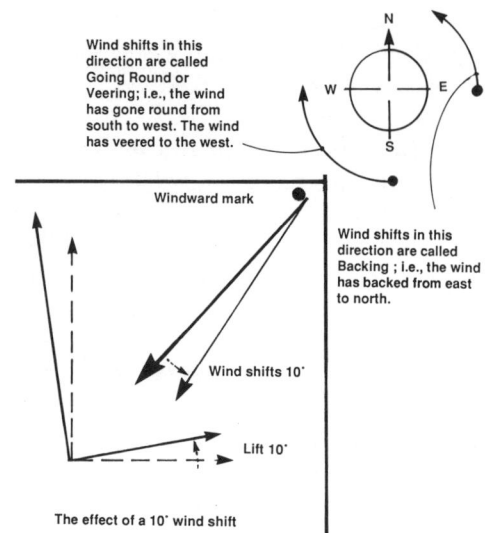

Diagram 3.3

board. It is a gamble, hoping that he'll find something that the rest of the fleet won't be able to enjoy. If that person is an excellent reader of the wind then fair enough, but don't you think if that was the case that the rest of the fleet would be following him? If you are at the very back of the fleet, it can, if done wisely, be a reasonable tactic. After all, in last position you have nothing to lose and everything to gain. Other than that it is most unwise — the odds are against you.

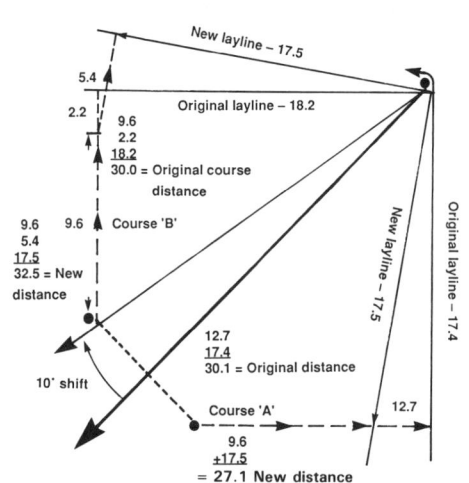

Diagram 3.4

34

Maybe one time out of ten it pays off, but racing is usually about winning more than the odd race. In a series it is overall consistent performance and good results that is going to win the series. As the wind varies in strength you are going to have to learn how your yacht behaves in such varying strengths of wind. Then you can respond appropriately to such gusts. If you are lucky and you have tuned up your yacht correctly, it will screw up into wind tighter as a gust passes through while holding or increasing its speed. If not you may need to ease the sheets out a little, while maintaining a close-hauled course. This lets some of the wind's increased pressure out of the sails, thus avoiding flattening the yacht too far over and increasing the drive. As I have already said, I like my yacht to respond to such increases in the wind's speed by gently heading up to her new close-hauled position and accelerating. I like to be able to sail up the windward beat without touching my transmitter except when I wish to tack. However it is worth noting that there are many different opinions as to how to tune your yacht and how to set your sails. Some just as good as others. Listen, read and experiment with your yacht so as you can form your own opinions as to what suits your yacht best!

Back to Diagram 3.1, we are yacht C managing to hold more or less the same speed as B, A, X and D. What happens next? All yachts will continue on starboard evaluating their relative speeds and positions. Yachts D and X will find it very hard to overhaul A because they are to some extent in the wind shadow of the boat to windward. What is wind shadow? Well, it is the area of space to leeward and slightly to windward that is affected by the wind passage over the sails, causing variations in wind pressure and direction.

Diagram 3.5(i) shows the worst position. When B tries to pass A to leeward it will slow B down and she will not be able to pass unless her relative boat speed was so much greater than A's to carry her through this turbulent area of weak wind. One solution is to ease off the sheets slightly and bear off to pick up more speed to clear A before sheeting back in and hardening up to windward again.

In Diagram 3.5(ii) the situation can be worse,

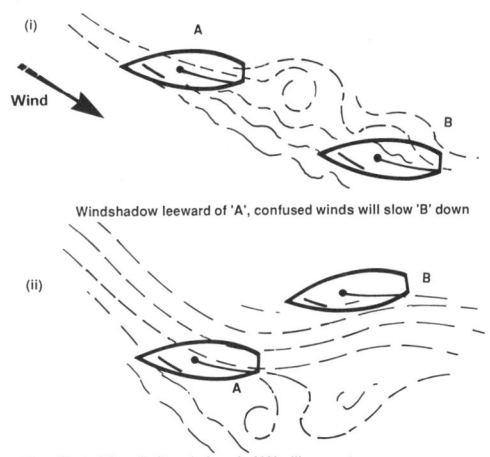

Windshadow leeward of 'A', confused winds will slow 'B' down

The effect of the wind to windward of 'A' will prevent 'B' from pointing quite so high as 'A' – be careful

Diagram 3.5

although the turbulence is much less it has the effect of heading the overtaking boat. The solution here is to work your yacht further to windward before you attempt to pass windward (easier said than done!).

Now going back to the basic concept of fairness being all important in yacht racing, I can explain **Rule 37** a little more. First, however, let us define the term overlapped. *A yacht must be either clear ahead or clear astern of another yacht or each yacht is overlapped.* Yachts are overlapped when they are both within two boat lengths of the longer yacht. Diagram 3.6(i) and (ii) should clarify things for you.

Rule 37.1: *When overlapped a windward yacht shall keep clear of a leeward yacht.*
That is surely fair? The leeward yacht is struggling to sail upwind clawing every inch to windward that she can. The yacht to windward, if on a converging course, either cannot sail so close to the wind or is in fact heading somewhere else in any event. In either case it does not seem unreasonable for her to take the stern of the leeward yacht. It is hardly going to inconvenience her much is it? If she really is sailing on the same leg of the course as the leeward yacht and thus towards the same mark, she ought to change her sail setting so as to be able to keep above and to windward of the leeward yacht. Her alternatives are simply to tack away onto the opposite tack or sail under the leeward yacht's stern. If she is

bearing down on the leeward yacht to dump some dirty wind on her — it is an odd tactic — provided she keeps clear of the leeward yacht while doing it, it is quite OK as far as the rules are concerned.

Rule 37.2: *When not overlapped a yacht clear astern shall keep clear of a yacht clear ahead.* Well that seems fair. If the yacht approaching from astern is closing the gap, she must be sailing faster than the boat clear ahead. She is in a better position to see what is in front of her than the skipper of the yacht clear ahead is in a position to see what is astern of her. The boat clear astern is thus in a much better position to choose on which side to pass the yacht ahead.

Rule 37.3 Transitional: *A yacht that establishes an overlap to leeward from clear astern shall initially allow the windward yacht ample opportunity to keep clear.*
Again that seems fair. The boat that was ahead must be given time to respond to the new situation and ample time at that. Once the boat that is now to windward has been given that opportunity though it has to be extremely careful indeed — if the overtaking boat is able to sail a slightly higher course than the windward boat without luffing, then pretty soon the windward boat is going to have to tack away to the opposite tack to keep clear of the leeward yacht. The overtaking yacht that is now to leeward should also be extremely careful to ensure that she can miss the stern of the now windwards yacht as it swings across to the new tack. This is because if the yacht has a centre fin and rear rudder it will tend to pivot about the centre fin, with the result that the stern of the yacht can swing into the side of the hull of any yacht that is too close to its leeward side!

All this paves the way for the last major rule I wish to introduce you to in this chapter. Please remember that you do not need to learn these rules parrot fashion. All that you do need to get into your head are the basics. The rule and its number can be looked up in a book after the race is over. During the race, you will not have the time to be looking at books. If you did, you would soon be sailing into another yacht! This rule is well worth knowing — it can provide you with lots of fun!

Rule 38: Same Tack — luffing after clearing the starting line. This is I'm afraid a lengthy rule, but since it provides you with your main defensive weapon as a boat clear ahead, you need to know it well. You also need to be prepared to respond to a luff when trying to overtake a yacht to its windward side. The definition of luffing is: altering course towards the wind. This means to just up to head to wind — remember once you pass through the head to wind position you are considered to be tacking! Tacking comes under **Rule 41** and most certainly cannot be done as a defensive measure right under the bow of another yacht, unless you really wish considerably to shorten the length of your yacht's hull!

Rule 38.1 Luffing rights:
After she has started and CLEARED the starting line, a yacht clear ahead or a leeward yacht may luff as she pleases, subject to the following limitations of this rule.

Rule 38.2 Limitations: (See Diagram 3.6(iii).)
(a) Proper course limitations. A leeward yacht shall not sail above her proper course while an overlap exists, if when the overlap began or at any time during its existence, the mainmast of the windward yacht has been abreast or forward of the stem of the leeward yacht.

(b) Overlap limitations. For the purpose of Rule 38 only: An overlap does not exist unless the yachts are clearly within two of the overall lengths of the longer yacht, and an overlap that exists between the two yachts when the leading yacht starts, or when one or both of them completes a tack or gybe shall be regarded as a new overlap beginning at that time.

(c) Hailing to stop or prevent a luff. When there is doubt, the leeward yacht may assume that she has the right to luff or sail above her proper course unless the skipper of the windward yacht has hailed—
(i) "Mast to stem" or words to that effect, or
(ii) "Obstruction" or words to that effect.
The leeward yacht shall be governed by such a hail and curtail her luff. When she deems the hail improper, her only remedy is to protest.
(d) Curtailing a luff: The windward yacht shall not cause a luff to be curtailed because of her proximity to the leeward yacht unless an obstruction, a third yacht or other object restricts her

ability to respond.

(e) Luffing rights over two or more yachts: A yacht shall not luff unless she has the right to luff all yachts that would be affected by her luff, in which case they shall all respond, even when an intervening yacht or yachts would not otherwise have the right to luff.

That, you will be pleased to read, is the end of the luffing rule. Once again please remember that you do *not* need to learn the rules off by heart. All you need is a rough idea of the rule to start with and after you have given it a few tries on the water you'll have a better idea of how it actually all works. Every time you are involved in a luffing incident you can look up the rule in your rule book after the race to clarify your understanding of the rule.

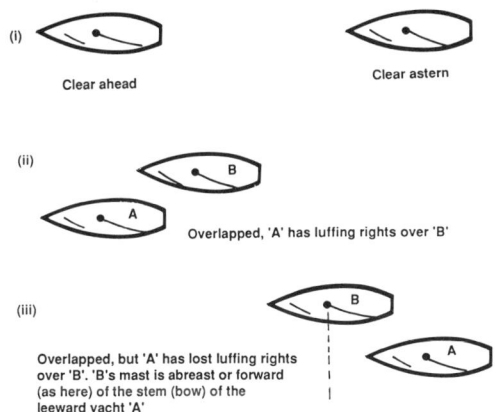

Diagram 3.6

As I said earlier **Rule 38** has an important defensive part to play — because it is difficult to overtake a yacht to leeward, it is natural to want to overtake a yacht to windward and steal its wind. I hope you can see the fairness of this particular rule which gives the yacht being overtaken a powerful deterrent. It allows the leeward yacht to try and stop a windward yacht getting into such a position as to steal its wind! A luff by the leeward yacht is going to force the windward yacht up into wind thus slowing it down. Certainly the luff will also slow down the leeward yacht, but she is in the position of being able to judge the best moment to return to her proper course. The yacht to windward can only respond to the actions of the leeward yacht and that always takes

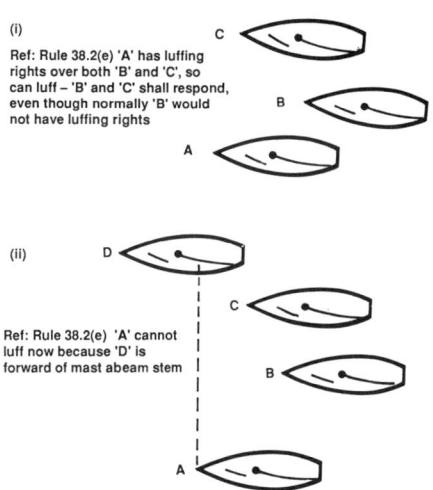

Diagram 3.7

a little longer. If the leeward yacht can really judge matters correctly she will wait until she can suddenly sharply luff up just enough to get the two yachts touching. There is not much danger of damage occurring in this manoeuvre because the relative speeds of the two yachts will be similar and also the courses much the same. Once touched, the windward yacht has an alternative penalty to accept and that should get it off the leeward yacht's back for quite a while! Remember that the luffing yacht must protest the windward yacht the moment contact occurs, repeating the call once more if necessary.

At the 1988 RM Nationals at Gosport, I remember seeing a yacht in very windy conditions literally luff so violently off the top of a little wave that the front half of the yacht leapt out of the water and onto the overtaking yacht's front deck! No damage was done and I have always thought of that little incident as the perfect example of the violent luff, quite legal and very effective! The other point is that as the luffing yacht, you must be most careful not to luff too high and get into irons, which can be very embarrassing. Even more importantly, do not get caught out by a sudden wind shift and find your luff turning into a tack! If that happens it will be you doing the penalty turns.

Here then is a wonderful gift — you can be as nasty to overtaking boats to windward as you like! You can actually touch them and impose a penalty on them if they are not wide awake! When I first discovered this rule I had to do the penalty turns! Well, I was the hopeful and ignorant overtaking speedy yacht! Once the rule had been explained to me and I had purchased a rule book and looked it up, I fell in love with it. My arch rivals and I would luff each other up and down the course everywhere. I'd even slow down a bit to find a new yacht to luff. What fun, at the back and middle of the fleet penalties were constantly being handed out! However I gradually began to notice that while I was having a lot of fun, other yachts that were not actually involved in these dramatics were quietly slipping through to my leeward from behind and gaining places. That is the danger of using this rule too much — it is not worth stopping one yacht getting by you to windward if, in the meantime, two other yachts sneak through to leeward of you. I suspect, however, that the only way to learn to use this rule to maximum advantage is to go out there and have some fun. Without doubt, used correctly it is a fine defensive weapon. So go on, get out there and have a luff or two.

Now with a little knowledge of **Rules 35, 36, 38** and **41** vaguely swimming around inside our heads let's tackle the windward beat a little further up the lake towards the windward mark. Remember once again that you do not need to be able to quote either the rule number or the complete rule while on the water — you merely have to remember for yourself the bare bones — so that you know what you can and can't do. When to accept penalty turns and when not to, but protest the other yacht instead. Don't worry at this stage if you cannot even remember some of the bare bones of the rules we covered so far. Just accept that until you do, if you are involved in an incident and you don't understand the ins and outs of it, you are going to have to do penalty turns right or wrong!

Look again at Diagrams 3.1, 3.2, 3.3 and 3.4. We are yacht C and it should now be obvious that none of the other yachts can tack at the moment without getting in our way and that is not allowed! (**Rule 41.1 Basic Rule**: *A yacht that is either tacking or gybing shall keep clear of a yacht on a tack*.) Plus of course we are on starboard so that

even if they have time to tack to port, they have to consider the fact that they are going to have to give way to us on starboard tack! (**Rule 36**.)

For the moment we are 'in command of the fleet'! I doubt very much whether you really wish to be in command of the fleet at this early stage in your racing career. It is likely to put a lot of pressure on you as to what should you do next. The decision will be yours and no one is going to help you. Well except me of course! The points to consider are these: if we and B, A and X tacked to port immediately, B, A and X would all then be to windward of C and in control of our immediate future, because we would not be able to tack back to starboard until they did. So while we have command of the fleet at present, we must use it to best advantage and progress up the course towards the port layline on starboard as at present. If you could retain the same sort of speed and direction as the remainder of the fleet of five, it would pay you to continue this course right up to and beyond the layline for the windward mark.

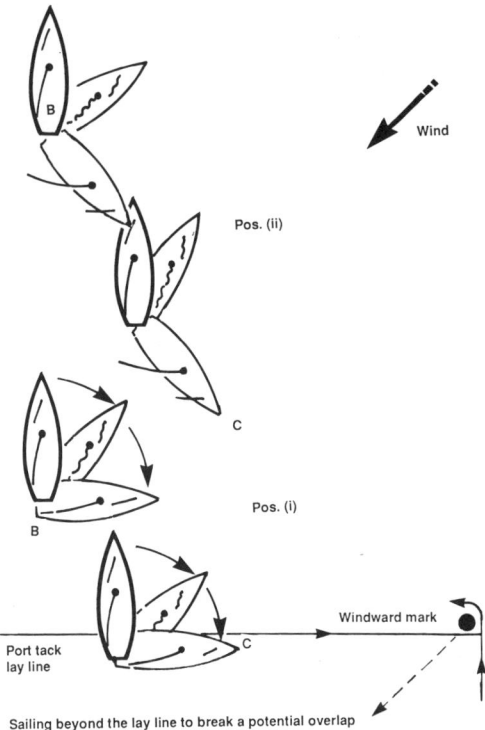

Sailing beyond the lay line to break a potential overlap
Diagram 3.8

Look at Diagram 3.8 — the reason for sailing beyond the layline is that if all the yachts retain roughly the positions as in Diagram 3.1, when you tack to lay the mark, B at least would tack also and promptly be on top of you to windward. By going beyond the layline it means that when you tack, you can bear off farther to gain speed while laying the mark. Since you also choose when to tack, you have a slight advantage over those who can only respond to your tack. This can give you a slight edge. That, combined with the different angles of approach involved, will increase your chances of getting to the mark clear ahead, but on port and thus having to tack to starboard to round the mark. This must be done without tacking in the water of any yacht coming up astern. We will be looking at this in the next chapter.

However in reality, going back to Diagram 3.1, as a complete novice our yacht C is not going to be moving quite as fast as the other yachts and they are slowly drawing ahead. We are possibly suffering a little from the leebow effect of B (Diagram 3.5(ii)), so we put in a tack to try and find some clear air and water. Sailing through another yacht's wake will slow your yacht down. The other good reason for doing this is that we want to be approaching the windward mark on starboard when we are about to round it not port! Once we have tacked to port the decision on what to do next lies with B, who is well placed to cover the rest of the fleet. Does she continue on her starboard tack covering the rest of the fleet? Or should she tack to port too so as to cover us? If we ignore possible wind shifts, basic theory says cover the majority of the fleet. If B tacks though she will be in clear air and ahead of the rest of the fleet anyway, able to tack back to starboard when she likes. Thus she is likely to consider what sort of threat C could present in the future

of this race as they beat up the course.

The major potential problem is that if B holds course on starboard and puts in, as she must some time, a tack to port, then there is a danger of C tacking back to starboard and forcing C back to starboard as their courses converge at a time that could present B with problems. Now if this happens on or beyond the starboard layline no problem, B tacks to starboard and lays the mark. But if B cannot lay the mark, then the situation in Diagram 3.8 can occur again and even worse for, if B cannot lay the mark, but C just can, then B is in a very bad position. If B is aware that C is a novice she might well continue on her original course from Diagram 3.1, concentrating on keeping herself between the windward mark and the rest of the fleet until such time as she wishes to tack to port. Otherwise she'd be wise to follow C's example and tack almost immediately to port, which would keep B to windward and in command of C and keep the rest of the fleet astern of B. By being in command of C, I mean that C cannot now tack back to starboard until B has tacked, because C would be tacking in B's water. (**Rule 41.1.**)

However C may well have luffing rights! C's tactics in this position have to be to try and sail as high into wind as she can, pinching up to windward in an attempt to out point B, thus encouraging B to tack. Or if B gets too close, a nice sudden luff might do the trick. In our situation though, being a novice, we will simply carry on sailing until B tacks back to starboard, at which time we will tack back to starboard ourselves. This will most likely be when B can lay the mark, so we have a good chance of rounding the first windward mark in second place!

4. Rounding the Windward Mark

The third chapter left us as yacht C of a racing fleet of five yachts, approaching the windward mark on starboard. Yacht B is ahead of C, slightly to leeward, also on starboard and able to lay the mark. Yachts A, D and X are all approaching the mark on port tack (see Diagram 4.1). This chapter, like the first two chapters, is going to include some large chunks of rules. I promise that it is the last chapter to have such large amounts of the rules quoted in it. The reason is of course, that we have to lay out the ground rules, so that you can get round the course safely and with some understanding of what on earth is going on. The next three rules are reproduced in full and lead on to reproduce one more as well. Just quickly scan over them for now and on to the text beyond, which will keep referring to little sections of the rules as we progress. You may then simply refer back to the section of rule I quote if necessary. So here we go...

Wind

Mark

Direction of next mark

Port tack lay line

Starboard tack layline

A

X

B

C

D

The 'Magic Circle' radius four boat lengths from the mark (See Rule 42)

Diagram 4.1

Before we can attempt to round the mark correctly we must look at the rules in section C of the *International Yacht Racing Rules: Rules that apply at Marks and Obstructions and other exemptions to the Rules of Section B.*

When a rule of this section applies, to the extent to which it explicitly provides rights and obligations, it overrides any conflicting rule of *Section B, Principal Right of Way Rules and their Limitations*, except **Rule 35, Limitations on Altering Course.**

Rule 42: Rounding or Passing Marks and Obstructions:

Rule 42 applies when yachts are about to round or pass a mark on the same required side or an obstruction on the same side, except that it shall not apply:

(a) between two yachts on opposite tacks:

(i) when they are on a beat, or

(ii) when one, but not both, of them will have to tack either to round or pass the mark or to avoid the obstruction, or

(b) when Rule 42.4 applies.

Rule 42.1 When Overlapped:

An outside yacht

(a) An outside yacht shall give each inside overlapping yacht room to round or pass the mark or obstruction, except as provided in Rule 42.3. Room is the space needed by an inside overlapping yacht that is handled in a seamanlike manner in the prevailing conditions to pass in safety between an outside yacht and a mark or obstruction, and includes space to tack or gybe when either is an integral part of the rounding or

passing manoeuvre.

(b) An outside yacht overlapped when she comes within four of her overall lengths of a mark or obstruction, shall give room as required, even though the overlap may thereafter be broken.

(c) An outside yacht that claims to have broken an overlap has the onus of satisfying the Protest Committee that she became clear ahead when she was more than four of her overall lengths from the mark or obstruction.

An inside yacht

(d) A yacht that claims an inside overlap has the onus of satisfying the protest committee that she established the overlap in accordance with Rule 42.3

(e) When an inside yacht of two or more overlapped yachts, either on opposite tacks or on the same tack without luffing rights, will have to gybe in order most directly to assume a proper course to the next mark, she shall gybe at the first reasonable opportunity.

Hailing

(f) A yacht that hails when claiming the establishment or termination of an overlap or insufficiency of room at a mark or obstruction thereby helps to support her claim.

Rule 42.2 When not Overlapped:

A yacht clear astern

(a) A yacht clear astern when the yacht clear ahead comes within four of her overall lengths of a mark or obstruction shall keep clear in anticipation of and during the rounding or passing manoeuvre, whether the yacht clear ahead remains on the same tack or gybes.

(b) A yacht clear astern shall not luff above close-hauled so as to prevent a yacht clear ahead from tacking to round a mark.

A Yacht Clear Ahead

(c) A yacht clear ahead that tacks to round a mark is subject to Rule 41, Changing Tacks — Tacking and Gybing

(d) A yacht clear ahead shall be under no obligation to give room to a yacht clear astern before an overlap is established.

Rule 42.3 Limitations:

(a) Limitation on Establishing an Overlap.

A yacht that establishes an inside overlap from clear astern is entitled to room under Rule 42.1(a) only when, at that time, the outside yacht:

   (i) is able to give room, and

   (ii) is more than four of her overall lengths from the mark or obstruction.

However, when a yacht completes a tack within four of her overall lengths of a mark or obstruction, she shall give room as required by Rule 42.1(a) to a yacht that, by luffing, cannot thereafter avoid establishing a late inside overlap

At a continuing obstruction, Rule 42.3(b) applies

(b) Limitation When an Obstruction is a Continuing One.

A yacht clear astern may establish an overlap between a yacht clear ahead and a continuing obstruction, such as a shoal or the shore or another vessel, only when, at that time, there is room for her to pass between them in safety.

Rule 42.4 At a Starting Mark Surrounded by Navigable Water:

When approaching the starting line to start until clearing the starting marks after starting, a leeward yacht shall be under no obligation to give any windward yacht room to pass to leeward of a starting mark surrounded by navigable water, including such a mark that is also an obstruction; but, after the starting signal, a leeward yacht shall not deprive a windward yacht of room at such a mark by sailing either:

(a) to windward of the compass bearing of the course to the next mark, or

(b) above close-hauled.

Rule 45 Keeping Clear after Touching the Mark:

45.1 A yacht that has touched a mark and is exonerating herself shall keep clear of all other yachts until she has completed her exoneration and, when she has started, is on a proper course to the next mark.

45.2 A yacht that has touched a mark, while continuing to sail the course and until it is obvious that she is exonerating herself, shall be accorded rights under the rules of Part IV.

Rule 52 Touching a Mark:

52.1 *A yacht shall neither:*

(a) touch:

(i) a starting mark before starting, or

(ii) a mark that begins, bounds or ends the leg of the course on which she is sailing, or

(iii) a finishing mark after finishing and before clearing the line and marks,

nor

(b) cause a mark or vessel to shift to avoid being touched.

52.2 (a) *When a yacht infringes Rule 52.1 she may exonerate herself by sailing well clear of all other yachts as soon as possible after the incident, and remaining clear while she makes two complete 360-degree turns (720 degrees) in the same direction, including two tacks and two gybes.*

(b) When a yacht touches a finishing mark, she shall not rank as having finished until she first completes her turns and thereafter finishes.

52.3 *When a yacht is wrongfully compelled by another yacht to infringe Rule 52.1 she shall be exonerated:*

(a) by the retirement of the other yacht (or by the other yacht accepting an alternative penalty when so prescribed in the sailing instructions) in acknowledgement of the infringement, or

(b) in accordance with Rule 74.4(b), Penalties and Exoneration, after lodging a valid protest.

Rule 74.4 Penalties and Exoneration:

When the protest committee after finding the facts, or the race committee or protest committee acting under Rule 70.1, Action by race or Protest Committee, decides that

(a) a yacht has infringed any of the rules, or

(b) in consequence of her neglect of any of the rules a yacht has compelled other yachts to infringe any of the rules, she shall be disqualified, unless the sailing instructions applicable to that race provide some other penalty, and, in the case of (b), the other yachts shall be exonerated. Such disqualification or other penalty shall be imposed irrespective of whether the rule that led to the disqualification or penalty was mentioned in the protest, or the yacht that was at fault was mentioned or protested, e.g., the protesting yacht or a third yacht may be disqualified and the pro-

tested yacht exonerated.

After all that you probably feel exhausted — relax, grab a drink and read on. Remember I did tell you that racing is great fun and so it is but, as driving a car requires some knowledge of the *Highway Code* to be able to relax and enjoy your driving so does racing. The good thing about racing though is that it requires very little knowledge of the racing rules before you are out there belting round with the best of them having fun and learning from your mistakes. There is no better way of learning the rules than by bitter experience. I am just trying to save you some of the heartache and to take some of the mystique out of racing. It is always very frightening for the newcomer considering racing. They notice all the shouts of "Overlap"; "Starboard"; "Protest" etc. and get the impression that it is going to take twenty years just to learn the rules. No way — we have now covered most of the rules used in the actual race and at a basic level we are almost there. So let's get on and try and get a basic understanding of what we need to know to round the mark safely and to let the other boats near to us round in safety too!

Back to Diagram 4.1. We are sailing as a novice yacht C and we are enjoying some of that beginner's luck that often annoys more experienced skippers. We had a good position on our start, being on starboard, right up by the starboard mark, crossing the line at half speed a few seconds after the gun. Being last over the line on the starboard end allowed us to tack across to the port tack, breaking clear of the fleet and finding clean air and water. B tacked across immediately after our tack and held command over us right up to the starboard layline. (We could not tack back to starboard, because we would have been tacking in B's water and that is not allowed — **Rule 41.1** *A yacht that is either tacking or gybing shall keep clear of a yacht on a tack.*) Once on the starboard layline, B tacked to starboard to lay the mark and of course we then immediately tacked to starboard to do the same. B had carried us a little beyond the layline, but not enough to hurt us. The thing that worries us is that although we are on starboard sailing on a fairly close-hauled course, there are three port tack boats A, X and D rushing towards us. D will clear our stern, but what on earth are these other two yachts going to do? The problem is, of course, very firmly *their* problem. (**Rule 36** *A port tack yacht shall keep clear of a starboard tack yacht.*) All the same it would be nice to hazard a guess. Let's look at it from the point of view of A and X's skippers. A has got a big problem. She is most definitely not going to be able to sail across B's bows — if she sails straight on then she will probably hit B on the port stern quarter. Even if A's speed is less than B's or if she slows down, there is the additional problem of C, hard on the stern of B, presenting a further barrier of a starboard tack boat! If A wants to bear off to miss B and C then there is yet a further problem in as much as X is leeward to A and A, as windward boat, must keep clear of X under **Rule 37.1**. (*When overlapped — a windward boat shall keep clear of a leeward yacht.*) To make matters still worse there is D even further to leeward of A. That is the situation, what are the options for A?

Before we look at those options, let me just point out that A is guilty of not thinking ahead, observing what other boats are doing and planning her course of action in good time to avoid getting into such a mess. The first option A has is simply to hold her course, but slow down enough to avoid hitting B or C. The problem with this plan is that X to some extent, and most certainly D, will be able to retain their boat speed and get to the layline, tack to starboard and present an even longer barrier of starboard tack boats to the by-now wallowing yacht A. So let's give that idea up if we can find a better one. She could immediately tack to starboard herself, accepting that she will not lay the mark and thus will have to tack back to port and back to starboard again. The problem once again is that X and D are likely to be able to position themselves on the layline behind B and C and get round the mark before A can even tack back to port to approach the layline. So A gives that idea a miss too. Now for the better options. Have a careful read of **Rule 42** and **42.1(a) & (b)**. Yachts B and C count as an obstruction; A and X are overlapped and so is D; three of them are well within four boat lengths of the obstruction.

At the four boats' length A could have called for "Water" to bear off under the sterns of B and C, at three boat lengths she could have called again, but to call for water in the position illustrated in Diagram 2.1 is pushing it a bit. Does it allow enough time for X and maybe D to hear the call and to respond to it? I think it is doubtful and I suspect that if an incident arose out of this situation that went to a protest committee, then the committee would find that the call was made far too late.

Let's just look at the position from X's point of view. X's skipper has a very good judgement of boats' relative speeds and likely intersection points when two boats are on converging courses. He can see that C is travelling at the same speed as X or possibly slightly faster. He reckons that if they were travelling at exactly the same speed then X will just clip the stern of C. Thus all X has to do for himself is to bear off just a touch and he can easily miss C. X does not have to worry about D, because all D needs or can do is to continue sailing on port, not coming anywhere near C, and only being able to tack once X has tacked (**Rule 41.1**). So X and D do not have a problem at all! If A did call for water in this position, it is quite likely that X would in fact just bear off a little more to allow A to duck under C's stern anyway, without any fuss. But if aggressive and highly competitive, skipper X might reply to A's call for water "No, too late you tack". Or he might bear off, but protest A's late call. The best solution for A — and she is lucky that there is one — is to start to tack to starboard immediately but planning it so that she can slip round to starboard right up the stern of B and as near as she dares to C, without forcing C to take any avoiding action to miss A, until A is on the new tack. (**Rule 41.2 Transitional**: *A yacht shall neither tack or gybe into a position that will give her right of way unless she does so far enough from a yacht on a tack to enable this yacht to keep clear without having to alter her course until after the tack or gybe has been completed.*)

Now once A has tacked to starboard she will be in the position shown in Diagram 4.2, with all the other four yachts in their new relative positions too. A paid due regard to **Rule 41.2** and did not

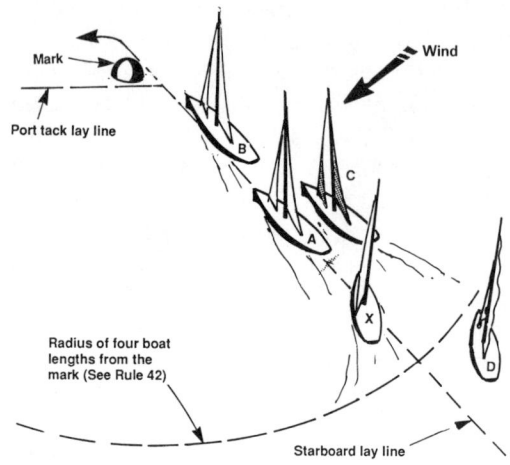

Diagram 4.2

get in the way of C or force her to change course while A was tacking. Now, however, A is firmly on her new tack and C, under **Rule 37.1** as windward boat, must keep clear. A also has luffing rights and so C must be fully alert to the distinct possibility that A, will at the very least, be pinching up a little to gain a bit of space to round the mark safely. It is unlikely that A would sharply luff C, because A would lose too much speed only having just tacked and she needs to gain as much speed as possible to be able to pinch up to lay the mark, but A does have the right too if she wishes. A point worth noting here is that A can only get room to round the mark in this situation provided C is able to keep clear. If there had been one or more boats close to windward of C forward of the mast abreast stem position, then C would not be able to move to windward very much, if at all. Under those circumstances A would have been pushing her luck to the limit, but as shown in Diagram 4.2, she would, I think, still have got away with it. Be very sure of yourself before you try such a manoeuvre, but be aware that others will do it to you.

You will notice finally in Diagram 4.2 that X is in the process of tacking from port to starboard to lay the mark, which in turn allows D to also tack. This brings us to the position in Diagram 4.3. B leads in nice clear water and wind. A slips through into second place and, because our yacht C has had to round the mark wide to allow A room, there is now a very good chance that X will

be able to round the mark tightly and gain some distance on us. X, as yacht clear astern, is under **Rule 42.2(a)**, but because we as C have to round the mark wide to avoid A, if X can slip round in the space we have left there is nothing that we can do. If we bear off to try and close the space we would hit A and as windward boat under **Rule 37.1** we cannot do that. This is the position in which we will leave our yacht C in this chapter. In the next chapter we will take up this race again to cover the two reaching legs and the wing mark.

We will now have a look at rounding the windward mark from the points of view of a fleet of five racing yachts, all approaching the mark on port and having to round the mark leaving it on their port side.

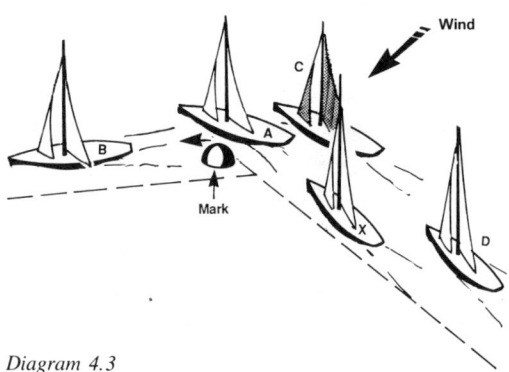

Diagram 4.3

Although I have previously said it is best to approach the windward mark on starboard, it often happens that a whole bunch of port tack boats approach the mark with no starboard tack boats to interfere with their passage around the mark. One example of how this could happen is that if all the yachts had started the race on the starboard tack, and all of them had continued on that tack until they had reached the port tack layline, then of course they would all be approaching the mark on port tack. Diagram 4.4 sets the scene, yacht 1 is clear ahead and close to the mark. Yacht 1 will have to remember **Rule 41** (basic rule, a yacht that is either tacking or gybing shall keep clear of a yacht on a tack.) The yachts clear astern however are bound by **Rule 42.2(b)** and thus must not luff up above close-hauled so as to prevent a yacht clear ahead from tacking to round a mark. Therefore as long as 1 pinches up

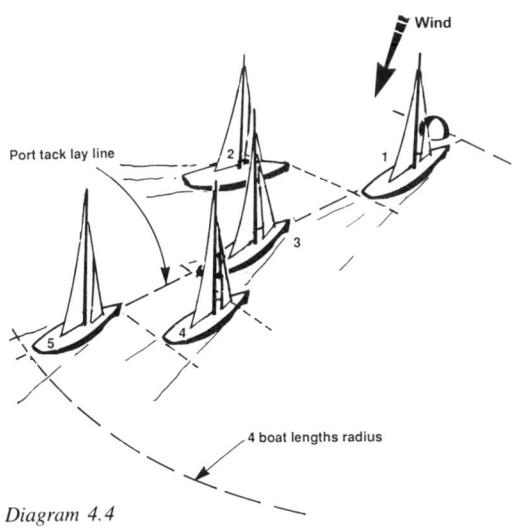

Diagram 4.4

The problem for boats 3 and 4 is that as they bear away, as they must to give 2 more room to round the mark, they are putting themselves into the positions show in Diagrams 4.5, 4.6 and 4.7. Boat 5 gains at least one position over 4 and looks likely to gain another over 3. Boat 5 had got an overlap over 4 before the four boats' length rule, but 5 had not got an overlap on boat 3. Boat 3 is in no position to be able to shut the door on 5 by closing the gap between 3 and the mark, because 3's bow is trapped to windward of 2's stern and by the time she had luffed up or slowed down so as to be able to clear 2's stern, I suspect 5 would be through. It is a dangerous manoeuvre for 5 to try — on this occasion 5 gets away with it but if 3 was not trapped by 2's stern and she was able to sail very close to the mark, 5 could be shut out or pushed against the mark with no defence.

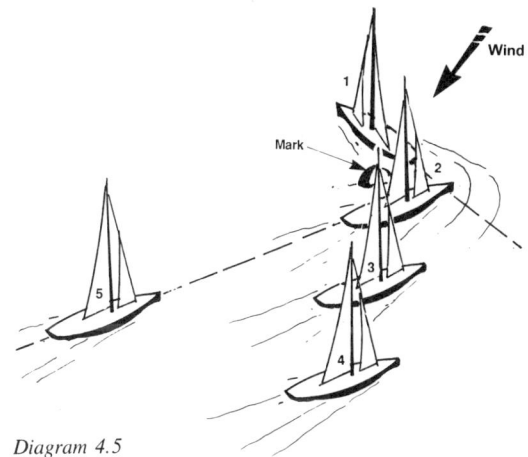

Diagram 4.5

very close to the mark and tacks smoothly around, she cannot possibly get in the way of the following yachts. This calls for fine judgement when the windward mark is a long way away from the bank from which you are controlling your yacht. If you are not sure if you can tack to starboard without getting in the way of a yacht close astern, it is better to continue on port, overstanding the mark, allowing the following yacht to tack to starboard before you do the same. You will drop a position or two, but that is better than losing lots of positions by incurring a penalty for tacking in another yacht's water. For the next three boats though, the position is not so easy. Boat 2 has overlap on 3 and 4 and she requires room from both boats so that she may round the mark safely.

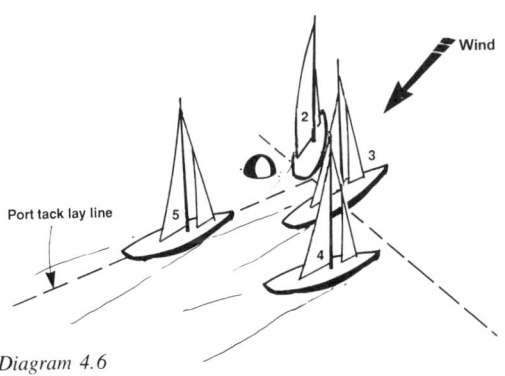

Diagram 4.6

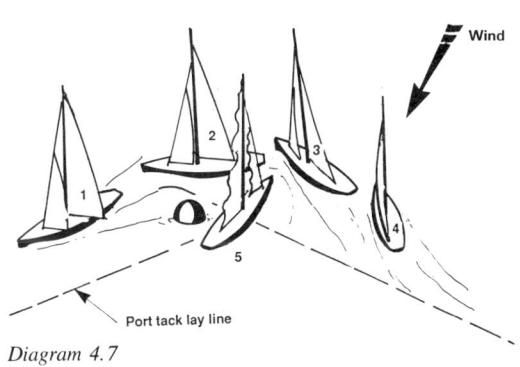

Diagram 4.7

5. The First Reach

Some of you may have been put off by the amount of cold, solid rule that has been quoted at you in the last three chapters. I apologise, but I can assure you that the worst is behind us now, and although we will be constantly referring back to various parts of those rules, we will not need to write them out again in full.

Rule 38 is a good example of a rule that is expressly there to help a yacht being overtaken to windward to defend its position by luffing. Use of the rules to defend position and to attack a yacht in front is quite legitimate and any yacht that tries to win by speed alone, unless leading from the start, is going to find the going extremely tough. If such a speedy yacht tried to overtake a yacht to windward, not knowing anything about luffing, then it would be taken completely by surprise when luffed. Contact would be made and our speedy yacht protested. It is highly likely that it would have no idea that it was meant to do penalty turns either and would be most indignant at the end of the race to learn that it had been disqualified! By the next race of course it would have a rough idea that luffing was something to look out for, but how much easier it would have been if speedy had spent a little time reading a book such as this. As I have said before you can learn as you go along.

You may recall that the last three chapters covered the progress of our novice skipper sailing yacht C in a fleet of five yachts around an Olympic course. Diagram 4.3 of the last chapter is now reproduced as Diagram 5.1 of this chapter, to show the actual position in which we left our intrepid yacht C. She is rounding the windward mark

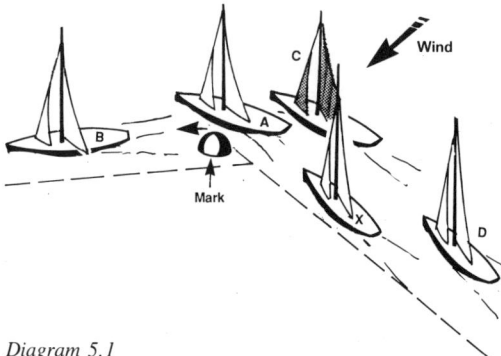

Diagram 5.1

after the first windward beat in third position, but with yacht X able to turn tightly around the mark and thus gain a better position than C. Let us look a little more closely at this, to justify why I think X will then be in a better position. What I am really thinking of already is the position the yachts are going to be in as they approach the magic four boats' length ring around the wing mark. (The distance from the next mark for establishing an overlap to leeward, so as to be entitled to space to round the mark.) It may be obvious from the positions in Diagram 5.1, that if X can round the mark tightly, she will be travelling less distance than C, which had to round the mark wide enough to allow A room. Thus the shortest route around a course will always be to round the mark as close as possible. The factors that make tightly rounding a mark difficult are: other yachts close to you; having an overlap to leeward; yachts immediately ahead rounding the mark at a speed slower than yours forcing you to go wide to avoid them and bad judgement by yourself as to the relative position of your yacht to the mark and thus over-shooting it. Every boat length you sail directly beyond a mark before turning to assume a proper course towards the next mark is, at the very least, a boat's length further that you are sailing than your more able competitors. At a leeward mark it becomes practically two boats' lengths lost for every single boat's length that you overstep the mark by! This is one of the main reasons why radio controlled model yacht skippers walk up and down the bank of the water that they are sailing on. Not for the exercise, but so as to be in the best possible position to see their yacht and to be able to judge its position relative to other yachts and the marks.

By the nature of the Olympic type of course being a triangle of marks, you are always going to have at least one mark across the water away from the bank on which you are standing controlling your yacht. There will often be flags or markers set upon the bank limiting skippers' travel in either direction along the bank. Race organisers are well advised whenever possible to allow skippers to get as near as possible to the windward mark, and to be able to walk back as far as possible to the other mark nearest the bank too. Skippers must bear in mind that they need to be in a position to hear other skippers' protests and hails, plus any calls from race observers. The skipper who does not bother to walk the bank rarely gains anything and stands to lose an awful lot.

However, since most of us cannot walk on the water, what are the clues to help us when rounding distant marks? Believe me it can be very very difficult when you are in a bunch of yachts approaching a distant mark. Yachts behind you tend to blanket your yacht from your view and the whole thing becomes very tense. Whatever you do don't panic! If you are a leeward-most yacht then keep shouting for overlap, move on the bank to get a better view of your yacht and keep a close eye on any yachts ahead to get an idea as to when to round the mark. Yachts being overlapped by other yachts to leeward can do nothing other than to keep clear of such yachts, only rounding when the inside yachts start to round, thus you can end up going very wide!

In less congested situations clues to help you judge your relative position to the mark are: shadows from your sails crossing the mark, if the sun is in the right direction; the wake of your yacht touching the mark; the mark moving because you have hit it! (this is not a very good clue, because it means that you have got it all wrong and now have one or two penalty turns to do!); lastly, part of your yacht being obscured by the mark shows that you have gone past it. If the bank that you are sailing from has some ground with height nearby, then it is often to your advantage to gain that height which will give you a much better view of distant marks. Come down again to bank level when approaching the marks near to the bank.

A few lines ago I mentioned that if you hit a mark you would have one or two penalty turns to do. This is true and **Rule 52 Touching a Mark**, sets out the conditions:

52.1 *A yacht shall neither:*
(a) touch:
(i) a starting mark before starting, or
(ii) a mark that begins, bounds or ends the leg of the course on which she is sailing, or
(iii) a finishing mark after finishing and before clearing the finishing line and marks,
nor
(b) cause a mark or mark vessel to shift to avoid being touched.

52.2
(a) When a yacht infringes Rule 52.1, she may exonerate herself by sailing well clear of all other yachts as soon as possible after the incident, and remaining clear while she makes two complete 360-degree turns (720 degrees) in the same direction, including two tacks and two gybes.
(b) When a yacht touches a finishing mark, she shall not rank as having finished until she first completes her turns and thereafter finishes.

52.3 *When a yacht is wrongfully compelled by another yacht to infringe Rule 52.1, she shall be exonerated:*
(a) by the retirement of the other yacht (or by the other yacht accepting an alternative penalty when so prescribed in the sailing instructions) in acknowledgement of the infringement, or
(b) in accordance with Rule 74.4(b), Penalties and Exoneration, after lodging a valid protest.

I will now expand upon this rule. 'Touching the Mark' means just that — please note that the slightest touch by any part of your yacht, booms, sails, flags etc counts as a touch and turns *must* be done. If you touch a starting mark before the start but during the countdown, you must do two turns. You may however do the turns immediately, you do not have to wait until the starting signal. (You must of course keep clear of other yachts while doing your turns.) The penalty for touching a starting mark can be as severe or light as the time remaining to you before the starting gun. If you touch a mark *that begins, bounds or ends the leg of the course that you are sailing* then you must do turns.

If you touch the wrong side of the mark *before* you have rounded the mark, then you must sail clear of the fleet and execute your two turns *before* you attempt to sail around the mark! If you simply touch the mark during the normal rounding of it or after having rounded it, then you must sail clear of the fleet and execute your two turns as soon as is possible. You keep all of your racing rights while sailing well clear of the fleet, you then lose them once it is obvious that you are executing your turns. *You must not obstruct any other yacht while executing your turns.* You have no rights and will, incur another penalty. (**Rule 45.1**) Before we get back to the race with yacht C let's just have a quick look at what you need to do if you attempt to sail round the mark in the wrong direction.

Every mark has a correct side, direction and sequence to be rounded. The course must be specified in the sailing instructions, which in turn must be in writing and made available for inspection before the start of the racing. At club level it is more common that the course will be called out before the start of the first race and any subsequent changes similarly called out before the next race. The easy way to see what is required is to look at **Rule 51.2** *A yacht shall sail the course so as to round or pass each mark on the required side in correct sequence, and so that a string representing her wake, from the time she starts until she finishes, would, when drawn taut, lie on the required side of each mark, touching each rounding mark.* So if you start to sail around

a mark of the course on the leg you are on in the wrong direction, you must turn around and go back on a reciprocal course so as to unravel your string before rounding the mark on the correct side. Diagram 5.2 helps to illustrate this.

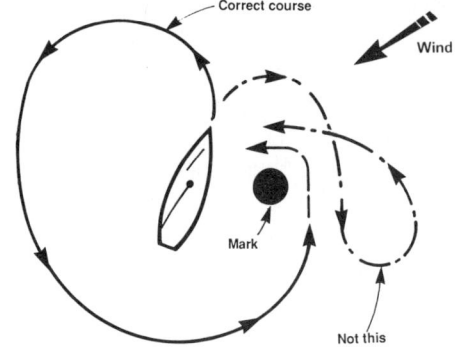

Diagram 5.2. Mark to be left to port

One last small point on all this, just make a note of **Rule 51.5** *It is not necessary for a yacht to cross the finishing line completely; after finishing, she may clear it in any direction.* A yacht finishes as soon as *any* part of it crosses the line. She may then clear the line by continuing to cross the line and sail off beyond the course or she may bear away and return to the course side of the line. In either event she must keep clear of the finishing marks while clearing the line and *must keep clear of other finishing and racing yachts.* Therefore it is prudent to continue on over the line and to keep well out of the way of other yachts until all yachts have finished. You can possibly be disqualified as a finished yacht if you obstruct yachts that are still racing.

Diagram 5.3 takes us past the windward mark, showing all five of our racing yachts on a broad reach sailing towards the wing mark. We are skippering yacht C and as we feared, X has gained an overlap to leeward. Why is that a problem? Well, if all the yachts were to retain their present relative positions right up to the wing mark, X would still have an overlap and would round the wing mark with a much tighter radius than C. By the time the mark would have been rounded X would most likely have drawn clear ahead. The other problem is that D might well be able to slip in to leeward as well, tightly rounding the wing

48

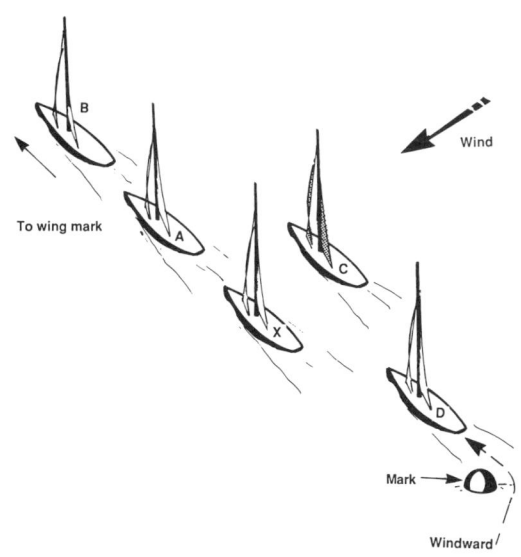

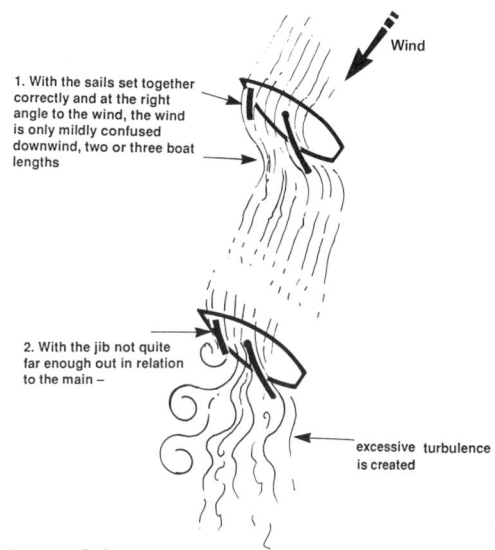

Diagram 5.3

mark and gaining distance on C. From this you might well gain the impression that there is some advantage in attempting to overhaul yachts ahead to their leeward rather than to their windward sides. In my opinion you would, generally speaking, be correct. However C did not really have any choice — circumstances at the windward mark have put her in the position she is and as previously stated, it was impossible for her to prevent X from getting an inside leeward overlap.

What can C do to make the best of her position? It is not all bad news — as the most windward boat, she is getting clean wind and is in a position to put dirty wind on boats to leeward. As the wind passes round and over a yacht's sails it becomes disturbed, an area of low pressure is formed to the immediate lee of the yacht's sails and, as the wind gradually fills in again to leeward of this area, eddies and other confusions occur. Diagram 5.4 may help to illustrate this to you. Any other yacht sailing in this area of confused wind will be at a disadvantage. It will not enjoy the same driving power as a yacht in clean wind. To a lesser extent, there is also the problem of sailing through disturbed water. It takes more effort to sail through another yacht's wake, than it does to sail through undisturbed water. Yacht C in Diagram 5.3 is probably only suffering from the wake of B and would be sailing inside the

main wave of her wake, which would be fairly dissipated by the time C reached it as well. So there is a good chance that she can proceed at a better speed than X and possibly A. Because A is probably suffering more from the effects of sailing in B's wake, C will have to remain alert to the possibility of A luffing C up, should C get too close to A. However, at the same time A has to remain aware of the fact that if she luffs up C too much then she might well put herself to windward of B and allow X to slip through to A's leeward.

Diagram 5.4

These are some of the main thoughts that should be passing through racing skippers' minds as they race up the reaching leg to the wing mark. The novice is probably much more concerned with being able to keep in sight of his boat and trying to keep the wind in its sails. How to keep the wind in your sails takes a bit of experience. As your yacht sails farther away from you, it is more and more difficult to see correctly what aspect the sails have to the hull and also exactly what direction the hull is travelling in. By keeping a close eye on the relative positions and directions of other yachts in your vicinity you ought to be able to spot quickly any deviation in direction by your yacht from the general direction of the next mark. As to the sails, if you notice that your boat speed is slowing down in relation to other boats near to you, then you need to check your

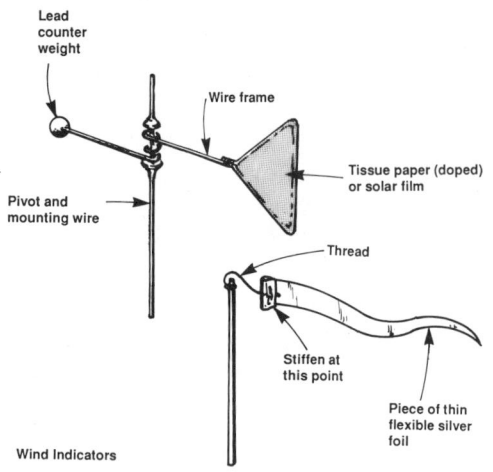

Lead counter weight

Wire frame

Tissue paper (doped) or solar film

Pivot and mounting wire

Thread

Stiffen at this point

Piece of thin flexible silver foil

Wind Indicators

Diagram 5.5

sail setting. If the sails are flapping a bit, you need to sheet in a touch to get the wind driving you properly again. If they are not flapping and you are slowing down, then it is likely that you need to sheet out a little. Try and get to know the approximate position of your transmitter control in relation to actual sail position. Ideally, with the control fully or nearly fully up, your sails should be fully sheeted out for running. Around the halfway mark (neutral) your sails should be somewhere near the reaching position, and fully down should have you sheeted in for a beat. Having a burgee on top of your mast can help you spot shifts in wind direction, although again it becomes an eyesight test the farther away from you the boat sails. The pattern of the wind upon the water is usually a much clearer indication of what is going on. Always keep an eye on the setting of the sails of yachts near to you. There are clues to be had. Again for the poor old novice it is all you can do to keep an eye on your own boat and six inches in front of its bow. This is understandable, but it does become rather worrying when another yacht pops up from nowhere into your narrow view — you have no time to take avoiding action and no time to think who is right or wrong. A collision is the usual result with you having to do the turns. So do spare time to look all around your yacht to keep yourself aware of what other yachts are doing.

We now need to look at a short rule that is most important when we are sailing on a free leg, that is a reaching or running leg of the course. **Rule 39 Same Tack — Sailing Below a Proper Course after Starting:** *A yacht that is on a free leg of the course shall not sail below her proper course when she is clearly within three of her overall lengths of a leeward yacht or of a yacht clear astern that is steering a course to leeward of her own.* If we look at this from the basic premise that yacht racing should be fair, then remember that if an overtaking yacht tries to pass to windward, then the yacht being overtaken has the defence of being able to luff. Therefore, if a yacht wishes to expose itself to the hazards of overtaking to leeward and into the windward yacht's dirty wind, that is considered handicap enough, without the overtaking boat having to put up with the boat ahead bearing off to make matters even more difficult. Therefore if the boat ahead is sailing straight towards the wing mark (or the leemark) then, as an overtaking boat to leeward, you can protest the leading boat if it starts to bear off to stop you gaining an overlap to leeward, once you are within three boats' lengths. A proper course is open to interpretation, but ignoring tides and river currents it may be described as the shortest course to the next mark. You would also have to consider any wind shadows that such a course might sail into. In such a situation, it could well be argued that a proper course in fact forced you to sail below a direct course so as to keep in the wind.

However, at this stage let us stick with the simple definition that a proper course off the wind is the shortest course to the next mark. Should the boat you are overhauling start to bear off, you must hail it first and give the boat a chance to respond to your hail. If it persists in sailing below a proper course, then protest it loud and clear twice. A collision is not necessary to prove an incident — the obstruction itself is enough if obvious. The protested yacht must either break clear of the fleet and accept the alternative penalty of two complete turns or simply continue to sail and attend the resultant protest meeting after the race, arguing its case. **Rule 39** is a most useful rule from an attacking point of view, because it allows you to gain the all-important overlap to leeward, which on an

50

Olympic course gives you the inside overlap at the wing and leeward marks. Thus it is quite natural that the boat clear ahead will want to do everything in its power to stop you gaining such an overlap. Its recourse is to anticipate what is going to happen and sail below a proper course *before* any boat astern comes within three boats' lengths of it. That of course is not always possible. That is where we are going to leave our intrepid yacht C in this chapter.

6. The Reaching Legs

Diagram 6.1 (which was Diagram 5.3 of Chapter 5) shows the position we had left our yacht C in the race we are participating in of five yachts belting around an Olympic type of course. We are not last so far and the five boats are still fairly close together. It must be said that in real life it would be highly likely that the boats would be more spread out by now. It is, however, much more convenient to be able to draw diagrams that include the positions of all five boats without using up all of the centre page each time! It also helps to illustrate various points easier. Anyway, in a large fleet of yachts racing, while the fleet might get well spread out there will often be little bunches of yachts having their own race within a race right round the course.

As skipper of boat C we have a problem! (Besides being a novice that is.) If we look ahead to rounding the wing mark, which we will be leaving to port (our left) as we round it, and if we remember about giving inside overlapping boats at four boats' lengths from the mark room to round the mark, we can see that X is likely to gain a place and possibly D as well. You can see that as we would have to round the mark wide enough to allow X to round it as well, D might slip through the gap we leave. What can we do? I'm afraid the answer is, at this level of racing, nothing other than try to sail faster than the other boats so as to be able to draw ahead of them enough not to have to give them an overlap at the wing mark. Go faster than the other boats? Us being complete novices! What is the alternative? Slow down enough to let X and D overhaul you and then duck under D's stern to try to get an

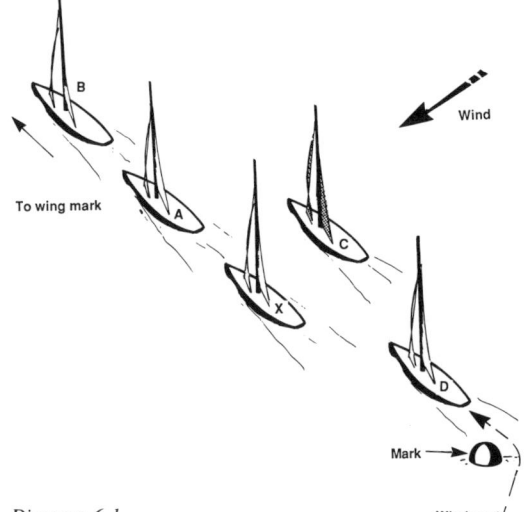

Diagram 6.1

inside overlap. To do that we'd be giving away three boats' lengths before we even started to fight back. If we did achieve that all-important overlap before and at four boats' lengths from the wing mark though we would certainly regain fourth position for the second reaching leg. So the alternative plan does have some merit, but let's stick with the immediate decision we made and try to gain speed or distance over X.

As we covered in the last chapter, usually as you have rounded the windward mark and proceed towards the wing mark your boat will be sailing farther away from your control point on the bank. Therefore it becomes more difficult to see accurately how your sails are set. Here are some clues to help you. Firstly when not racing, practise doing complete turns of your yacht near to the bank. Practise keeping the sails full and driving through all points and also feed into your memory bank the relative positions of your transmitter's control stick for the winch for all the various settings of the sails. Then you will have some idea of the angle your sails are at when too far away to judge by eye. Next, when on the reach, study the behaviour of your yacht's sails — if they are flapping they need to be sheeted in a bit. If the boat is going slower than others around it and is heeling over too much then the sails need easing out a touch. Be gentle with your adjustments and constantly study the effects of your adjustments to your boat's relative speed.

As yacht C in Diagram 6.1 we have the benefit then of clean air, i.e. there are no boats to windward of us confusing the wind's direction. We may also just be in clean water, keeping just ahead of the wake yacht A is producing. If we get caught in A's wake it will very likely slow us down. B's wake will have spread far enough to reach beyond the water we are sailing through, but it will have largely dissipated and our objective here should be to keep inside of the leading edge of B's wake anyway. This is how we shall proceed up the first reaching leg. Now let's just have a think as to what rules are most likely to affect us on the reach. Firstly if we start really to gain distance on yacht A there is the very real danger of A luffing us! Remember luffing, where A might suddenly change course heading up as tight as she likes into wind but not beyond, causing us as the overtaking boat to windward to respond to her luff and have to luff up as well. That usually has the effect of slowing us down more than the luffing boat and if, heaven forbid, the luffing boat caught us unprepared and managed to touch us there are going to be penalty turns to do! Remember the number of this rule? No nor do I, who cares, we can both look it up at the end of the race if we need to — the important thing is that we remember the actual workings of the rule. Do you remember the way to curtail a luff? If the boat you are overtaking is slow to spot the danger or is not very interested in luffing you, once your mast is abeam the stem (pointed bit or bow) of the boat being overtaken to windward, you as overtaking boat can shout ''Mast abeam'' which immediately removes the luffing rights

from the leeward boat! If it was in the process of luffing you, it immediately has to stop luffing any higher, and if it was not luffing you at all it must retain its proper course. Yes **Rule 38** covers all these points and more.

Should we be lucky enough to pull clear ahead of yacht X, we might well be tempted to ease across to leeward and assume a course more directly in front of X. In this case we must be mindful of **Rule 39 Sailing Below a Proper Course after Starting**. Do you remember we covered it in the last chapter? I'll quote it again because it is only a short little rule.

A yacht that is on a free leg of the course shall not sail below her proper course when she is clearly within three of her overall lengths of a leeward yacht or a yacht clear astern that is steering a course to leeward of her own.

While it is only a short little rule, as I previously stated it is a very useful rule for the yacht over-taking to leeward on reaching and running legs. However, for us in the present situation being discussed it works against us to some degree. Notice that the rule says that we must not sail below a proper course. Since we are a yacht ahead and to windward of X, our proper course to the next mark will be a converging course with X's projected course. Therefore it is possible to ease our boat nearer to a position where we are actually more or less dead ahead of X, but we must *not* sail below that proper course! The reason for doing this would be firstly, to ensure that X did not get an overlap at the wing mark and secondly, had absolutely no chance of trying to nip into any gap we might leave as we round the wing mark. All of the above should give you some useful clues as to some of the thoughts that will be going through a competitive club skipper's mind. Some of them might even go through your head as you are lying in bed after a tough day's racing wondering what went wrong. In fact, it is very useful to cast your mind back after the racing in a peaceful place and rerun the races, trying to learn from your mistakes and the mistakes of others that you spotted.

Back to the race — our yachts are rapidly approaching the wing mark and the magic four boats' length circle. Why magic? Well remember

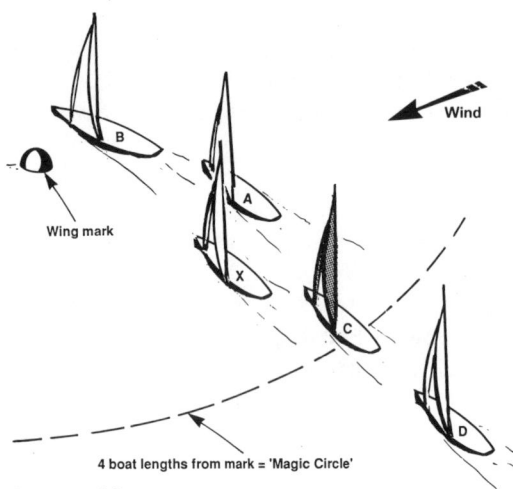

4 boat lengths from mark = 'Magic Circle'

Diagram 6.2

that is the point at which you must have established or held an inside overlap to be able to retain that overlap as you round the mark. **Rule 42** covers overlaps and mark rounding. It is such a long rule that anyone that can remember it word for word can't possibly be sailing — they would still be studying the rule book! Diagram 6.2 shows the up-to-date position in our imaginary race — although we tried hard to maintain good speed on the reach, we did not manage to overhaul X. However, we did manage to keep clear ahead of D and at the four boats' length circle from the mark we do not have to worry either about giving an overlap or maintaining one. All we have to do is to judge when to round the mark! This is easier said than done and often becomes an eyesight test. Here are one or two clues to help you judge for yourself when it is safe to round that distant mark. Boats ahead are a good guide — you can easily see if they hit the mark or miss it on the right or the wrong side. Their wake will also give you a clue as when to turn. Your own yacht's wake will also give you a clue — when it touches the buoy you will be well past. Sometimes the sun will be obliging and cast a shadow from your sails on to the mark. That then gives you very useful feedback. In Diagram 6.2 yacht X has an overlap on A and had it at the all important four boats' length from the mark. Thus A *must* allow X enough room to round the mark in a seamanly manner. There is often discussion as what constitutes seamanly-like rounding. Most people

would agree that it means you must round the mark fairly tightly and assume a proper course towards the next mark immediately. The variables are that some allowance must be made for skippers' varying sailing skills and eyesight. Also, much depends on the weather and, in particular, the wind strength. It is one thing to round a mark well in a breeze and quite another in a gale. In the gale you would be quite entitled to give the mark a wide berth. But, remembering the fair sailing principle, you must do your best according to the prevailing conditions.

One thing you should try to avoid, although it is very difficult, is giving too much room to inside overlapped boats at the mark. Let's look at Diagrams 6.3 and 6.4 drawn with only two boats' lengths of progress being made from 3 to 4. Look at what A has done! Not only has it given away

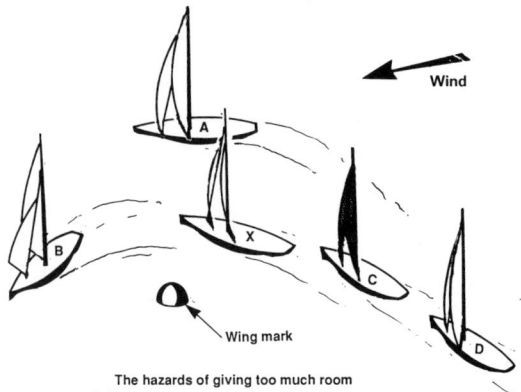

The hazards of giving too much room

Diagram 6.3

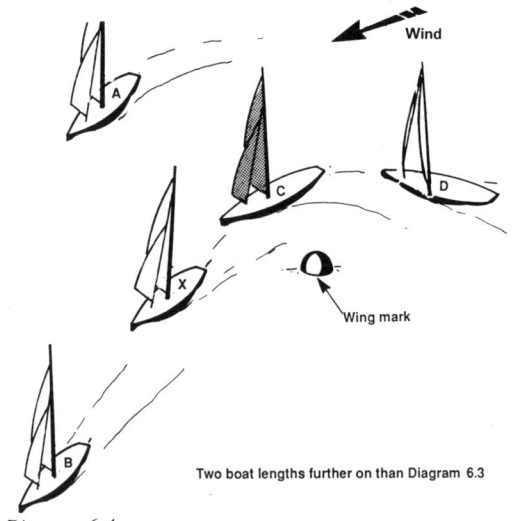

Two boat lengths further on than Diagram 6.3

Diagram 6.4

a place to X as might have been expected, but it has also given away a place possibly to our boat C. In fact it is even possible that D might gain an inside overlap on A by the time they get to the leeward mark! All because A went far too wide rounding the wing mark. Do remember that every boat length you sail beyond such a mark is another boat length you have to sail back just to get back to where you were before! Therefore it costs you two boats' lengths to sail one length beyond a mark in the wrong direction! Boats very often give away five to ten lengths and more while rounding distant marks. Again, before the start of a day's racing, if you have the opportunity it is well worth your while to get your boat on the water (having checked your frequency with race control, and taken your peg) and sail around the course. Practise sailing right around the distant marks and even try to bump into them to get their positions fixed into your mind.

Do remember however that when actually racing the only thing worse than overstanding the mark is hitting it! If you hit it then you have to immediately clear the fleet and execute your two complete penalty turns before resuming your course. Remember that if you hit the mark before rounding it, then you do your turns before rounding the mark. If you brush the mark as you round it, then you do your turns after rounding the mark. You must keep clear of racing yachts while you are doing your turns. Doing turns usually means that you lose places on the water! So try to avoid hitting marks. One point that not too many skippers know is that if another yacht forces your yacht onto the buoy, you may protest the other boat and thus not have to do any turns for hitting the mark. Under **Rule 52.3** you will be exonerated provided the protested yacht retires, accepts its alternative penalties or lodges a valid protest after the race. The third thing, of course, that can dramatically slow your progress around the mark is having a collision with another yacht since that is highly likely to mean you are going to have to accept the alternative penalty of doing two complete turns. If the wind is fairly light, or if the race organisers want to save themselves a lot of protests, it will often be put in the sailing instructions that the alternative penalty will be

reduced from two complete turns to one complete turn. **Rule 52.2** will also be reduced from two complete turns to one complete turn in this case.

Back to the race and Diagram 6.4. Yacht A is feeling a bit sore — by her own stupidity places have been lost. What can she do now to try and salvage something? The first thing she can do is to head up to wind more on a converging course with C and hope that will accelerate her a little bit faster than C is travelling. She can then close and try to engage in a little luffing match. However, by the time she draws close, C has got her mast abeam of A's stem and calls "mast abeam" curtailing A's attempts to slow C down. (Our novice skipper must have been reading this book!) A's skipper gives up and falls back on purpose and comes up under C's stern manoeuvring into a position just behind and to windward of C's stern. Yacht A also now has full luffing rights over D, so all is not lost. This brings us to the position shown in Diagram 6.5. The reason why everyone is very busy trying to get an overlap to windward on the boat in front is that they will be rounding the next buoy leaving it as usual to port, thus the inside overlap required to round the leeway buoy is a windward one. If you can have just a bit of an overlap over a leeward boat established at the magic four boats' lengths circle from the mark, then that boat has to allow you room at the mark, and because you will round the mark on a tighter radius than the outside boat you should come out clear ahead! That is the theory and as I ask in the diagram, there is the not inconsiderable possibility of being luffed as you try to establish your overlap on the boat in front. In

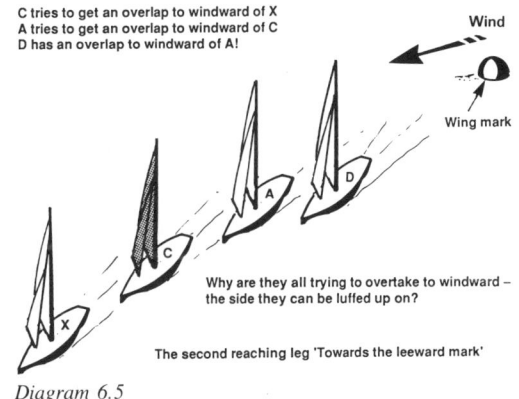

C tries to get an overlap to windward of X
A tries to get an overlap to windward of C
D has an overlap to windward of A!

Wind

Wing mark

Why are they all trying to overtake to windward – the side they can be luffed up on?

The second reaching leg 'Towards the leeward mark'

Diagram 6.5

fact, the correct defensive tactic for the reaching boat in front having a pursuing boat nibbling her windward stern quarter is to initiate a luff followed by a rapid return to course which will hopefully push the overtaking boat clear astern again. This is a leg that can see some very interesting luffing tactics ranging from the tactic just described to long length luffing matches that have the participants sailing more towards the windward mark than the leeward mark! All good fun, but do remember to keep an eye on what the rest of the fleet are doing meanwhile, otherwise as mentioned before you may find back markers (those behind the luffing pair) slipping through to leeward whispering 'thank you very much'!

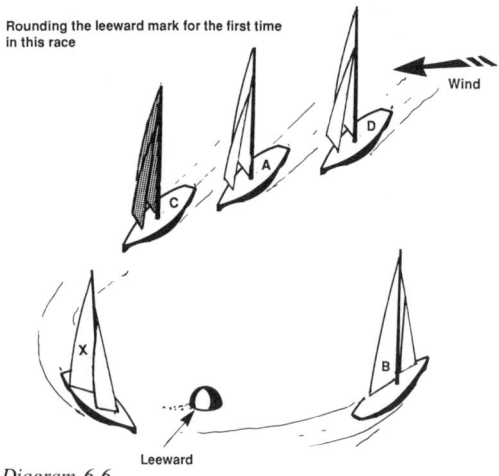

Diagram 6.6

The rounding of the leeward mark can be quite interesting or even stressful depending upon the number of racing yachts near to your yacht as you round, your experience and state of your nerves! The higher the strength of the wind the more interesting it gets! Imagine, you have a crowd of yachts hammering down towards the leeward mark on a good reach, all wanting to whip round that mark immediately hardening up to a close-hauled course towards the windward mark. Remember that we are rounding the mark to port. Some of the yachts as they round will want to tack across to starboard and some will perhaps continue on port. All yachts are likely to slow down as they are rounding the mark depending upon the varying abilities of skippers to maintain full drive in their sails. (This requires

excellent co-ordination between rudder control and winch control — it takes a bit of practice and concentration. The concentration can easily be lost in the excitement of the moment!) One or two yachts may even seem to engage reverse gear which can be a bit disconcerting if you happen to be the poor boat screaming along behind them. If there is a bit of wind blowing you most definitely need to be thinking ahead and to be hyper-alert. Yachts that are clear ahead of you as you enter the four boats' length circle have to be allowed room to round the mark — you have a duty to keep clear of them in anticipation of their rounding manoeuvre. Why? Go back to **Rule 42** and in particular **Rule 42.2** and I quote *When not overlapped a yacht clear astern a) A yacht clear astern when the yacht clear ahead comes within* four *of her overall lengths of a mark or obstruction shall keep clear in anticipation of and during the rounding or passing manoeuvre, whether the yacht clear ahead remains on the same tack or gybes. b) A yacht clear astern shall not luff above close-hauled so as to prevent a yacht clear ahead from tacking to round a mark.* So there you have it, however, let us continue to read the same rule as it goes on to cover what the duties are of the yacht clear ahead. *A yacht clear ahead c) A yacht clear ahead that tacks to round a mark is subject to Rule 41. Changing tacks — Tacking and Gybing. d) A yacht clear ahead shall be under no obligation to give room to a yacht clear astern before an overlap is established.* So, once again, as is often the case by digging into one rule we find that we have to refer again to another rule if we are to understand entirely what the rule is getting at. Here is **Rule 41** reproduced. **Changing tacks — Tacking and Gybing. 41.1 Basic Rule** *A yacht that is either tacking or gybing shall keep clear of a yacht on a tack.* **41.2 Transitional** *A yacht shall neither tack nor gybe into a position that will give her right of way unless she does so far enough from a yacht on a tack to enable this yacht to keep clear without having to begin to alter her course until after the tack or gybe has been completed.* **41.3 Onus** *A yacht that tacks or gybes has the onus of satisfying the protest committee that she completed the tack or gybe in accordance with* **Rule 41.2. Rule 41.4 When**

Simultaneous *When two yachts are both tacking or both gybing at the same time, the one on the other's port side shall keep clear.*

"Good heavens!" I hear you cry, "by the time I've remembered all that lot I'll be right up someone's transom!". Relax, you do not have to remember all of that or even have to quote it all at someone on the water. You do not even need to remember the rule number! If you need to look up the rules after the race all you need to remember is that you were rounding a mark, so you need to look for the rule that applies to rounding marks (**Rule 42**) and that will lead you on in turn to any other rule you may need to check on. Back on the water, however, this is roughly what you need to know from a bare survival point of view.

Yachts clear in front of you need to be missed — if they slow down and get in your way steer to go round them, not through them. Remember that you are rounding the mark on port, there will be yachts in front of you that will rapidly tack to starboard. Be prepared for this, because once they are pointing in a starboard close-hauled position relative to the wind direction, they are considered to be on starboard whether or not their sails are full and drawing. At that stage you must take avoiding action!! So plan your action. Are you clear ahead enough of a boat astern to be able to tack to starboard yourself to avoid a tacking boat ahead or do you need to duck under the tacking boat's stern? If there are several boats ahead all tacking to starboard, you may not have any choice but to tack to starboard, if so, call immediately for water to tack to miss obstruction. Any yacht close to your stern must then allow you room to tack to miss that obstruction which in this case is one or more starboard tacked boats. That's it really, keep clear of boats in front and do not tack in the paths of boats behind unless you have time to get across on to starboard tack *before* they have to take avoiding action. They do then need to have a bit of room to take that avoiding action, so bear that in mind if you value the port side of your yacht.

7. Rounding the Leeward Mark

In the last chapter we left yacht C about to round the leeward mark for the first time in third place, but with two other yachts claiming overlap on her. That means that C has got to leave enough room for A and D to round the mark in a seamanlike manner (see Diagram 7.1).

Yacht C, as she alters course towards the mark, picks up a bit more speed than A and D, the two boats she is obliged to leave room for while rounding the leeward mark (because A had an inside overlap on C at the magic four boats' lengths and D at that time had an inside overlap on A). Thus C draws clear ahead of A and D with that little bit more speed and cuts close to the mark, hardening up to close-hauled and proceeds to beat up the windward beat still on the same tack. Now C as a novice did not know any better, but the fact of simply drawing clear ahead of an inside boat that had established an overlap at the four boats' lengths from the mark does not remove C's obligation to allow room at the mark for A and D. As long as she managed to keep clear ahead with slightly better speed she can risk cutting close to the mark, *but* if while executing this manoeuvre she slows down, and A and D catch up without there being any room left for A and D between C and the mark, then there is most definitely going to be trouble! At the very least A and D will have to bear off to avoid hitting C and will protest her, or more likely, they will try to squeeze in with much shouting for water and contact will be made and again protests will be shouted. Yacht C will be the guilty party either way, so do be very certain when closing the gap on yachts that have a legitimate overlap on you.

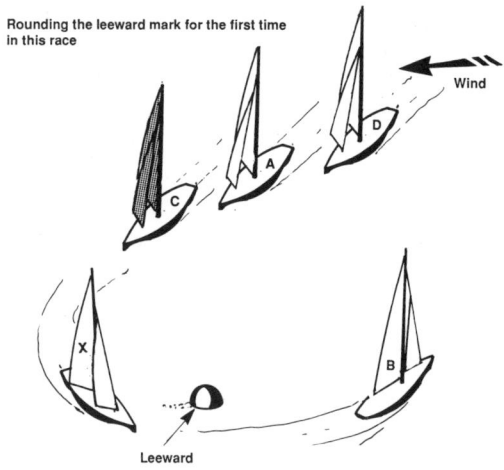

Rounding the leeward mark for the first time in this race

Wind

Leeward

Diagram 7.1

If you don't get it right it can be very expensive in position terms — by the time you have done all of your penalty turns the fleet will be disappearing into the sunset!

As we said earlier C had beginner's luck and got away with it, D retained her actual inside overlap on A and so we get to the position in Diagram 7.2. You will notice that D has got 'command' over A. That is to say that at present A cannot tack to starboard without tacking in the water of D, forcing D to tack to avoid A. This of course is not allowed. Remember the rule? No, well here it is again to refresh your memory.

Rule 41 Changing Tacks — Tacking and Gybing.

41.1 Basic Rule
A yacht that is either tacking or gybing shall keep clear of a yacht on a tack.

41.2 Transitional

A yacht shall neither tack nor gybe into a position that will give her right of way unless she does so far enough from a yacht on a tack to enable this yacht to keep clear without having to begin to alter her course until after the tack or gybe has been completed.

41.3 Onus

A yacht that tacks or gybes has the onus of satisfying the protest committee that she completed her tack or gybe in accordance with Rule 41.2.

41.4 When Simultaneous

When two yachts are both tacking or both gybing at the same time, the one on the other's port side shall keep clear.

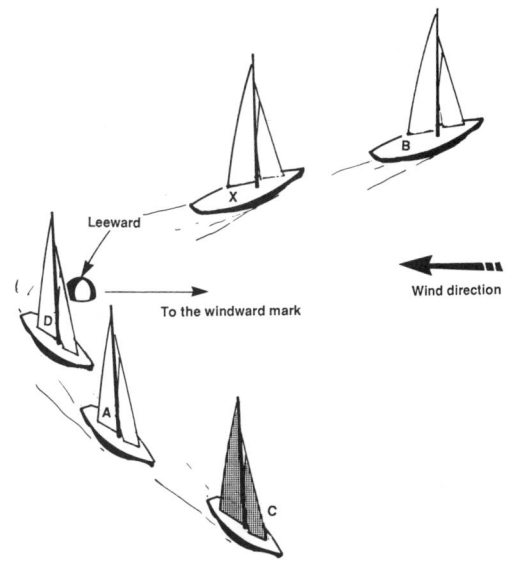

Diagram 7.2

There you are, **Rule 41.1** and **Rule 41.2** cover the situation we are talking about. Thus A cannot tack on to starboard until D tacks to starboard, or until A cannot only pull clear ahead but slightly to windward as well. In the positions shown in Diagram 7.2 even C has got to be very careful if she is considering tacking to starboard because you must remember that if you alter course sharply a fin boat will pivot about the fin. The fin being somewhere near the centre of the boat on the fore to aft plane means that, as the bow swings around to the new starboard course, the stern is swinging backwards and to leeward right into the path of A. The trick is to execute the tack to starboard very gently to start with — this should have the effect of taking your boat slightly to windward of any yacht following close behind directly in your wake. Once you have gained that little bit of space to windward you can speed up your tack, swing across to starboard and drive away.

Talking of driving away, one of the very common mistakes novices make is stalling the boat immediately after tacking. There are several ways of achieving this rather disastrous state of affairs. Giving the boat full rudder and swinging it violently round will stop it very effectively. Full rudder will mean different things on different models — some rudders can swing through ninety degrees either side of straight ahead, these will be the best sort of brakes you can use — others may swing through forty-five degrees

either side of straight ahead or less. The only time having a lot of rudder movement is useful is before the start in tight manoeuvring positions or when trying to avoid a collision. The disadvantage of having so much rudder movement is that in the tension of racing you simply tend to apply full rudder whenever tacking or altering course, especially for the poor old novice of course. As time goes by you remember to be a bit gentle with the rudder control stick. So that is one way to kill all boat speed while tacking. The next favourite way is to tack into a head to wind position or into such a close-hauled position, say twenty-five degrees to the wind, or so that the wind cannot possibly supply you with motive power. Tacking into irons is a very expensive mistake because it certainly does take a little while at least to recover. There is no easy way out of being in irons. If your boat is sitting there with no way on, then moving the rudder is going to have little effect — the wind pressure being the same on each side of the sails is likely to keep the boat in irons for several seconds at least. As soon as you see the boat beginning to fall off to one tack or the other, encourage it to continue in that direction with your rudder, ease the sails out a little until you can spot some forward motion, bear off a little more, get up speed, sheet back in and assume a proper course towards the back of a rapidly disappearing fleet. *Do not get into irons*. In fact the best thing to do is practise getting into irons and finding your own solution to the problem. Once you've done that, practise tacking again and again in all strengths of wind, so that you don't *ever* get into irons again! Getting into irons just before the start is always a good one, think ahead all the time to avoid being forced into such a situation. The final favourite way of killing all speed while tacking is to slam the boat across losing all speed, and assume the same close-hauled direction as boats ahead, but boats that have way on. (Way by the way, excuse the pun, means motion i.e. the boat is moving at a speed greater than the current of the water in some direction or other. A boat normally thus will have 'way on' as it proceeds forward in the direction it wishes to go. If it is beating up to windward it will also have a certain amount of leeway, i.e. the wind tends to push the boat not only forwards but sideways towards its lee. Leeway is resisted by the action of the hull biting into the water, the fin and the rudder.)

The boat that has assumed a close-hauled windward course immediately after tacking without any forward motion will simply make an awful lot of leeway with very little forward motion if any. The trick here is to let your sails out just a little so that the wind can flow over the sail more easily and start to push the boat forward. As the boat picks up speed you can sheet in the sails to their normal close-hauled position again. Do remember that a normal close-hauled position does not have the main boom yanked right tight into the centre of the boat. The actual position will vary from boat to boat according to the set of the sails and type of rig. However, as a rough guide perhaps around five degrees off the centre-line for the main boom and ten to fifteen degrees for the jib boom.

In light to medium winds the best method of tacking is to be very gentle in turning through through the first half of the tack, then give slightly more rudder for the second half of the tack. You will then find it is possible to retain quite a bit of the boat's speed right through the tack and into the new course. This then dramatically cuts down the chances of going into irons and also the

chances of losing so much way that leeway is all that is being made. In heavy winds you have to pick your moment much more carefully. The first thing to try and choose, if you have any choice in the matter, is a moment when the wind is not at its strongest. Try and look ahead on the water for those telltale signs of a gust coming — dark patches on the water rippling towards you. Then either tack before the gust or wait until the gust has passed. Next study any wave formations that may be about, a wave can either help you round to the new tack or simply push you back onto the old tack — it all depends on the angle of attack. Sailing into the wave at less than forty-five degrees may push you back, at over forty-five degrees there will be more chance of it helping you around. The final thing is maintain good boat speed or get good boat speed by bearing off a touch, sheet the sails out a little and throw the boat around to slightly beyond a close-hauled course on the new tack, gently sheet the sails back fully in gaining speed at the same time and resume a close-hauled course.

Having mastered the art of tacking a little more, the next thing we have to do is start to think ahead. We have successfully rounded the leeward mark and, therefore, have mastered to some degree all of the basics required to get our yacht around a course in one piece. We are now entering our first full length windward beat and there are a number of options open to us as to how we zigzag our way up the length of the course to the windward mark. More by luck than judgement, our trusty yacht C would appear to be third at present in our little fleet of five. As such we have positions to lose and possible positions to gain. We are at least in the thick of it and have the opportunity to think things out a bit rather than simply be tagging along at the end of the fleet following the rest of them.

From the leeward mark, if the course has been laid correctly, the windward mark should be directly upwind! That of course is rarely the case because of wind shifts, but since we are on the novice level of rounding the course let's assume for the moment that the wind is remaining in a constant direction, coming directly from the wind-ward mark to the leeward mark. What are the

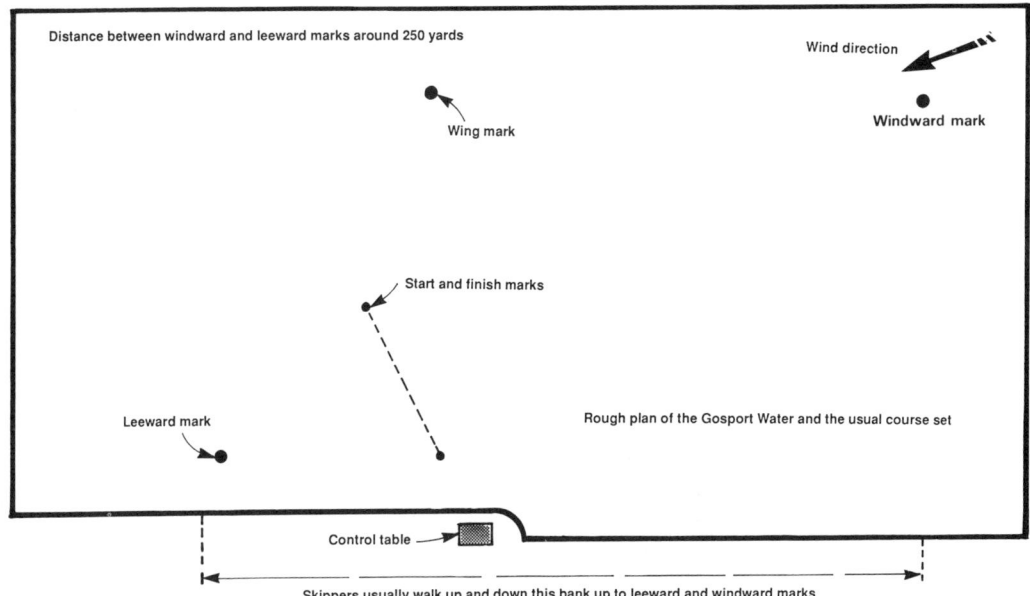

Distance between windward and leeward marks around 250 yards

Wind direction

Wing mark

Windward mark

Start and finish marks

Leeward mark

Rough plan of the Gosport Water and the usual course set

Control table

Skippers usually walk up and down this bank up to leeward and windward marks

Diagram 7.3

things we need to think about before making a decision to tack? The first point is that tacking most definitely is going to slow us down a bit, some more than others. The second point is what boats are around us? Can we even tack if we want to? The third point is what obstructions are approaching or are we approaching. Obstructions approaching us could be other yachts crossing our intended course on starboard and the most usual obstruction we would be likely to be approaching is the bank or edge of the lake!

The usual way courses are laid out on lakes and ponds tend to have the start near to the bank and the leeward and windward marks nearer to the control bank than the wing mark, which is usually right over the far side of the water or a fair way away from the control bank. Diagram 7.3 shows the sort of typical layout you might find. This is a very rough layout of the Gosport Model Yacht Club's water, a purpose-made pond constructed early this century for the racing of vane controlled model yachts. The pond is around 900 feet long and two hundred feet wide. In its time the club has hosted all of the major National and International events. It is a marvellous facility and is without doubt the best water available in the south of England. The entire area around the lake is paved and it enjoys fairly open aspects on

all sides. There are, however, various banks and buildings in the middle distance that influence the direction of the wind, causing local bends etc. which are enough to test anyone's awareness.

The point I am trying to illustrate here though is obstructions. Let's imagine Diagram 7.2 on the Gosport water at the leeward mark and you will see that an obstruction in the form of the bank soon presents itself to boats that, having rounded the leeward mark, stay on port. (Not for long if they wish to keep their bows looking pretty!) This now brings in a new dimension for our novice skipper to consider and one that he needs to consider fast! All choice of tack is removed from him or her, there is only one thing to do and that is tack to starboard to miss the bank. We have already pointed out to the skipper of C that he must not tack in A's water and suggested a few tips to avoid that happening. Therefore C swings across to a starboard tack and misses the bank. However what about A? Yacht A has a big problem, she cannot tack to starboard because she has D sitting on her windward stern port quarter and under **Rule 41** she cannot tack in D's water. What is she to do? Well, as you have no doubt guessed, since the racing rules are all about fairness, there has to be a rule to cover this situation, otherwise poor old A could just be

61

forced into the bank!

A quick flip through the racing rules enables us to find a rule that mentions obstructions — **Rule 42**. Desperate reading of the rule sheds no light on our awful plight, however, just as we are about to fling the rule book at the skipper of D for being such an inconsiderate so and so, we notice **Rule 43 Close-hauled, Hailing for Room to Tack at Obstructions**. This is the rule we now need to study and since we are now sixteen feet high and dry up on the bank, let's take a little time off from the nail-biting action and study this rule in its entirety.

43.1 Hailing

When two close-hauled yachts are on the same tack and safe pilotage requires the yacht clear ahead or the leeward yacht to make a substantial alteration of course to clear an obstruction, and when she intends to tack, but cannot tack without colliding with the other yacht, she shall hail the other yacht for room to tack and clear the other yacht, but she shall not hail and tack simultaneously.

43.2 Responding

The hailed yacht at the earliest possible moment after the hail shall either:

(a) tack, in which case the hailing yacht shall begin to tack immediately *she is able to tack and clear the other yacht; or*

(b) reply "You tack" or words to that effect in which case:

> *(i) the hailing yacht shall immediately tack and*
> *(ii) the hailed yacht shall give the hailing yacht room to tack and clear her.*
> *(iii) The onus of satisfying the protest committee that she gave sufficient room shall lie on the hailed yacht that replied "You tack".*

43.3 When an Obstruction is Also a Mark

(a) When an obstruction is a starting mark surrounded by navigable water, or the ground tackle of such a mark, and when approaching the starting line to start and after starting, the yacht clear ahead or the leeward yacht shall not be entitled to room to tack.

(b) At other obstructions that are marks, when the hailed yacht can fetch the obstruction, the hailing yacht shall not be entitled to room to tack and clear the hailed yacht, and the hailed yacht shall

immediately so inform the hailing yacht. When, thereafter the hailing yacht again hails for room to tack and clear the hailed yacht, the hailed yacht shall, at the earliest possible moment after the hail, give the hailing yacht the required room. After receiving room, the hailing yacht shall either retire immediately or exonerate herself by accepting an alternative penalty when so prescribed in the sailing instructions.

(c) When, after having refused to respond to a hail under Rule 43.3(b), the hailed yacht fails to fetch, she shall retire immediately or exonerate herself by accepting an alternative penalty when so prescribed in the sailing instructions.

That's it — this chapter's dose of straight hard rules is out of the way. You imagine trying to read all that lot as you approach an obstruction and you'll see why it is better to have some idea of the bare bones of the rule, so here they are.

Rule 43 only applies to yachts that are close-hauled i.e. beating to windward sailing as close to the wind as possible and on the same tack. Next it applies to the boat clear ahead or to the leeward yacht that is going to hit the obstruction first unless it puts in a rapid tack. This is the boat that hails "Water to tack". In our racing situation that we left a few dozen lines ago it would be up to A to hail "Water to tack". Yacht D is now obliged either to tack immediately or to reply with an instruction such as "You tack" or "You tack and take my stern". Let us look at these alternatives a little more closely. Take a look at Diagram 7.4(i) — in this situation D as boat clear astern has two options, the first is to tack to starboard immediately without making any verbal reply. In this case as soon as A sees that D is tacking she *must* immediately start to tack herself. If she simply holds on her original course she opens herself liable to being protested and would be obliged either to retire or to accept an alternative penalty (720-degree turns). The second choice D has is to reply "You tack" or words to that effect — again A *must immediately* tack. Yacht D is obliged to keep clear of A as she tacks, but D now has the advantage of being able to sail a little nearer to the obstruction before tacking and thus get into a position where she is

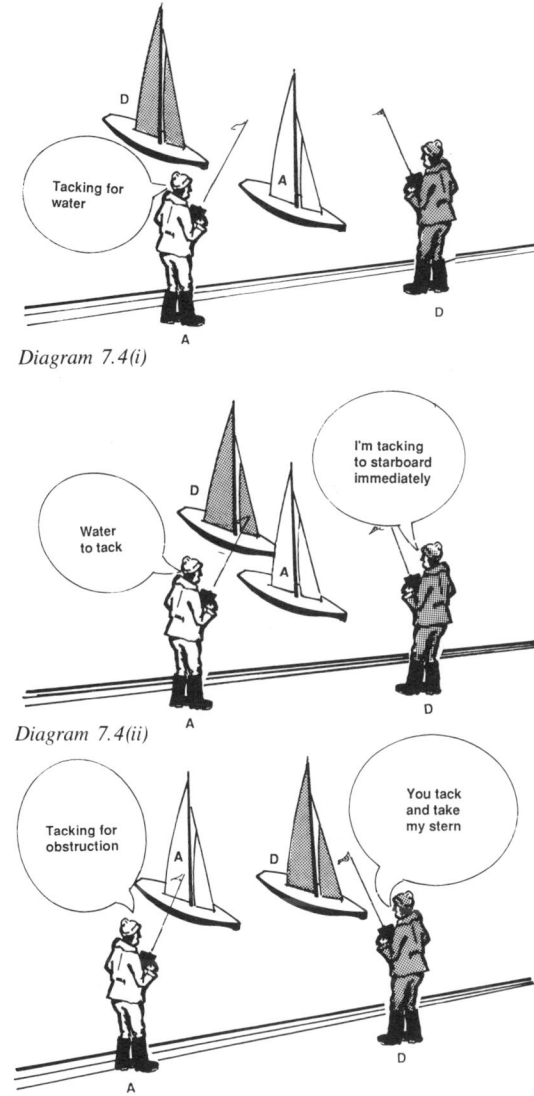

Diagram 7.4(i)

Diagram 7.4(ii)

Diagram 7.4(iii)

sailing a starboard course slightly to windward of A which, in theory at any rate, gives her command over A. In Diagram 7.4(ii) the only practical option D has is to tack immediately and hope to keep slightly ahead to leeward in clean air. The alternative of trying to slow down enough to duck under A's stern would not really work because as soon as D replies ''You tack'', A has to do just that. She would consequently slow down somewhat and D has nowhere to go except to tack to miss A anyway with the additional handicap of being in the wrong if there is now a collision!

In Diagram 7.4(iii) D could tack immediately with no reply in which case A again is obliged to immediately tack herself which would keep her astern and slightly leeward of D. The better option of D is to reply ''You tack and take my stern''. Yacht D has to be sure when making this reply that A will in fact be able to miss D's stern if she tacks immediately she hears D's instructions as she is obliged to do. If, as a result of obeying D's instructions, A touches D then D is in the wrong. This is not to say that A can simply aim at D in an effort to penalise D. Yacht A must simply execute a normal tack from the close-hauled course of port to the close-hauled course of starboard in this case.

You may notice that A hailed something different in every example above — this is simply to give you an idea of the common hails you will hear. Any of those hails would have done in any of the situations illustrated. The replies however are pertinent to each particular situation. *The most important point about* **Rule 43** *is that after having made your hail you cannot do a thing until you hear a reply from the hailed boat. If you do not hear a reply then hail again.* The common mistake is simply to make the hail for water and to immediately tack without waiting to hear what reply the hailed boat wishes to make. This mistake will render you immediately liable to being protested either by the hailed boat, race observers or other racing yachts. This is an important rule — use it wisely. The other point about this rule that is commonly misunderstood is that the onus is solely upon the yacht clear ahead or to leeward to determine what is and what is not an obstruction. This usually again concerns approaching the bank, where it is known that the water gets shallow. Once the boat clear ahead or to leeward thinks that it needs water to tack to miss whatever it may hail, the hailed boat *must* respond as set out above. It *cannot* reply ''Rubbish there is plenty of water there,'' it must respond. The hailed boat's only recourse is to protest the hailing yacht after the manoeuvre has been completed for making an incorrect hail. This is a pretty difficult protest to make successfully, so the hailed yacht had better be sure of its facts and be certain that a race observer was watching the incident otherwise she stands little chance of getting the hailing boat penalised. Do bear in mind that weed growing in the shallows near the side of the pond can also be considered to be a legitimate obstruction. All other sorts of obstructions come under **Rule 42** as does the shoreline when not approaching it close-hauled.

Having got to grips with the basic problems of calling for water at the bank or other continuous obstruction, let us return to consider the options that are before us immediately after rounding the leeward mark. There is always the ever popular choice of swinging immediately onto the starboard tack and away. I think it seems to be a natural progression from the sweep around the leeward mark. To my mind there are two things wrong with it. Firstly you are in great danger of losing all of the acceleration that can be gained as you sweep around the leeward mark and onto a close-hauled course. Secondly, you are, by tacking immediately onto starboard, sailing a course that will put you through all of the wakes that have been, or are being created, by boats still reaching down to the leeward mark. Even if you are the only boat on the water, you will put yourself through your own wake. This has the effect of slowing your boat down to some degree and therefore should be avoided. I guess, perhaps, the big worry to immediate starboard tackers is that a boat hard on their heels might gain an overlap to windward and thus hold command over them. The trick to stop that happening is harden up and sail a very high course for a few seconds before reverting to your normal close-hauled course — this should make it very hard for the following boat to get above you. So, in my opinion, you are far better off simply to continue on the tack you round the leeward mark on, making the most of the little turn of speed you can get if you co-ordinate the rounding of the leeward mark with the correct speed of sheeting in your sails. This is quite a difficult manoeuvre to execute correctly and is certainly worth practising. The easy way of getting into the groove is to use very little rudder and let the sheeting in of the sails swing you round and up to the close-hauled position. Obviously, if you can do this better than your surrounding opponents you are going to gain some ground.

When you have sailed some little distance from the leeward mark and you are proceeding at a normal close-hauled speed for the prevailing conditions, that is the time to make your choice of course up the windward leg (provided there is enough water available for you to stay on your existing tack).

Having retained good boat speed, we are now in a position to look ahead and wonder what we are going to do to get ourselves up to the wind-ward mark and still be in the race. In a moment we will rejoin yacht C in our imaginary race, but before that a useful tip for the novice skipper would be to copy whatever the club star is doing. If you are so new you don't even have a clue who the club star is, copy the boat that is leading. Follow the sort of course he or she is following and you will have a better chance than simply worrying yourself silly as to which tack you should be on. Do keep an eye out for what the boats around you are doing, and do remember if you are on port or starboard so that you will know if it is you that has to give way to a boat on the opposite tack or vice versa.

Have a look at Diagram 7.5 which again shows the prevailing course at Gosport. You will see that I illustrate three courses, all of which cover more or less the same distance. In theory, they will all be exactly the same distance if the wind holds a steady direction. The course up the middle of the lake sailing fairly close to the rhumb line (i.e. the direct line from the leeward mark to the windward mark) would be the recommended course from a safety point of view, because you would be well placed to take advantage of any wind shifts that might occur. However, you would put in two more tacks, which would have the effect of making the course a bit slower. If I knew the wind was that steady (it never is) I would opt for the course that had me approaching the windward mark on starboard. Why? Because then, at the important time, by approaching the mark on starboard all other boats coming in on port will have to give way to me. This leaves me free to concentrate on rounding the mark without hitting it.

One of the lucky things about model yacht

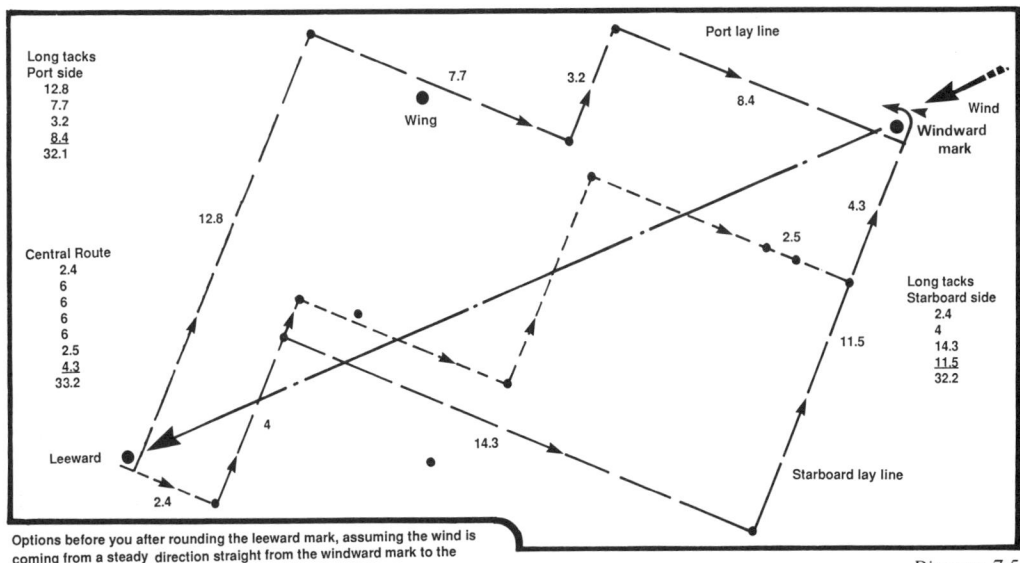

Long tacks
Port side
12.8
7.7
3.2
<u>8.4</u>
32.1

7.7   3.2   8.4   Wind
Windward
mark
Wing   Port lay line

12.8   4.3   2.5

Central Route
2.4
6
6
6
2.5
<u>4.3</u>
33.2

Long tacks
Starboard side
2.4
4
14.3
<u>11.5</u>
32.2

11.5

4   14.3

Leeward   Starboard lay line

2.4

Options before you after rounding the leeward mark, assuming the wind is
coming from a steady direction straight from the windward mark to the
leeward mark - a very rare occurrence!

Diagram 7.5

racing is that we have lots of races happening in one meeting. Therefore, if you have your memory banks in gear, you ought to be able to remember from the immediate past race what sort of things the wind is up to and what sort of course to the windward mark appeared best last time. This does not always help since the wind does swing about, but it should give you some clues. It certainly should help you to identify who is sailing their boat best and therefore is the best person to try to get near to copy their course.

Now let's cast our minds back to our imaginary race which, for the sake of realism and to tie in with some of the diagrams in this chapter, might as well be situated at Gosport. Have another look at Diagram 7.2 — you may recall that our yacht C had caught a lucky gust right just before rounding the leeward mark and managed to draw clear ahead of yachts A and D. Yacht C's only option now is to tack to starboard to miss the rapidly approaching bank. Because there is an obstruction approaching, C might as well hail for water to tack to make quite sure that she is not going to be tacking in A's water. Yacht A replies "You tack" and C immediately starts to tack. Yacht C does not have to execute a super rapid tack — she may simply tack at her normal speed — but she *must* start that tack *immediately* she has heard the hailed yacht's response to her call. Yacht A has

decided to sail under C's stern and to sail on a little further before tacking so as to try and get possible command of C farther up the beating course. One of the dangers of trying this at Gosport, with a course laid out as Diagram 7.5, is that the water is quite shallow at that particular point near the bank and also there is weed on the bottom. Yacht A is so keen to try and get back a position or two that she is prepared to gamble, also there is a fair wind blowing so she is heeling over nicely thus drawing less depth of water — with a quick tack she stands a good chance of getting away with it. Yacht A, of course, must bear in mind that she has D sitting upon her port stern quarter. Thus she must leave enough room to sail on her present course towards the bank to allow time for her hail for water to tack to be answered *before* she can actually tack. So a couple of boat lengths from where she wishes to tack, A calls for water to tack, D immediately tacks to starboard without any reply. The moment A sees that D is definitely tacking she *must immediately* start to tack herself, even if there is a dramatic windshift that would favour A to continue on the port tack. In that case she would still tack to starboard as obliged, regain speed and tack back to port to make best use of the change in wind direction.

We are not going to cover wind shifts in any

65

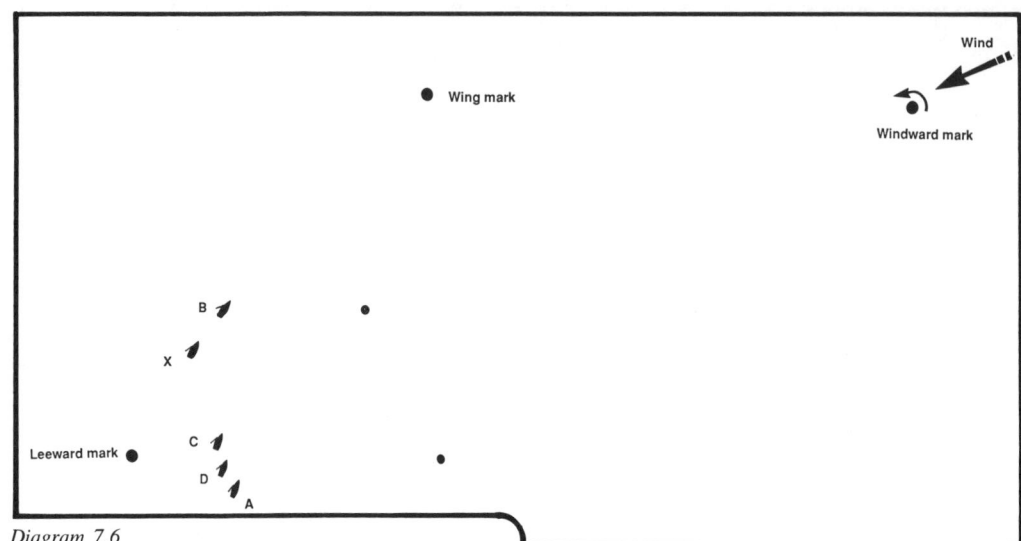

Diagram 7.6

detail but be aware that such things exist, and as suggested, keep an eye on what the hot shots are doing. The important thing to appreciate at this stage is that the best gains are to be made on the windward beat. However the best gains of all are to be had by reading the wind correctly.

We need first to sharpen up on our tacking ability and our general awareness of what is going on around us. It is so easy to become totally wrapped up in your own boat when you are first racing that the rest of the lake and the racing fleet fade into obscurity. You are so busy trying to make the thing go! Sails in, sails out, twitch the rudder, bear off, head up, try and remember what bear off means etc. etc. All of a sudden a boat appears in your little bubble of concentration and whacks your boat for six. You haven't a clue where it has come from and the incident is over before you have time to work out if you were on starboard or port. Believe me, it happens. So, if for the remainder of this race we concentrate on getting the basics right, it will help to get them set in your mind until they become second nature. Then you will have spare thinking time to consider other aspects of trying to win.

We now have our five racing yachts all on starboard spread over quite a distance. Diagram 7.6 gives an idea of how it might look superimposed on our outline plan of Gosport's water, which by the way is not to scale, but roughly gives the general idea. The other point I am at present taking licence with is that most radio Marbleheads can sail closer to the wind than forty-five degrees — at the moment it makes for easy drawing and frankly whether the angle of attack to the wind is forty-five or thirty-five degrees is a bit academic, the theory is the same in either case. You will notice that in Diagram 6 our yachts look a little bit lost, but they are roughly to scale. It is a long way up that windward beat which is good because it gives people a chance to demonstrate their skills in clawing back lost positions. Before we leave the windward beat until the next chapter let us just consider as a novice the main points we have to bear in mind.

1) Don't get into irons.

2) Nice smooth tacks.

3) Remember what tack we are on.

4) Remember to call for water when approaching obstructions close-hauled.

5) Remember to wait for a response or tack from the hailed yacht.

6) Remember then to tack immediately ourselves.

7) Try and get 'command' over boats just ahead.

8) Think about sailing in 'clean-air' and 'undisturbed water'.

9) Keep an eye on what is happening around your boat.

10) Keep an eye on the hot shots now and then.

11) Use the rudder as little as possible.

8. The Second Windward Beat

I want to start off this chapter repeating the list of eleven points with which we finished the last chapter, expanding upon them to remind you on some of the basics that ought by now to be well fixed in your mind.

1) Don't get into irons (i.e. stuck head to wind, sails flapping with no forward motion).

2) Nice smooth tacks. (To avoid getting into irons and to maintain good boat speed. Because if you turn your rudder too sharply it acts not only to alter your direction but as a very good brake!)

3) Remember what tack you are on. (This is very important because of **Rule 36** : *Port tack boats give way to starboard tack boats*.) The tack you are on is the same as the side of the boat *opposite* to the side that the main boom is nearest. While beating it will be the windward side of the yacht, that is the side nearest to the direction the wind is coming from. If you were a dinghy sailor sitting on the side of your dinghy facing the sails to stop it from heeling over too much then your right arm would be nearest to the bow if you were on a starboard tack, or your left arm would be nearest the bow if on a port tack.

4) Remember to call for water when approaching obstructions close-hauled (i.e. as you are approaching the bank or shallows and there is a yacht close to you that in normal circumstances would prevent you from tacking, you call ''Water to tack to miss — bank, shallows, etc.'').

5) Remember to wait for a response or an immediate tack from the hailed yacht (such as ''You tack'' or ''Take my stern'').

6) You then must follow the hailed yacht's immediate tack by tacking yourself immediately they have or immediately obey their instructions, tacking immediately if so instructed, either in front of the hailed yacht or behind if instructed to take their stern. In either case your tack is immediate and if you then hit the other yacht then the fault is with the hailed yacht.

7) Try and get 'command' over boats just ahead. This means trying to get to windward of a boat clear ahead so that it cannot tack (because if it did tack it would be tacking in your water) until you tack.

8) Think about sailing in 'clean air' and 'undisturbed water'. Clean air is air that has not been disturbed by the passage of other yacht's sails through it. If you remember, as the wind hits a yacht's sails its direction is altered as the wind is split to bend in front of the sail and to flow along the sail and off its leech. There is then an area of low pressure downwind of the sail with confused wind vortexing and filling in the low pressure area. There is also a high pressure area on the windward side of the sail which bends the direction of the wind. The area of influence is approximately half a boat's length to a boat's length to windward and three boats' lengths to leeward. Disturbed water is the wake moving through the water of yachts that are ahead of you or sailing on another course near to you. Usually sailing through such water will slow you down — the exception is when the wake approaches your yacht from astern it is possible to gain speed from the wake if you can 'surf on it'.

9) Keep an eye on what is happening around your boat. By keeping an eye out you should not be caught unaware by any starboard close-hauled boat that you have to give way to. Do remember that if you are on port, with another port tack boat near to you, that a starboard boat approaching on an intersecting course is considered to be an obstruction and you can call for water to tack to miss the starboard boat.

10) Keep an eye on the 'Hot Shots' now and then. 'Hot Shots' come in all shapes, sizes and varying abilities. They are the ones that are winning all the races or most of the races that particular day. They may show you a good course to sail up the windward beat and they might respond to wind shifts first, but don't bank on it. In fact, as you get better it can pay to do the exact opposite on rare occasions. For the moment they can provide some useful pointers for the struggling novice.

11) Use the rudder as little as possible.

You will probably notice throughout this book that we spend more time on the windward beats than any other point of sail. This is because the windward beats are the major battleground, more positions are gained and lost on the windward beat than any other leg of the course. Why? There are obviously more opportunities for errors to be made, the sort of errors that I have just warned you about in the eleven points listed. It is the leg of the course that boats will most meet each other on port and starboard tacks as they zigzag up the course towards the windward mark. As soon as you get three or more yachts converging on opposite tacks there is always the distinct possibility of an incident occurring, resulting in penalty turns for someone to do. The wind shifts will play a major part in the changing fortunes of a yacht's beating. In fact, in normal conditions, the windward leg is the only leg where playing the wind shifts properly can gain you enormous advantages. Be aware that the wind can, and normally does, shift direction fairly regularly, such shifts being measured in minutes rather than hours. The wind also bends depending upon obstructions that lie in its path! Look around your local sailing water — there are bound to be objects within a mile of the water that will influence the direction of localised wind. For

example, a solitary tree will cause the wind to split each side of it and to rise up to go over the top of it. The result is confused wind way downwind of the tree. Air behaves much like any other fluid that is flowing — have a look at a stream or a river sometime and study the way the water flows around obstructions. It will give you some clues as to how air behaves as it rushes along in a wind. Just be aware that such things exist and understand that the wind will not behave in the same way all over your local sailing water, even if it is coming from a constant direction. I can certainly remember when I first started sailing a dinghy finding it quite difficult to keep track of where the wind was coming from. Later, learning to windsurf, it was even more annoying to discover that not only was it shifting in direction all over the place but its strength was up and down like a yo-yo. When you are hanging onto a sail to keep yourself up, you tend to get rather wet until you learn to respond automatically to all the wind's little idiosyncrasies.

When you are watching a race that you're not taking part in, concentrate on watching the pattern of the wind on the water as it passes over — this will help you to understand the sort of things I have been writing about. It is also very helpful in any case to learn how to read what the wind is up to by watching the patterns it makes on the water's surface. You will notice in time that different strengths of wind leave different patterns.

Now let's return to our mythical race and take a look again at Diagrams 8.1 and 8.2. We, as usual, are skippering yacht C with yachts D and A behind us, but to windward. Yachts X and B are several boat lengths ahead of us while being three or four boat lengths to leeward. They both had rounded the leeward mark well ahead of C, D and A, but lost a little of their advantage by tacking quickly to starboard and sailing through the wake of C, D and A as those three had approached the lee mark from the wing mark. Yachts C, D and A had also tacked to starboard after approaching the bank as described in the last chapter (see diagram 7.6). What options do we have? The straight answer is not many — we have even less in fact since D and A hold 'command' over us.

That is, we cannot at present tack to port until D and A tack to port because we would immediately get in the way of D and A. That is not allowed because we cannot tack in another yacht's water. **Rule 41.1 Basic Rule** : *A yacht that is either tacking or gybing shall keep clear of a yacht on a tack*. Therefore it would seem that the obvious thing to do is to stay on starboard.

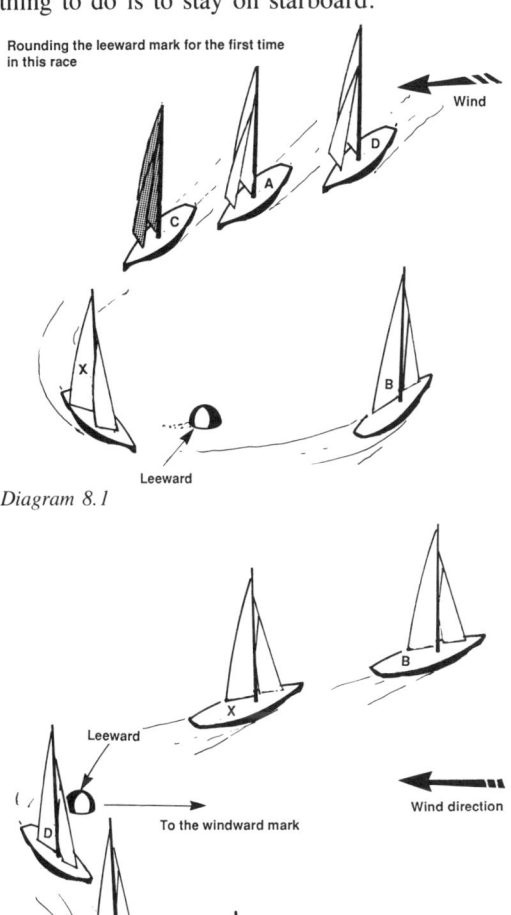

Rounding the leeward mark for the first time in this race

Wind

Leeward

Diagram 8.1

Leeward

To the windward mark

Wind direction

Diagram 8.2

The next thing we want to think about then is how to keep D and A behind us. The best thing that could probably happen would be for D and A to engage in a luffing match. That would slow the pair of them down and would allow us to draw well clear. That is rather grabbing at straws

though. It might be more positive to actually encourage them to engage in a luffing match by violently luffing up D should the opportunity arise. Another tactic we could consider would be to first gain good boat speed relative to the conditions and then to pinch up to windward as hard as we can, easing off a little as we begin to slow down. This could have the effect of slowing D and A down as they in turn have to pinch up to try to retain 'command' over us. Something else we could consider is to free off our sails slightly and go for maximum speed sacrificing direction to windward slightly in the process, in an effort to get better boat speed than X and B and to try and shake off D and A.

This will then perhaps become a test of concentration — how quickly will D and A spot whatever tactic we try? They will notice very quickly any pinching up that we attempt. If it came to a violent luff then there is a chance that we could catch them by surprise. The slight easing out of the sheets and very slight bearing off for more speed might take them a little longer to spot. I suspect it would probably take yachts X and B even longer to spot. They would most likely be feeling safe in the knowledge that they rounded that last mark several boat lengths ahead. They are likely to be engrossed in their own private battle for what they see at present as first and second place. (Depending very much on their level of experience. Let's remember that this is simply an imaginary club race, and not even a club cup race at that, so it is likely to be serious racing of mixed abilities with plenty of room for errors. It must be, we are a complete novice, remember?) Would we, as a novice, consider all the options I have just mentioned? Not unless we had read this book I suspect. We have, however, read the previous chapters and therefore we are well aware of the powers of luffing to defend our precious lead. We are also aware that it can be dangerous to get engaged in a luffing match with one other boat that allows other boats clear astern to overtake to leeward while we are engaged in the heavy luffing action that slows us both down. In this situation there are no other boats behind to slip through, so provided we can slow down both D and A it is worth a crack.

In reality the most common problem for the novice is getting the boat heading on a nice course to windward with reasonable speed. I'm afraid the usual temptation is to pinch the yacht far too high up to wind, losing much too much speed and dying. The other favourite trick is to pull the sails in far too tight after tacking, before good boat speed has been regained. The result is that usually, all forward motion comes to a halt and leeward motion increases dramatically. Let us pretend that we have progressed enough to overcome these absolute beginner's problems and we are progressing with good speed in more or less the right direction. The next observation is that novices rarely manage to keep the boat going well to windward even when they have been astute enough to gain good boat speed and direction after a tack. Obviously the tension of having two boats snapping at your heels is off-putting. However, having a guiding hand to help us, we manage to progress holding that all-important speed and direction. Having achieved that, it now gives us a chance to spare a glance at boats D and A to see what sort of speed and direction they are making. After all they could be relative newcomers to the sport too. They do not seem to be doing any better than ourselves, mainly because, I suspect, D is suffering a bit from our dirty wind to windward and A has the same problem with D's wind. D, of course, not only has to consider ways of overhauling us, he also has to keep A firmly astern if possible. In some ways A is in the best position because she has 'command' on both D and C. Yacht A can choose when she wishes to tack to break away to find clean air and water. The thing she then has to consider is that if she does tack away to port, it is quite possible that D and then C will tack to port also and thus acquire 'command' over A. There is a definite tendency amongst racing yachts to act a little like sheep. One tacks so they all tack — this applies especially to any little groups that bunch up near to each other during the course of the race. Sometimes there is a good reason for the tack, such as the layline has been reached or a wind shift has been correctly read by the yacht first to tack — other times it is simply the herd instinct at work. If you have the option

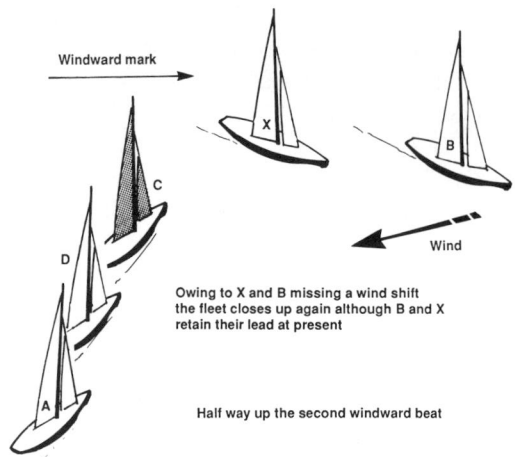

Windward mark

Wind

Owing to X and B missing a wind shift the fleet closes up again although B and X retain their lead at present

Half way up the second windward beat

Diagram 8.3

think before you follow a mass tack — why are they all going and do you really want to go too?

While all this has been discussed we have travelled halfway across the Gosport water still on starboard and still just ahead, but to leeward of D and A. Suddenly X and B tack across to port and a sudden surge of excitement flashes through our veins. A chance to chop them in half as we race towards them on starboard! Yelling "starboard" we inch towards them, only to see them easily slip across our bows and away. The only encouraging thing is that it would seem that we have definitely closed the gap somewhat between X, B and ourselves. However, most annoyingly D and A stay on starboard stopping us from tacking to port to give chase. There simply is nothing that we, as C, can do! We are a bit too far leeward of D to try any luffing tricks and too near to tack to port, even if we wanted to lose a bit of ground and go under D and A's stern. (Which would be a crazy thing to consider anyway. We would lose far too much ground and would be in a bad position for tacking back to starboard in due course to lay the mark.)

The only happy thought we have is that before long we will be approaching the bank. At that time we will be able to call for water and force D and A to tack to port themselves. We should then be in a fairly good position to gain an overlap at the windward mark or, at the very least, hold a position near to D and A to windward that they cannot tack to starboard to lay the mark without tacking in our water. (**Rule 41** remember.)

Let us have a look at the manoeuvres involved as we approach the bank. Diagram 8.4 sets the scene. Can you remember what to do? **Rule 43** is the rule that applies: **Close-hauled, Hailing for Room to Tack at Obstructions**. Well, we are close-hauled and we certainly need room to tack, so at a distance from the bank that allows both D and A time to respond we hail ''Water to tack please''. We then wait continuing on towards the bank. Yacht D hails A in turn, by which time over a boat's length has been travelled. Yacht A responds to D's hail by tacking — A could have simply responded to our hail, without waiting for D to hail, but perhaps she did not hear our hail. If neither A nor D had responded we would have had to hail once more very loudly before taking emergency action and protesting both yachts. As it is, as soon as we see D starting to tack, we *must* start to tack ourselves, even if we would rather have gone on right up to the wall before making our tack. We cannot — we must

tack immediately we see or hear a response to our call. You will see from the diagram that the situation has changed the relative positions of the three yachts quite a bit. Whereas before on the starboard tack all three yachts were almost abreast with C having her nose in front, the positions are reversed. Yacht A is almost clear ahead, with D ahead of C. However the difference is now that C has command over both D and A — neither of them can possibly tack to starboard without tacking into someone else's water! Thus C holds the all important command over D and A. As it stands she is in an excellent position to round the windward mark in third position at least. Yacht A and D will try every trick in the book to get into a position whereby they can tack to starboard without fear of tacking in C's water.

Before we consider their possible tactics further, let us just go back to Diagram 8.4 again and for the benefit of 575 and 590 skippers, who sail without the use of rules, consider what would happen to C if **Rule 43** was not available to use. I suppose the first option would be a violent luff

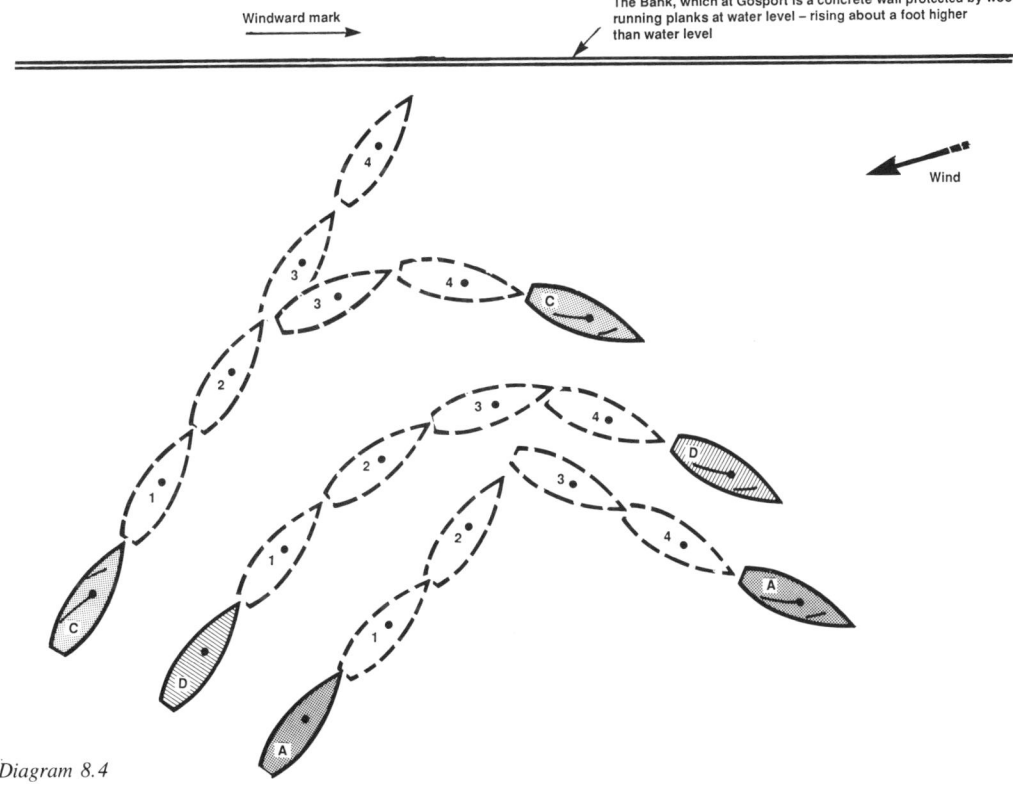

Windward mark

The Bank, which at Gosport is a concrete wall protected by wooden running planks at water level – rising about a foot higher than water level

Wind

Diagram 8.4

71

to encourage D and A to tack, but of course if sailing to 575 or 590 (with almost non-existent rules), D and A do not have to respond to a luff, so contact is likely with all the risk of hooking up and all three boats sailing straight into the bank! Yacht C could let the wind out of her sails and then tack under D and A's stern, losing way and position in the process, plus putting herself in a very bad position for later rounding the mark. She could gybe away maintaining perhaps greater speed and go under D and A's stern with the same resulting bad position. Or she could simply carry on and just hope that D and A would tack before getting to the bank, leaving C just enough room to tack right on the bank and gain some sort of command over D and A on the new tack — very risky!! So **Rule 43** is a rule that puts safety first — in full-sized racing there is very much more at risk than just damaging your yacht as someone forces it into the bank, lives could be lost! This situation illustrates yet again that whenever a situation arises that potentially offers danger to a racing yacht there will be a rule to cover it, to allow the endangered yacht to take action to avoid the hazard while still retaining some sort of course in the direction of the next mark. The rules almost always manage to find a solution to a problem that resolves it in the fairest possible way, so that the yachts involved do not lose their relative positions to each other or so that one yacht is not favoured at the expense of another. In the situation that developed in Diagram 8.4, if we had taken away the bank and the three yachts could have sailed on into infinity, sooner or later they would have reached a point beyond the layline to the next mark and A would have tacked, closely followed by D and C, and they all would have ended up in much the same sort of relative positions as in the diagram anyway. Although, of course, the farther beyond the layline they had gone the more C and D would have fallen clear astern of A as they tacked to starboard. Against that C and D would then be able to sail a slightly faster course to the mark and ought to still to be able to retain their command over A.

Going back to the race, A's objective now is to try and find a way of pinching up to windward higher than D and C, so that by the time it comes

to tack to starboard again she can do so without tacking in the water of D and C. In other words she wishes to break out of the command that D and C at present hold over her. The problem is that pinching up slows you down! The trick is to gain best possible boat speed then to gently pinch up until the speed drops off a bit, then, ever so slightly, bear off to regain speed and pinch up again etc. etc. The problems are the boats behind might just do the same, or worse, one boat might simply bear off a little with better speed and break through A's windshadow to leeward and thus overtake A to leeward to break clear ahead!

The other trick A has up her sleeve is simply to sail on with speed, but lose just enough speed to allow D's bow to draw level with the middle of A's boat, then a sudden violent luff will, with any luck, work wonders. D is going to have to respond with an equally violent luff possibly catching C out. Yacht A as the instigator of the luff is in total control and can plan to bear off smoothly at the end of her luff to regain speed and direction. Yachts D and C can only respond to A's alteration of course back towards the mark once they see it, so have to be slightly behind A in bearing off themselves to regain speed and course. If the luff was very violent it is quite possible that C or D could have been put into irons or even across to the other tack, which is all time delaying stuff. Those are the sort of thoughts that ought to be going through the mind of the skipper of A.

Yacht D has the problem of considering what tactics A might employ against her and what she can do to keep C behind herself and to gain space to windward over C. Sailing in the wake of A and being slightly in the back wind of A is likely to slow D down slightly, but provided she can retain command over A it will not matter much because at the windward mark she will be able to tack to lay the mark before A. Being a truly competitive skipper, D would like very much to round the windward mark before C as well! However if D engages in luffing warfare with C it will possibly allow A to break clear enough ahead to be able, when the time comes, to tack to starboard and complete the tack before coming into D's water. Then, of course, D would have to give way to A, and if A had tacked right on the layline then D would probably have to take A's stern before tacking herself. To make that problem even worse, if C was still in command of D, D would have to let C have enough water to avoid A as well and still would not be able to tack to starboard until C tacked.

Now as C's skipper, once again we have had some insight into the thoughts running through the minds of the two skippers close to ourselves. As a racing skipper you must develop the ability to look ahead, to be able to evaluate the possible tactics of the boats that are near to you and to be able to project forward to imagine what might happen at the next mark. Because what can look like a losing position in isolation on the water can become a winning position when the next mark is taken into consideration. When trying to overtake boats it is vital that you attempt to overtake on the side that is going to offer you an inside overlap at the next mark, unless you have such speed and are so far away from the mark that you know with certainty that you can overtake on the other side, and be clear ahead and more by the time the next mark is reached.

9. The Windward Beat Continued

We have taken a long time covering this particular beat because it is on the windward beat that much of the action takes place. I think it is fair to say that more positions are won or lost on the windward beat than anywhere else. At the end of the last chapter we had bounced off the bank at Gosport, tacking onto port with yachts D and A in front of us but to leeward. We have a slight overlap on D and feel confident that we could hold command over the pair of them right up to the windward mark. Diagram 9.1 should refresh your memories!

Yachts X and B are some little away ahead on the same tack and also to leeward, with B clear ahead and to windward of X. At present B and X do not need to be considered, but D and A most certainly do.

More by luck than judgement we, as yacht C, have managed to get into a good position. While we only just have an overlap on D at present, we most certainly do hold command over yachts D and A because neither yacht is going to be able to tack to starboard as long as we can retain the relative positions of all three yachts. At present D cannot tack to starboard because she would be guilty of breaking **Rule 41.1 Basic Rule** *A yacht that is either tacking or gybing shall keep clear of a yacht on a tack.* Likewise A cannot tack to starboard in the water of D, so both A and D at present will have to wait until C tacks to starboard before being able to follow suit.

Needless to say, neither yacht D or yacht A are going to feel too happy about this situation and they will want to try to extract themselves from this predicament as soon as possible. If they could manage to get clear ahead of C and to windward, they would then be able to tack to starboard to lay the approaching windward mark when it suited them rather than when it suited C. Yacht C needs to be aware of this possibility and prepared to meet any squeezing up to windward by D and A with a similar squeezing up to windward herself. In this kind of situation the winner is often going to be the boat that can point highest to wind while retaining reasonable boat speed. The other way A and D can push themselves into a clear ahead and to windward position of C is by a series of little luffs, trying to push C clear astern and at the same time gain distance to windward of C. Again C must be prepared for luffing tactics to be employed against her. The only way she has of stopping D from luffing her up is to bear off very slightly to gain relative speed over D and to try and establish a quick mast abeam stem position at which stage she can curtail D's luffing chances. She might then be able to retain speed to go on to do the same to A. This, however, is a very difficult manoeuvre and not likely to be accomplished by a novice since it requires good spatial judgement and that only comes with plenty of racing experience. However, there is nothing to stop C just trundling along behind D and A but slightly to windward. As long as she can retain that windward position relative to D and A they are not going to be able to tack to starboard to lay the windward mark until C chooses to let them. In that situation the only letout for A and D will be if X and B cross their paths near to the windward mark on starboard, forcing A and D to tack to starboard to give way to them. In that event A

Windward mark →

The Bank, which at Gosport is a concrete wall protected by wooden running planks at water level – rising about a foot higher than water level

Wind

Diagram 9.1

would call for water to tack to miss an obstruction to D, and D would in turn call for water to tack to give water to A who requires to tack to miss an obstruction. The obstruction being two approaching yachts on a converging starboard tack, X and B. This still might not help D and A too much because such a situation would almost certainly put A, D and C all on to the starboard tack before they were able to lay the windward mark. Thus all three would need to tack back to port to approach the mark again and C could easily regain her position of command over D and A. Therefore it would be more likely that A and D while on port tack, meeting X and B on starboard tack, would simply duck underneath X and B's stern. In which case they would be obliged to allow enough water for C to also duck under the sterns of X and B.

Does C have any alternative plan to gain places by the time she reaches the windward mark? Not that I can think of. The only alternative plan that might be considered is that if D and A do get put about onto starboard before they can lay the windward mark by X and B, then C ought to consider ducking under the sterns of D and C and tacking to starboard the moment she reaches the starboard layline, that way she will not be slowed down by putting in two extra tacks, although of course she will have lost some distance to windward by ducking under D and A's sterns.

As it happens that alternative is removed from C's consideration for as A, D and C continue on port towards the starboard layline for the windward mark, they plainly see yacht B sailing up the layline on starboard. Diagram 9.2 sets the scene. Off the diagram but in sight of A, D and C is yacht X, slightly to windward and clear astern of B also on starboard. Yacht C is four clear boat lengths away at least from the starboard layline by which time both B and X will have cleared that section of line with B at the mark. As already explained C's only hope is to hold that vital command over D and A. With the short distance left to go before reaching the starboard layline in this instance it will not be a problem. So C now concentrates on making sure that she has reached the layline before tacking.

It is very easy to write that! How easy is it in

75

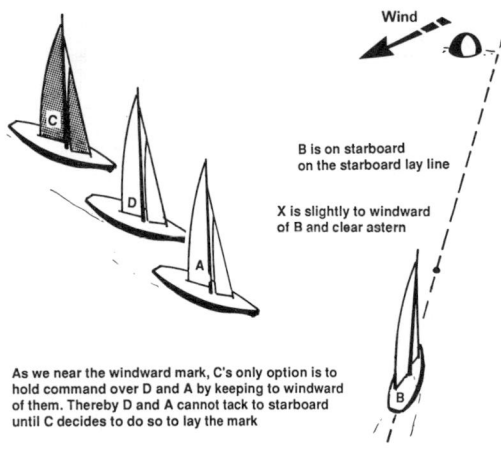

Wind

B is on starboard
on the starboard lay line

X is slightly to windward
of B and clear astern

As we near the windward mark, C's only option is to
hold command over D and A by keeping to windward
of them. Thereby D and A cannot tack to starboard
until C decides to do so to lay the mark

Diagram 9.2

fact to calculate that you have reached the layline on either tack? Looking at boats I see sailing on the water I would say not very easy. All too often I see yachts tacking before they have properly reached the layline and then have to pinch up to try and struggle round the mark. This is an expensive mistake, firstly because other yachts that have calculated their layline tack correctly, or even gone a little higher than their layline before tacking, will simply sail round the pinching yacht with better speed and gain places. The second danger for the pinching yacht is that she does not pinch up quite high enough and finds herself hitting the mark or, even worse, laying on the mark with no way on. To lie on the mark with no way on is almost certainly going to put you firmly at the back of the fleet. We all have done it in our time and learnt the consequences. So let us try to avoid doing it in the first place.

Take a look at Diagram 9.3. The diagram shows two yachts sailing close-hauled at forty-five degrees to the wind. Each skipper as he is sailing his yacht projects a line straight along his yacht's transom (that's at the stern or back of the yacht). That projected line should thus be at right angles to the course of the yacht through the water. Yacht B's projected line is still the wrong side of the mark. Yacht A's projected line though has just passed the mark on the side it is to be rounded (mark left to port), therefore the skipper of A now knows that provided the wind does not shift or bend he should be able to lay the mark in one. Then he or she smoothly tacks and proceeds with

speed towards the mark. You get no prizes for seriously overlaying the mark — that is sailing well beyond the laymark before tacking — because it allows yachts behind you to come up and lay the mark correctly and gain an inside overlap over you and thus you lose yet another place! Neither do you get any prizes for tacking that little bit too soon and find you have to continually pinch up to try and lay the mark in one! If you do make the mistake of tacking that little bit too soon, or the wind shifts a bit after you have tacked and you find you can no longer quite lay the mark — don't panic! Concentrate on gaining the best boat speed you can in the conditions and accelerate towards the mark or slightly to leeward of the mark. At the last moment before hitting the mark luff up and use the momentum of the yacht to carry you round, ease the sails out just a touch at the same time. If there are yachts to windward of you and you have an overlap it is best to give them warning of your intentions so that they keep clear. Whatever you do in that situation do not tack to port, or you are likely to be in big trouble! Of course if there are no other yachts around at the time it does not matter — you will just lose a little time and distance over those yachts you are trying to overhaul and any yachts astern of you will come that little bit closer!

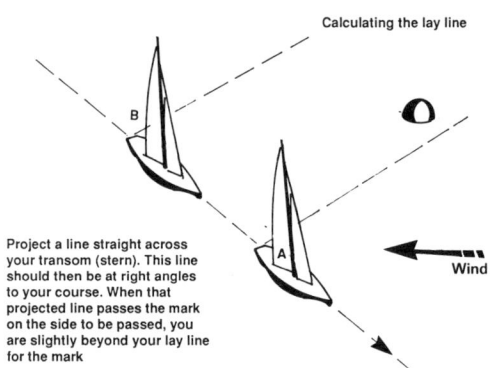

Calculating the lay line

Wind

Project a line straight across
your transom (stern). This line
should then be at right angles
to your course. When that
projected line passes the mark
on the side to be passed, you
are slightly beyond your lay line
for the mark

Diagram 9.3

The same trick of projecting the line over the transom can be used to calculate if you are being headed or lifted by the wind while beating up towards the windward mark. In this situation, if the projected line ends up nearer towards the mark than your projected course line you are being headed! That is you are sailing further away from the mark than you would be if you tacked. If your course line projection ends up nearer to the mark than the transom line then you are being lifted i.e. you are sailing more directly towards the mark than if you were on the other tack. If there is no difference between either projected lines' distance from the mark then the wind is blowing in the same direction as the course layer planned.

These very basic geometric tricks can gain you more places than you can imagine if you use them correctly. Do make careful note of them and go out and try them. You must get them into your head!

No doubt some of my more experienced readers will be dying to point out to me that a modern radio Marblehead points much higher to wind than forty-five degrees. So it does, but at this stage we are looking at ways of helping the new-comer to our marvellous sport enjoy the basics of racing and, in particular, to start to enjoy beating the odd boat on the water. As time passes we can refine the geometry to suit the particular yacht's pointing ability. Every yacht and every skipper will perform slightly differently and in the end, the successful skipper knows his yacht and his own capabilities well.

The other obvious bit of information available to our intrepid skipper of C in the current situation is the course that has been sailed by B and X to the mark. Once C is in the middle of their wakes she is pretty sure to be on or above the layline to the windward mark (provided of course that B and X got round it without pinching!). If C had seen B and X pinching up to round the mark she would be well advised to sail on a little further before tacking to lay the mark so that she does not experience the same problem.

Now at long last we are approaching another mark, we have to try and remember all about overlaps and who does what at marks. The easy bit to remember perhaps about overlaps and all that is . . . if you are the inside yacht at the four boat lengths magic circle all those boats on the outside of you have to give you room to round the mark. Diagram 9.4 helps to show what I mean. Yacht 4 is inside of yacht 3 at the four boats' length from the mark. Even if yacht 3 now pulls

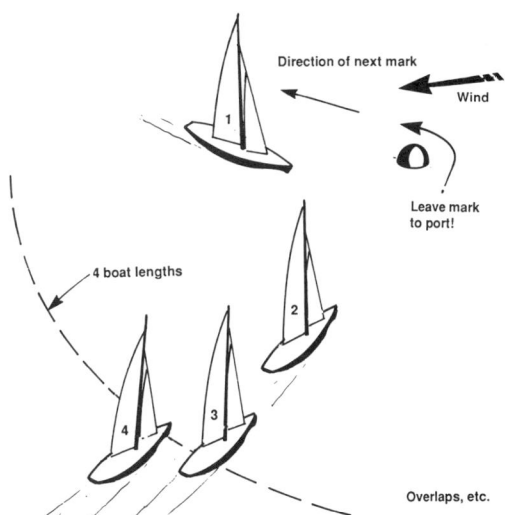

Diagram 9.4

ahead she must still give yacht 4 room at the mark if required. Yacht 2 is clear ahead of yachts 3 and 4. Yachts 3 and 4 cannot get an overlap on 2 now even if they somehow gain extra speed than 2. They would have to pass 2 to windward and keep clear of her. If that did happen then yacht 2 would be quite entitled to luff them up as violently as she likes at any stage during the rounding of the mark until yacht 3 or 4 had called mast abeam stem. Yacht 1 at present is obliged under **Rule 36**. **Rule 42** does not come into play until yacht 1 tacks to starboard, because this rule only applies to yachts on the same tack when the yachts involved are on the beat. If yacht 1 wishes to tack to starboard and under yacht 2's port bow, she must execute her tack so that 2 does not have to alter course to miss 1 until after 1 has com-pleted her tack. Once 1 has completed her tack 2 must try to keep clear. If yacht 1 has completed her tack with yacht 2 clear astern or behind mast abeam stem position, then yacht 2 had better look out, because once 1 has given 2 room and oppor-tunity to keep clear she may luff as hard as she cares.

If yacht 1 had managed to cross yacht 2's bow on port before tacking to starboard, and yacht 2 was unable to avoid establishing a late inside overlap, then 1 would have to give that overlap to 2 and leave room for 2 to round the mark inside 1. Yacht 2 only has to respond once 1's tack has been completed — if she can avoid 1 by slowing

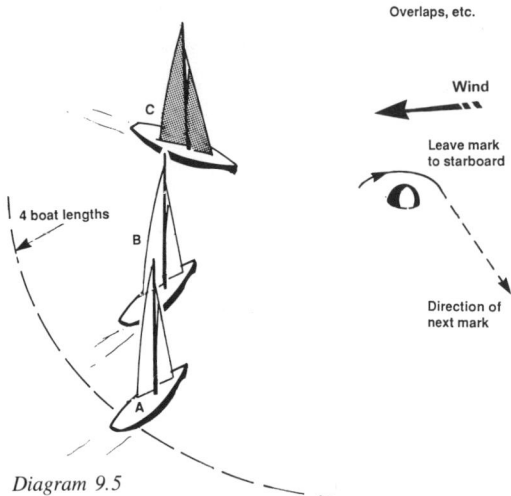

Overlaps, etc.

Wind

Leave mark
to starboard

4 boat lengths

Direction of
next mark

Diagram 9.5

down or luffing to windward she must. It is only if she is travelling at a speed greater than 1, and to leeward of 1, that she can legitimately call and gain that late inside overlap. If 1 tries to shut the door on 2, 2 should hit 1 rather than hitting the mark and should protest 1 loudly twice. Do not go the wrong side of the mark and simply protest 1, it will cost you places and the best you can expect is to get 1 disqualified. Yachts 3 and 4 must keep clear of 2 while 2 rounds the mark.

Now let's look at the whole situation again at the windward mark but this time leaving the mark to starboard. Believe me it is a whole different game, with much more potential for incidents to develop!

Diagram 9.5 sets the scene. Yacht A is clear astern of B and thus enjoys no overlap as inside boat BUT ... under **Rule 42.2(c)** *A yacht clear ahead that tacks to round a mark is subject to* **Rule 41 Changing tacks — Tacking and Gybing**. That is the rub, because A now holds command over B! Although clear ahead B cannot tack to port to round the mark if by doing so she gets in the way of A. Yacht A under **Rule 42.2(b)**: *A yacht clear astern shall not luff above close-hauled so as to prevent a yacht clear ahead from tacking to round a mark*, has certain obligations, but she has no need in the situation set out in Diagram 9.5 to luff up at all, B dare not tack until A has tacked, thus A takes the lead even though she was clear astern.

The next point to consider is C's situation. She

cannot cross the bows of starboard tack B therefore she has to tack to starboard. While tacking she comes under **Rule 41** — she must keep clear of B until her tack is completed. Yacht B does not even have to begin to take avoiding action until C's tack is complete, at which stage she shall take immediate action to keep clear. In the situation shown in Diagram 9.5, C has no choice except to tack immediately, B will have no choice except to gain an inside overlap within the four boats' lengths circle under **Rule 42.3(a).ii**. This is an important section of **Rule 42** that can be used to advantage at starboard windward mark roundings — it is more difficult to use it on port windward mark roundings because the keyword in the rule clause is luffing. I reproduce the rule section which comes under **42.3 Limitations on Establishing an Overlap**. *A yacht that establishes an inside overlap from clear astern is entitled to room under Rule 42.1(a) only when, at that time, the outside yacht:*

(i) is able to give room, and

(ii) is more than four of her overall lengths from the mark or obstruction. However when a yacht completes a tack within four of her overall lengths of a mark or obstruction, she shall give room as required by Rule 42.1(a) to a yacht that, by LUFFING cannot thereafter avoid establishing a late inside overlap.

With a little bit of thought, or perhaps a lot of careful thought, it should be clear to one and all that different strategies and tactics need to be employed when approaching and rounding starboard windward marks.

Hopefully you may now have a little bit more understanding of what goes on around the windward mark. Going back to our race for a minute, for anyone who hadn't guessed we leave the race with B in first place having X hot on her heels, and then C leading D and A round the windward mark and onto the running leg straight before the wind and down to the leeward mark. In the next chapter we'll be covering that leg and discussing more tactics for rounding leeward marks plus how to handle bargers — those naughty skippers who go charging in where angels fear to tread — inside at the leeward mark *without an overlap* established at the four boat lengths!!!

10. Running Before The Wind

Without rules yacht racing can at best become a shambles, and at worst serious damage can result. In full-sized racing, of course, the other major element comes into play — that of lives being risked! So it was that rules evolved, and anyone who thinks that they can simply race and ignore the rules is in fact denying themselves the opportunities that the rules offer the racing yachtsman to defend his position or safely to attack a yacht ahead, so as both parties have some idea of each other's reactions.

Running is perhaps rather a paradox in as much as at first glance it appears very easy and even rather boring. Perhaps that is the first danger, because in reality it is far from easy and if you allow yourself to get bored by the relatively slow moving yachts you will surely be in danger of losing a place or two! Being novices however at this stage of studying racing techniques, the most important thing to remember is to concentrate. As I have mentioned many times before, keep a good eye on what the other boats near to you are doing. If you are not too sure which is the best course to follow running down towards the leeward mark, don't be afraid simply to follow the crowd. If we continue to ignore the effects of wind shifts, it is in fact quite interesting that widely differing courses taken by yachts that round the windward mark together down to the leeward mark usually have all the yachts converging again in much the same order as they approach the leeward mark! Indeed taking it to extremes, I have even witnessed a yacht that forgot that it did not have to round the wing mark, round the wing mark and still get to the

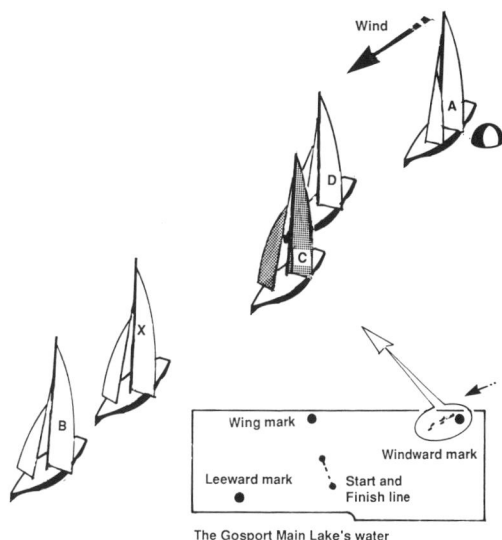

Diagram 10.1

leeward mark at much the same time as those yachts that simply sailed directly to the leeward mark from the windward mark!

Have a look at Diagram 10.1 for this chapter. This diagram simply reminds you of the positions that we left our fleet of five in at the end of the last chapter. We will now have a look at the basic thoughts that should be going through the various skippers' minds.

Yacht B in front is feeling rather pleased with herself so far, leading the race with not much farther to go. At the same time her skipper is biting his nails — any increase in the wind's speed will be felt firstly by the boats behind and they will come rushing up towards B with any such stronger wind. He is also worried about X who is hovering about just behind B trying to steal B's wind. At present X seems to be trying to get to windward of B, something that B will try and encourage given half a chance.

The skipper of yacht X has only one thought on his mind — how to get past B! He has not been sailing that long and is still obsessed by trying to overtake everything to windward — he thinks he is going to get better wind, and thus better speed, and is convinced that he can respond quickly enough to any luff that the overtaken boat throws at him. I doubt that he has seen a violent luff yet, so he has a lot to learn!

Our skipper struggling along with C is rather overwhelmed by the closeness of D and A, besides trying to make sure that the sails are set in the right position and, more importantly, that the jib goes across to the opposite side to the main. You will notice that in Diagram 10.1 all of the yachts have their mains out over the port side and are all running on starboard! That is because they all rounded the last mark leaving it to their port and were all on starboard as they rounded it. It is therefore much easier to leave the main out on starboard and run for the leeward mark. If the wind is doing what it should be when the course was laid, i.e. blowing straight down the lake from the windward buoy to the leeward buoy, then that is fine. In such a situation it is also always to be favoured to be running on starboard. Why? Well if you remember the rule about starboard boats having right of way, it means that a running boat on starboard does not have to give way to any boat on port. So any boats that are still beating up the windward leg of the course, either to round the windward mark from the last leg or, as we near the leeward mark those yachts that have already rounded the leeward mark and are beating up the windward leg towards the finish line that are on port, will have to give way to any starboard running boat. So it is one less thing to worry about. The other nice thing about running on starboard is that if any boat in front of you is running on port, it is going to have to keep clear of you or waste time gybing back to starboard! If it gybes back to starboard in your water and a collision occurs, then the boat doing the gybing will be in the wrong! (**Rule 41.2**.)

In real life the wind is hardly so kind as to be blowing in that steady constant direction. Often you will find that you will have to gybe to the port tack after rounding the windward mark because the wind is a little biased in that direction. Whatever tack you are running on, the quickest thing you need to sort out if you are using conventionally rigged sails is to get the jib out the opposite side to the main. Having let the sails out to a good running position all that is usually needed is for you to give the rudder a little wiggle bearing off slightly to flip the jib across and then back to your steady course. Easier said than done, but it usually only takes a few practice sessions to get this simple manoeuvre to move the jib across every time.

Once you have the sails out and goose-winged you can take a moment to take stock of the situation. First, how is your boat speed relative to the other boats around you? If you are moving at the same speed as the others, fine. If you are going faster don't complain! If, as is often the case, you are moving slower, don't panic! Try and see why? Are you pointing in the same direction as everyone else? Are your sails set more or less at the same angle as the other boats around you? Is there some nasty boat between your boat and the wind, hogging all the wind? If none of these things, is the bow of your yacht being pushed down into the water too far for the weight of wind on the sails? (Perhaps you've picked up a bit of weed!) Is the twist in your mainsail all wrong? So that the top of the main has moved forward far beyond the best setting to catch the wind and the wind is consequently just brushing straight past. If this is the case sheet in the sails a little. Unless the wind is really honking, it pays to be a little gentle with your movements while on the run. It is the slowest point of sailing and violent movements are only going to slow you down some.

You may recall I said a little earlier that the skipper of C was a little overwhelmed, partly because he'd managed to get back in front of D and A, but mostly because they were now sitting firmly on his tail. In fact things are not too bad for C. Yacht D has been forced to go to the windward of C, and while D might be taking some of C's wind, all C has to do is to bear off a little for clear air. Of course yacht D might simply follow C, but all the time C bears off, the blanketing effect of D's sails will be mostly lost. The fact that C will, by this time, be sailing by the lee will not help her. Sailing by the lee is when really you should be gybing across to the other tack to get the full benefit of the direction of the wind in your sails. It is only possible on the run, and when sailing by the lee it pays to let your main out as far as it will go. Not a thing to do for long, but it can be useful as a short term tactic. When you consider, gybing for what may be a very short period on the opposite gybe would waste too much time and possibly lose too much speed.

Yacht A, as last boat round the windward mark, has the luxury of seeing exactly where the other boats are heading and what all the other boats are doing. Although no doubt, he'd rather be up in the front looking backwards at what all the other boats are doing! However, he knows that all is not lost and that now more than ever he really must concentrate and try a few tricks to gain places. He knows that his windshadow will be affecting D and C to some extent and he also knows that any increase in the wind's strength will come to him first! His main preoccupation at this time is to be sailing through as clean water as possible. No doubt he will therefore sail right up the middle of the wake left by C. At some stage he may well bear off to try and break through the wave of the wake and into clearer water. The problem with doing this however, is that any windshadow effect on C and D will be lost.

All of the skippers at this stage should be thinking about which side they are going to round the leeward buoy. As we know they are going to leave it to their port — this is the usual side in Olympic type of courses. Race officers always, if they have the choice, should lay a course that allows all marks to be left to port. The reason for this is that it avoids many of the complications that can arise when rounding a mark leaving it to starboard. At the windward mark this often arises in yachts clear ahead tacking to port just in front of starboard tacked yachts approaching the mark, with all the dangers that involves.

I'm afraid not all race officers appreciate the potential dangers involved and I must admit I've sailed in some meetings all day long with starboard roundings all the way, without an incident. It does however call for fine judgement on the skippers' part and a good knowledge of the rules. Occasionally you will get courses set with both starboard and port roundings involved which can make life very confusing indeed. The course then becomes a memory test as well and does throw up the potential for the always very interesting situation where you get a yacht rounding one mark in each direction and meeting halfway round! Because we sail from the pond side and often can only use one side of the water to sail from, these are problems that a race officer has to try and resolve as best he can. The main thing is to get the yachts racing! At club level this is fine. At open and above levels a more careful approach is needed.

Anyway, all of the skippers in this little race of ours know that they are going to leave the leeward mark to their port. This knowledge immediately allows them, if they think about it, to plan which side is the best side to try and overtake any yacht in front. On this run it will pay to try and overhaul yachts in front passing them on their port side, leaving them to the starboard side of the overtaking yacht. This way the overtaking yacht is gaining a potential inside overlap for rounding the leeward mark. There is nowhere else an overtaking yacht should be. The yacht that is trying to overtake a yacht in front to its windward is crazy! It runs the risk of being luffed all over the pond and, worse still, it is going to be on the outside when rounding the leeward mark unless it is going so fast that it will have passed the other yacht long before coming to the magic four boats' lengths from the leeward mark.

The other thing is that there is a little rule that actually helps us when trying to overtake a yacht ahead to its leeward. Remember it? I used to love this one when I first discovered it. At club level of racing it is very common for the yacht in front that is being overtaken to its leeward to simply bear off so as to make the task of overtaking almost impossible. This used to frustrate me — I'd think if I try to pass it to windward it will luff me up and if I try to pass to leeward it bears off! How do I get past? As usual there was something in the rule book to make this manoeuvre fair. **Rule 39** which, for the benefit of those of you that are still being frustrated by this sort of ungentlemanly behaviour, I'll quote in full: **Rule 39 Same Tack — Sailing Below a Proper Course after Starting**. *A yacht that is on a free leg of the course shall not sail below her proper course when she is clearly within three of her overall lengths of a leeward yacht or of a yacht clear astern that is steering a course to leeward of her own!*

The meaning of a 'free leg of the course' within this rule is entirely related to the actual wind direction at the time *not* the leg of the course originally set by the race officer. In other words it is possible that the original windward leg can become a free leg of the course if the wind swings sufficiently so that the previously close-hauled windward beat simply becomes a reach!

For our purposes though, all we are worried about is that we are on a proper run and we do not want the boat in front bearing off as we attempt to overhaul it. If it does we will most definitely be hailing it to stop sailing below its proper course and, if that doesn't work, we will be protesting it loud and clear twice! So there! You do however have to be a little careful as to what is a proper course. Normally in model yacht racing we tend to think of a proper course as being the shortest distance between two marks, in other words a straight line between the two. It can also be reasonably argued that a yacht that sailed below that course to avoid sailing into a windshadow cast by a tree or a bank etc. is sailing a proper course. Should that be the case, the yacht being hailed to not sail below her proper course ought to immediately reply to the hailing yacht the reason she is sailing below an apparent proper course, so as to defend her position should the hailing yacht decide to protest her. Normally the hailed yacht simply stops bearing off and you can continue to attempt to overhaul it to leeward, accepting the fact that you will have to sail through her windshadow to do so. It is not so important to get right past her anyway — you simply want to have a good overlap established by the time the four boat lengths is reached at the

leeward mark. Unless of course, you are so far behind the rest of the fleet that you are trying to gallop through the fleet! Easier said than done, I might add! However I have seen it done on rare occasions even in world class fleets! So never give up. The only time to give up is when you have crossed the finishing line — until then no matter where you are in relation to the rest of the fleet, you must keep concentrating and trying your hardest.

I remember that during the 1989 RM Nationals I had been up in the A Fleet all through the first two days. During the final day I had the misfortune to drop into B Fleet. The pressure is then really on you to get into the top four positions in the B Fleet race so as to get promoted back up to A Fleet. Well, I was so keen to get away that I had an excellent start, or so I thought, until I was called over the line a second or two later! This was in light winds! I returned and recrossed the line thus being well behind the rest of the fleet. I was now looking at the very definite prospect of being relegated to C Fleet! Progress up the windward beat was slow and painful, by the time the windward mark was reached I had just caught up with the back markers! By the time we reached the wing mark I was no longer in danger of being relegated. Then coming up to the leeward mark I was involved in an incident — I have forgotten the details except that it was most likely my fault! Thus I did my turn, only one was required. I was now again in last position going around the leeward mark for the final time. The prospects were looking grim! The wind was getting so light as to be non-existent, the fleet were spread out from near the leeward mark right up to ten boat lengths from the finish line. Those near the finish line were on the side of the lake farthest away from the bank we were controlling the yachts from. I had a little forward motion being on the tack opposite to the rest of the fleet. I continued on that port tack right up to our controlling bank. I could feel the faintest breeze upon the back of my neck, so I knew that right up close to the controlling bank was the place to be — despite the fact that you would expect the bank, and the skippers standing upon that bank, to blanket that tiny breeze. I tacked to starboard and crept along the bank. I drew level with the leaders stuck in the middle of the lake and as the breeze filled in slightly from over my right-hand shoulder, I continued on my starboard tack to take the race! Most people probably thought it was jam, I call it concentration and never giving up whatever the odds.

Back again to our little race. As shown in Diagram 10.1, X is at the moment trying to pass B to windward, however there is just about enough room for X to swing across, ducking under B's stern to try and either pass B to leeward or to attempt to get an inside overlap on B by the time the next mark is reached. Yacht B at the moment has the option of bearing off, so as to make that choice of plan by X unworkable. Why can B bear off at the moment? Well X is not steering a course to leeward of her own, so she may bear off as much as she likes! Until such time as it is obvious that X is steering a course to overtake B to leeward when, of course, B must hold a proper course to the next mark. By this time the actual proper course to the leeward mark may well be a broad reach which is sailed at a faster speed than a dead run. It would then be very difficult for X to even gain an overlap to leeward.

Our yacht C has exactly the same sort of considerations to make regarding D. The only complication for C is that A is within three boat lengths of C as well. As shown in Diagram 10.1, A at present is not sailing a course that aims to overhaul C to leeward. So C's immediate plan should be to bear off, so as to encourage A to attempt to pass to windward and to keep D well and truly to windward too. The additional advantage of this plan is that if C gains any speed relative to boats A and X, she will be well placed to attempt to pass them at leeward as well.

A favourite dodge by the way, is immediately to sail below a proper course to an off the wind mark the moment you round the last mark. At that time no one can possibly be trying to overtake you to leeward and by the time they are, you ought to be well in command of the situation so as to respond to any threat the best way you see fit at the time.

I have given you now the basic thoughts that ought to be going through your mind as you enter the downwind leg. These considerations will remain your objectives throughout the running leg. You must keep a sharp lookout for boats that are beating to windward across your projected course. You must identify what tack they are on and you must also check the tack that you are on as well! If you are running on port you must give way to everything! If you choose to gybe to starboard so as to gain some rights, you must do so sufficiently clear of other yachts so that they have time to respond to any right of way you gain, *after* you have completed your gybe! If you are running on starboard, you must remember that you are windward of any close-hauled starboard yacht that is on a converging course and as such it is your obligation to keep clear.

Consequently, you must keep fully alert for these developing situations. If you don't you can find yourself forced to harden up suddenly and assume a course in a very different direction to the one you would like to pursue. This will become a very real problem as you approach the leeward mark unless you are leading the fleet. Many yachts will round the leeward mark and shortly after tack to starboard on a close-hauled course beating to the finish line. They have absolute right of way. They are not allowed to tack in your water to gain such rights, but do be aware that the environment around the leeward mark will be rapidly changing as you approach. Have your alternative plans of action ready in your mind and be prepared to call for water to avoid an obstruction to any nearby yachts that restrict your manoeuvring abilities.

Diagram 10.2 sets up a typical situation : B has, immediately upon rounding the leeward mark, tacked to starboard and straightaway A has a problem. Yacht B has probably lost a lot of speed by tacking so quickly and also because she is now sailing through the disturbed wind and water that the remainder of the running fleet have caused. (She'll also be sailing through her own wake too!) However A will be taking a big chance if she tries to sail across B's bows — her better course of action is to aim to sail very close to B's stern. If she points straight at the mark now, she'll probably achieve that and still be able to round the mark without too much inconvenience.

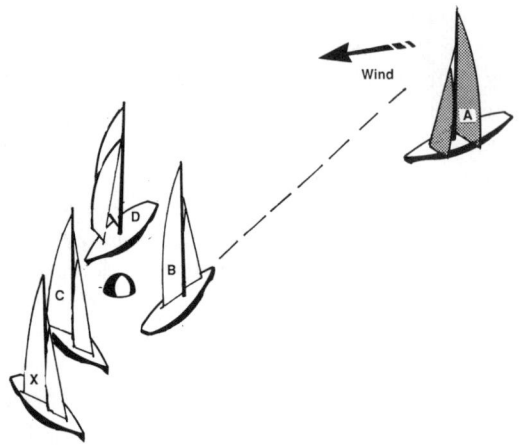

Diagram 10.2

Yacht A's problems could get worse if any of the remaining three yachts also decide to tack quickly to starboard. She may end up having to sail under the sterns of all those yachts that do tack to starboard, which will certainly slow her down somewhat. There is no easy solution to this problem other than to be leading the race! As I said before, be alert and ready with alternative plans to evade close-hauled starboard boats. As stated in earlier chapters, it is not in B's interests to tack immediately having passed the leeward mark. It immediately puts her on a course to cross her own wake which will slow her down! The other fault is obvious in Diagram 10.2, i.e. C and X, when they tack to starboard, will quite likely be in a position to take command over B, stopping her tacking back to port to lay the finish line!

We will continue with our mythical race in the next chapter, which might even see the end of the first race! In the meantime it seems an opportune moment to explain how to deal with 'BARGING', that is when a yacht, with no overlap rights established at the four boat lengths distance from a mark, sees a gap and slips through gaining places on yachts that were previously ahead. It is quite a problem at the leeward mark, because it is a longer, wider procedure rounding the leeward mark since no yacht can turn on a sixpence. Some yachts can turn tighter than others though and some skippers plan their entry and exit lines better than others.

Firstly please note that there is *no* rule against barging other than at the start (**Rule 42.4**). If a

yacht that is clear astern within the four boat lengths wishes to take a chance and dive through a gap it does so at its own peril! If it gets away with it all well and good, but... if it fails and contact is made either with the buoy or with any yacht that was clear ahead, then the result is all too clear — the barging yacht has turns to do or face being disqualified! So the onus is firmly upon the yachts clear ahead to stop other yachts clear astern barging through. How do they do this? By sailing properly and rounding the mark in such a manner that there is not room for a yacht clear astern to poke its nose in where it is not wanted. At the leeward mark the favourite way of doing this is by entering wide and coming out tight to the mark. However, if a yacht has an inside overlap over another yacht it cannot practice this particular manoeuvre, because **Rule 42.1** states that an outside yacht that is overlapped by an inside yacht shall: *give each inside overlapping yacht room to round or pass the mark or obstruction, except as provided in Rule 42.3.* Room is the space needed by an inside overlapping yacht that is handled in a seamanlike manner in the prevailing conditions to pass in safety between an outside yacht and a mark or obstruction, and includes space to tack or gybe when either is an integral part of the rounding or passing manoeuvre. It does not provide for the inside yacht to be able to enter wide and come out tight in a fast rounding manoeuvre — the rule only provides for the inside yacht to make as tight a turn as possible around the mark. The fact that it will often slow her down a bit more than a wider sweeping rounding is tough.

So if you are an inside overlapping yacht at the leeward mark — be careful. If you can enter wide, without pushing the outside yacht farther out do so and be grateful. If not, you must come in tight to the mark, turn as tight as you can and assume your new course. If that manoeuvre allows another yacht that was clear astern to poke its nose in as you are coming out from rounding the mark what can you do? Firstly luff it up and into the mark! That is always a good one if possible! The trouble is it is often not possible simply because you are already turning as hard as you can and thus there is no rudder left to luff up higher than you are already turning. The second problem can be that you do not have enough speed to luff up any higher either. If so, just bite the bullet and congratulate the better turning ability of the barging yacht. You can work out later how to improve the turning circle of your own yacht! However all may not be lost because as you build up speed on your new course, you may still have the opportunity to give the barger a violent luff, which with any luck, will hit him or at least force him across onto the other tack, which will then allow you to tack also and hold command over him should you so wish. Do remember that even if you are annoyed with the barger there are a lot of other yachts in the race, and it is a waste of time engaging in a private war with your new enemy. The barger only did what any sensible racing yachtsman would do and that is to take an opportunity that was there to be had. However, you do have to be rather careful and this is where it pays to know your opposing yachtsmen because some more experienced skippers will purposely leave what is known as a 'sucker's gap'! You've got it — as soon as some innocent sticks his nose in between the experienced skipper's boat and the mark wham — the door is shut and the innocent ends up at best touching the mark and at worst touching the mark and being hit by the luffing skipper. Ho ho ho, possibly two lots of penalty turns to do!! What fun, one barger firmly taught a hard lesson.

Barging at the wing mark is often possible, usually because the wing mark is far away from the controlling bankside and skippers' judgement of their yacht's position relative to the mark varies enormously and there are often large gaps to be dived through. Again be very careful because it is very easy for the outside boat to luff up hard after gybing to the new course coming out from the mark.

11. The Final Beat to Windward

After you have read this book you will know quite enough about the rules to survive. The best way of reinforcing the knowledge of the rules is by actually getting out there and taking part in some racing. Every time you are involved in an incident you can quietly refer to your own copy of the rules after the race to find out who was right and who was wrong. Listening to other people's protest hearings is always educational if allowed. As long as you keep quiet there is no reason why you should not be allowed to sit in listening to a hearing. You will not be allowed to hear the protest committee discussing the case after having heard all of the evidence, but you should be able to hear the presenting of the evidence by parties concerned and witnesses. Then the result of the hearing will be made public immediately after the committee have reached a decision and notified the skippers involved. It is a lot easier to simply do penalty turns on the water than get involved in a protest hearing. The catch is that you have to know a bit about the rules in order to know whether it is you or the other boat involved that ought to be doing the turns. When observing races I often see the wrong boat do the penalty turns, presumably because the skipper of the boat doing the turns does not know enough about the rules to know that in fact he was in the right. How on earth a skipper like that expects to win races I do not know. Perhaps he doesn't, but he just enjoys joining in and sailing round with the fleet.

You will find that when a lot of top quality skippers are racing amongst themselves, that while there may be quite a few calls on the water,

there are in fact very few incidents and even fewer protests. Everyone knows the rules fairly well and consequently know what their obligations are in a developing situation. Extremely complex situations can develop that at a normal club level of racing would be frightening. These at higher levels simply unfold into dramatic close quarter manoeuvres without contact. Of course occasionally even the best misjudge it and there is a collision, usually resulting in the offending boat immediately acknowledging the fault and breaking clear of the fleet at the first opportunity to execute a penalty turn or two before chasing back up towards the rear of the fleet. Now and then both skippers think that they are in the right in such an incident and that is when a protest hearing ought to and does take place. If the protest committee are lucky it is an interesting and unusual situation that has them all desperately leafing through the various rule books with their different interpretations to find some previously heard case that is similar. All too often the incidents are quite straightforward, once the evidence has been given and the facts established. The hardest job of all is establishing the facts! Each skipper usually has a quite different idea of what occurred and it is necessary to get the race observers to give their versions of what occurred. You can end up with half a dozen different stories from which you have to try and find the common threads to establish a set of plausible facts. Once these have been established you can apply the rules. Sometimes both skippers will agree the circumstances which makes the task much easier — it is simply a matter of rule interpretation or applying the correct rule.

This should give you an idea of how rules are applied. As I have already said the main reason for having rules is firstly safety, and secondly to make the racing as fair as possible. In fact you will not go far wrong if you always apply those two criteria to any situation. A judgement based on safety and fairness is likely to be very near to whatever rule applies.

Model yacht racing is about enjoying an outdoor pursuit, being near water and enjoying the magnificent spectacle of a group of model yachts quietly working their way around a set course. In my opinion the best racing to watch is the race that has plenty of close tight manoeuvring with places changing throughout the race as first one and then another take the lead, with similar exchanges taking place throughout the fleet. Drawn out processions are equally boring to the leader, back marker and spectator. The cut and thrust of the close encounter is where the thrill is and tremendous satisfaction can be gained in seeing someone pull off a good manoeuvre, even if that manoeuvre beats you! After all now someone has demonstrated a new idea to you, there will come a time when you may be able to use it yourself to equal devastating effect!

Others may enjoy their racing more because they have designed the boat, sails or rig themselves and are pleased to see it hold its own against other competitive boats. Some may just enjoy the companionship of yachty types or model freaks. Still others simply enjoy offering up their valuable free time to help run events or record results. The main thing, I hope, for all people involved whether sailing, organising or simply watching is that they are for the most part enjoying it.

This brings us nicely back to the imaginary race that we have been following to date, wherein five radio controlled yachts have been battling it out around an Olympic type of course. We are on the downwind leg of the sausage about to round the leeward mark. Yacht C is the yacht we are supporting, skippered by a complete novice, who has, however, been reading this book. Luck, common sense and the author have all been on C's side and she is at present lying in third posi-

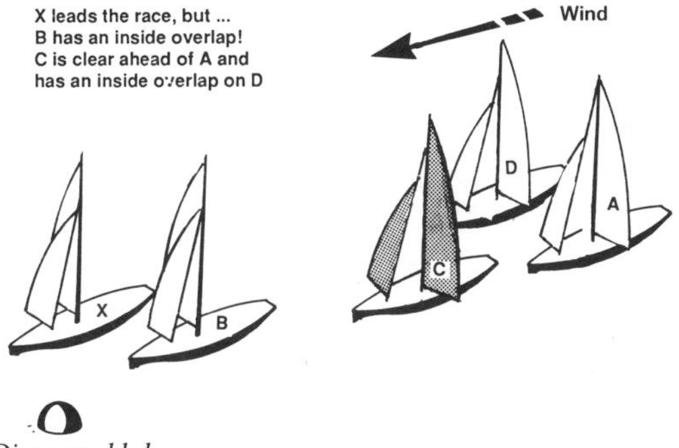

X leads the race, but ...
B has an inside overlap!
C is clear ahead of A and
has an inside overlap on D

Wind

Diagram 11.1

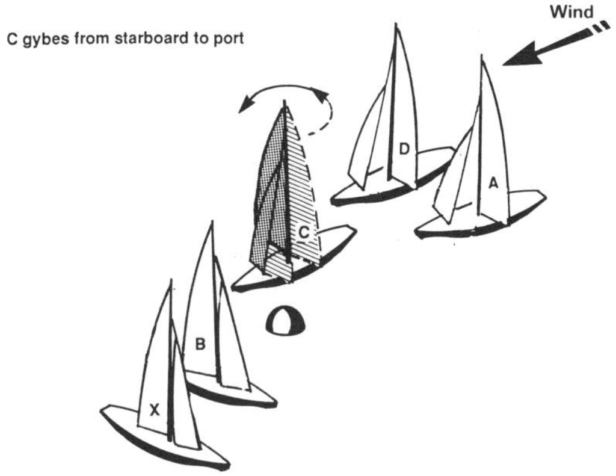

C gybes from starboard to port

Wind

Diagram 11.2

tion. Diagram 11.1 sets the scene. Yacht X has managed to gain ground over B, but B still holds the inside overlap at the mark so she is not worried about X at all. Meanwhile C has managed to keep D on the outside and A has not managed to gain an inside overlap by the time the four boat lengths from the mark was reached. This is how it looks at present so C should be able to hold third place around the mark. She will have to watch out for either B or X slowing down and keep clear of them if they do. It is a hazard that is quite often encountered at the leeward mark and if you are not prepared for it, you simply end up in trouble either hitting the boat in front or hitting the mark as you attempt to avoid the boat with the brakes on. Diagram 11.2 shows the progress of the yachts as they go round the mark with C gybing from starboard to port. Diagram 11.3 shows the start of an interesting development: C has not made the best of her rounding having made quite a large turn, A is definitely going for the large gap C has left and D is almost committed to having a bash as well. What is C to do?

Diagram 11.3

Neither A or D have any rights, but of course are quite welcome to take the risk of diving for the gap at their own risk. Yacht C has lost some speed having recently gybed and is in the process of hardening up to find her close-hauled course. She hardly has the speed to luff D or A up into the mark. Meanwhile X has not given up the idea of trying to win this race. She is gently luffing B up in an effort to encourage B to tack to starboard so as to get B off her back.

Diagram 11.4

By the time we get to Diagram 11.4, B has tacked across to starboard to avoid further luffing contests with X and also to get into some clear air, since she was being slowed down by the disturbed air around X. Meanwhile C has swung up as far as she can to windward and has closed the gap somewhat. She cannot stop A since she does not have enough way on to point up any higher. If she had gained more speed she could have luffed A right into the mark where she deserved to be. As it is we have to smile graciously, however D has had the good sense to realise that there certainly was not going to be room for her as well as A, so is swinging down and around C's stern. Yacht D has it in mind to try and gain speed over C and A as they have their little battle and to slip underneath the pair of them and come out in front enough to be able to tack to starboard

in front of the pair of them which, if it works, would seem like a good idea!

Diagram 11.5 shows D that she was lucky — A has tacked across to starboard in an effort to get away from C only to have C immediately follow suit and tack to starboard herself. Yacht X has tacked across to starboard also to keep a loose cover on B. All boats are now firmly on the final windward beat and there is still plenty of time for fortunes to change. A lot of places are often given away on the final windward beat by skippers who simply do not follow a few basic rules.

If we take B and X in isolation for a moment or two their objectives are easy. Yacht X had rounded the leeward mark in a fairly bad position, in as much as it would have been much better to have been the inside boat. However she managed to retain her speed throughout the turn so as to be in position to harass B by luffing her up, thus encouraging B to tack away to starboard and allowing X to choose when to tack to cover B. The very basic objective for a yacht that believes itself to be in front of another is to keep the other boat between itself and the finish line. If it can achieve that it is almost certain to win. This is almost the sole objective in match racing and it certainly holds true for the two leading yachts *provided* that they are both well ahead of the rest of the fleet. Their problems start when the third placed boat is also close on their heels because if the second and third placed boats choose to beat up towards the finish line on different tacks, the leading boat cannot cover them both. The leading boat will have to make a choice which usually is to cover the largest threatening group of yachts. That way you stand to lose the least number of places should things go wrong.

If you are in third position or so you have to balance between trying to beat the two boats in front and trying to stop the boats behind overtaking you. It all depends on how many boats are racing, or at least how many boats are racing near enough to you to have a chance of beating you or of you beating them. It is always better to try and stop a big group of boats overtaking you on the final beat than it is to overtake one or two boats yourself, only to see a larger group take the line from behind you on the opposite tack. When you are at the back of the fleet the opposite applies. All you have to do is to take the opposite tack to the majority of the fleet in front of you and hope for a friendly wind shift. Gambling on doing the opposite to the majority of the fleet is always a risky business and the odds are never in the favour of the gambler, but on the final beat with nothing to lose and everything to gain, what the heck — it is the only option left to you to try in any case. If it fails you were last anyway, if it works you may gain at least a place and maybe more.

Now finish lines come in all shapes and sizes, the one thing that is constant about them is that you always must approach them from the direction of the last mark, and that if two boats on opposite tacks are converging upon the line the starboard tack boat has right of way and is going to put the port tack boat about. Thus to approach the finish line on starboard can be an advantage in close finishes. No leg of the course shows up better the speed that can be lost on tacking, or how nervous tension in the skipper freezes up the thinking and reaction abilities. Mistakes made on the final leg are terminal, there is no longer any time to romp after the fleet and overtake them all again after having done two turns for a penalty. You will drop places and it will hurt. It hurts even more to be actually crossing the line on port and have a starboard tack yacht clip your stern and protest you. You have to do your two turns and recross the line from the direction of the last mark in order to finish again! Expensive!

So going back to Diagram 11.5, when I said that X has tacked to maintain a loose cover over B, I mean that X has tacked so as to maintain a position over B that effectively stops B from tacking back to port. This is because although B has just enough room to tack back to port, she would then immediately be on a collision course with X and would have to tack immediately back to starboard, which would of course be a waste of time and speed for B. Yacht B could always tack slowly and go under X's stern, but all X would have to do is tack across to port herself as B is taking X's stern and thus remain with then close cover over B. The difference between loose cover and close is just that. When you are covering

the other boat at close quarters, you do suffer from the windshadow or disturbed backwind created by the boat you are covering. The advantage of the tight cover is that the option of tacking and tacking the covering boat's stern is removed. Under a tight cover the covered boat has only the options of bearing away and gybing, which is time and distance wasting. Slowing down and trying to tack once X is clear ahead is also time wasting and of course the covering boat can slow down also if it so chooses. The other options are to luff the covering boat up, which is where a loose cover is an advantage, or to sail on until the covering boat tacks for the line and then tack immediately also.

Other factors that come into play on the last windward beat to the line are how the line is laid — does it have a favoured end? The favoured end may be because that end of the line is nearest to the leeward mark or it may be that the favoured end enjoys a better wind. There is also the very real consideration that the end of the line nearest to the line judge is likely to be the end to go for in a tight finish, because it is nearer to the judge's sight and your boat may obscure the opposing boat's finish!

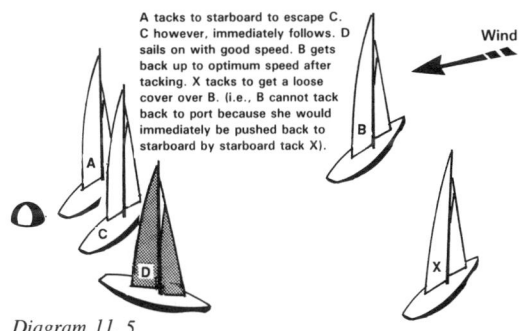

A tacks to starboard to escape C. C however, immediately follows. D sails on with good speed. B gets back up to optimum speed after tacking. X tacks to get a loose cover over B. (i.e., B cannot tack back to port because she would immediately be pushed back to starboard by starboard tack X).

Wind

Diagram 11.5

Let's take a quick look at Diagram 11.6. This illustrates the ideal aspect the line should take in relation to the rhumb line from the windward to the leeward mark, that is at right angles to it. Ideally the finish line marks should be placed equal distances from that rhumb line (i.e. the shortest distance between two points in a straight line). The line from the windward to the leeward mark should also be the exact direction of the wind. On a day when the wind is blowing from a constant direction this might be possible, but

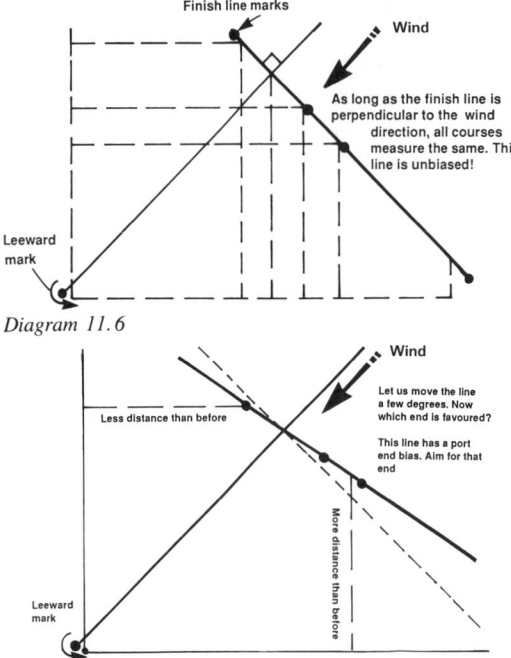

Diagram 11.6

Diagram 11.7

the wind rarely obliges novice sailors or course layers in this way.

Diagram 11.8 shows the dramatic effect of a small ten-degree wind shift. Immediately the two outer layline courses become different lengths to each other. If the wind backs it will favour the port end of the line and if it goes round it will favour the starboard end of the line! All of a sudden wind shifts become rather important, because the result of being headed or lifted becomes rather obvious.

Diagram 11.7 simply shows what happens if the course layer gets it a little wrong — once again the line has a bias. It is very difficult to set a good course that is going to last the day. The course setter is usually laying the course early in the morning before the wind has set in for the day. A wise course setter will have looked at the shipping forecast for the areas around his district and will also have looked at the local forecasts as well. They should give him some idea of the expected wind and possible wind speeds. This has to be balanced against the time of year, local features and the possibilities of a sea breeze setting in later in the day. If thunder is expected, you can be prepared for some dramatic swings in

the wind's direction and strength as such storms move across the area. If such weather is expected it is worth laying some extra buoys to use as the wind swings. A lot depends as to whether it is simply a club race or a rather more important open event. At internal club level some clubs are quite content to simply sail around permanently laid buoys. If it is an open every effort ought to be made to lay a proper course and if required, that course should be altered as the day progresses. The windward beat part of a course is essential as a tactical arena where developed skills come into their own. It is much easier for everyone to simply sail a course that only involves reaching and running.

Now that we have some idea of what we are looking for as we leave the leeward mark for the last time to beat back up to windward and the finish line, let's go back to our little race. As we left them in Diagram 11.5, B, X, A and C were entering into their own little battles. This left D able to continue to sail at optimum speed on the port tack into clean air and undisturbed water. The other reason D continued on this tack instead of following the herd, was that she did not want to tack until she could tack and lay a course that put her above all of the other boats. Luck then played a part — the wind backed ten degrees as shown in Diagram 11.8. This immediately lifted D's course putting her on a course sailing more directly towards the line. The other two pairs were too engrossed in their own battles to notice immediately what was going on. The two pairs of battling yachts were now approaching the layline to tack to lay the finish line in any event, so both pairs tacked to port (X and B to lay the port end of the line and A and C to lay the starboard end of the line) and at much the same time D tacked to starboard. Now of course D was being headed and the other boats were enjoying the lift, but you've guessed it ... the wind rounded to its original direction! Thus we get to the position shown in Diagram 11.9.

Yacht X has left it too late to bear off under D's stern so calls for water to tack to miss a starboard tack boat. Yacht B immediately responds by starting to tack to starboard. While X in turn starts her tack but is lucky enough to be able to poke her

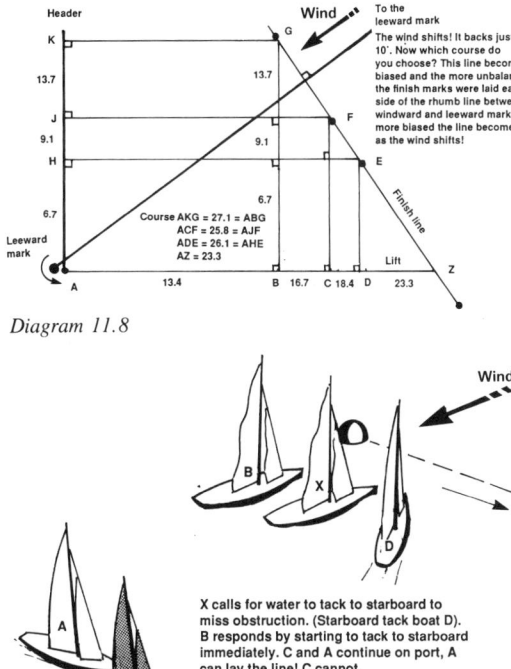

Header

K

13.7

J

9.1

H

6.7

Leeward mark

A

Wind

G

To the leeward mark

The wind shifts! It backs just 10°. Now which course do you choose? This line becomes biased and the more unbalanced the finish marks were laid each side of the rhumb line between windward and leeward marks, the more biased the line becomes as the wind shifts!

13.7

9.1

F

E

6.7

Course AKG = 27.1 = ABG
ACF = 25.8 = AJF
ADE = 26.1 = AHE
AZ = 23.3

Finish line

Lift

Z

13.4   B 16.7 C 18.4 D   23.3

Diagram 11.8

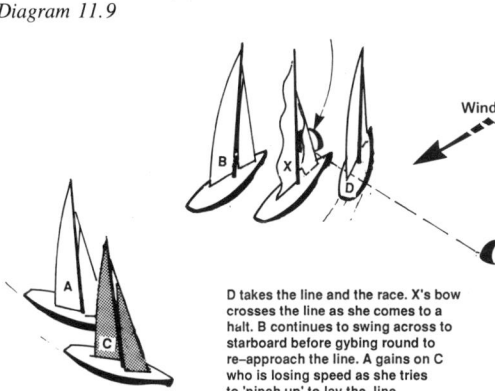

Wind

B

X

D

A

C

X calls for water to tack to starboard to miss obstruction. (Starboard tack boat D). B responds by starting to tack to starboard immediately. C and A continue on port, A can lay the line! C cannot.

Starboard finish mark

Diagram 11.9

Wind

B

X

D

A

C

D takes the line and the race. X's bow crosses the line as she comes to a halt. B continues to swing across to starboard before gybing round to re-approach the line. A gains on C who is losing speed as she tries to 'pinch up' to lay the line.

Diagram 11.10

bow over the finish line as she heads up into wind with such little forward motion left that she comes to a halt before drifting back off the line and falling back onto a starboard tack. (Diagrams 11.9 & 11.10.) Yacht B circles round and comes back to the line on port ahead of A but C, who had misjudged the layline (calculating it before the wind swung back), cannot lay the line and thus has been pinching up above a close-hauled course in an effort to lay the line and to beat A. She lost such speed though that A was easily able to sail

past to take fourth place.

Poor old C — from third to last. Some people might think D was lucky to go from last to first but was it really luck? She first made a sensible decision to swing round wide at the leeward mark and to go for speed and remaining on the port tack. The other two pairs got too engrossed in their own little battles. So engrossed in fact that they did not even notice when the wind shifted. The wind shifting was a lucky break for D — but only if the other boats did not take advantage of the shift. If the other four boats had tacked to take advantage of the wind shift they would have probably still beaten D to the line. Yacht C's inexperience was against her and her skipper did very well to keep up with the fleet in any case. I think as a novice any readers who had been sailing C could quite justifiably feel pleased with themselves.

Hopefully this last leg will have given you a taste of some of the skills that need to be developed in order to get the most out of a constantly varying situation. The wind varies in strength all the time and its direction rarely stays still for many minutes — it usually swings from side to side of an average direction and that average direction may swing round or back as the day progresses. The wind does not even behave the same over the area of water you are sailing on. Surrounding trees, hedges, bushes, buildings, hills, banks and people all divert the course of the wind to some degree. There can even be holes in the wind — patches on the water where for some moments there is no wind at all. The water itself can behave differently in different areas, especially if there is any sort of current or tidal effect involved. Luckily in this country we usually sail in ponds or lakes and thus do not have to worry too much about that sort of thing. However, if the wind is blowing hard it is bound to be pushing the water up hard against one bank resulting in larger waves at that point, the smoother water elsewhere will be easier to sail through.

Different strengths of wind will require different sets of sails with different types of settings to suit the conditions. Some people will vary the weight they have upon the keel of the yacht if the class rules allow it, according to the expected wind strength. The general theory being lighter fin weights in light weather and heavier weights in heavy weather. On top of all this is the constantly changing pattern of the racing yachts themselves. Thus the need for intense concentration. It is no good just concentrating on your boat though — you must be constantly aware of what is going on around your yacht and with the fleet in general. You should be keeping an eye on the wind direction and any local lifts or headers that are being caused by local obstructions to the wind.

These are some of the factors that contribute towards making yacht racing one of the most demanding and challenging sports. The one major advantage we have as radio controlled model yacht racers is that we do not have to be super fit, and we are in a much better position to protect ourselves against the elements. If you want to enjoy a lovely sunny day and get some good racing in, then you cannot beat a good model yacht race meeting.

12. Summing Up

I wonder how many of you are heartily relieved that our first race is over? I hope not too many, although of course I realise that this book cannot hope to please all of those who for one reason or another sail model yachts using radio control.

I realise for example, that 575 and 590 skippers are not very interested in the International Yacht Racing Rules, but they ought to be interested in the tactics I set out to gain places during a race. The tactics employed at the start and the tuning hints might also be of interest.

What I have in mind by club races is literally internal races open to club members only. In my experience these races are very different to open races where skippers from other clubs come along to the host club to do battle. Club races offer you a fairly protected environment where it should be reasonably easy for you to soon recognise the pecking order and the various skills displayed by the racing members. Existing club members in turn recognise even quicker the skills of the new member and adjust their sailing when close to the newcomer accordingly. For example, it is easy to spot the complete novice and a wise racing club member gives the novice's boat lots of room on the water. Club members will, if asked, give their help and advice to the novice newcomer. Most people within the radio controlled model yachting fraternity realise that we desperately need more people within our sport and will go out of their way to offer all manner of help and support.

We usually find that anyone who gives our sport a week or two of hands-on experience is hooked. It really is a wonderful hobby/sport with enough challenges to satisfy the most demanding appetite. There are plenty of levels within the sport to satisfy most tastes. Not everyone has the ambition to try to become National Champion but there is plenty of satisfaction to be gained from doing what the vast majority of model yachtsmen do and that is sail or race at their own club with perhaps the odd visit to a neighbouring club. I certainly enjoyed enormously the first two or three years of my model yacht racing simply sailing all the time at Gosport.

Gosport Club has possibly one of the best water facilities in the country and I feel I was very lucky to be living within twenty miles of it. Every week I would be there dying to have another go. During those years I gradually got to understand the basics of the rules that we have been covering in this book. I tried to find books to read to help me improve but, it proved impossible to find one book that was able to give me much help. The best I could find was little bits in a number of different books. That is because perhaps at that stage I wanted pretty basic advice. These days of course I'm still looking at various books and building up a library. It still is the case though that you need to pick out little bits from here and there.

At the end of this book I shall give a list of all the books that I have referred to in this book, both to help readers wanting to investigate further any aspects of sailing and to give due credit to those worthy people whose efforts in the past to put pen to paper helped me to acquire my knowledge and to develop my experience. After all there is nothing very new in sailing, except the modern benefits of high tech materials. You dream up some new rig or gizmo and it is odds on that the Victorians or before had taken it up and then forgotten it. Man has been harnessing the power of the wind for many centuries to provide motion in boats, controlled with varying degrees of success.

Before we finish this book, I think it should be of help if we take the time in this chapter to review everything that we have covered to date and perhaps to enlarge on one or two points. The first thing any novice wants to know is how to make the thing go. After all the first thing we want to do with a new toy is get it out and use it — it is just the same with a model yacht. You assemble it, put all the electrics in, connect everything up, check it all works and then off to the water. In it goes and, wonder of wonders, off it moves as the wind catches the sails. Usually very soon however, it stops moving and drifts around for a while while you struggle to get your pride and joy to move again. Let's suppose that you have never sailed before and have never built and flown model aircraft either. You realise, of course, that it is the sails that provide the power to shift the yacht along but that is about it. If you have never had occasion to use the power of the wind before you are in for a few surprises. I don't suppose too many of us gave the wind much thought other than being something that varied in strength from day to day and occasionally blows trees down or worse. In reality as we all soon find out, it swings around all over the place sometimes and rarely blows from a steady direction, preferring instead to swing some degrees each side of a mean direction. Its strength can go up and down like a yoyo. You learn that the wind can be blowing in different directions over very localised areas. The wind on your check may not be blowing from exactly the same direction on your yacht's sails that is only a few yards away.

Having got a rough idea as to where the wind is coming from, the poor old newcomer then has to work out at what angle the sails should be set to the wind. Thus we arrive at our first refresher diagram (Diagram 12.1) that simply shows the points of sail that a modern yacht can obtain forward motion from. You can immediately see

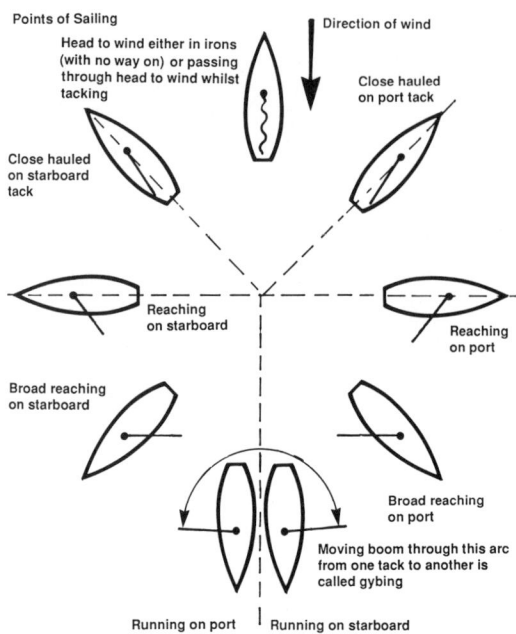

Diagram 12.1

that there is an area roughly forty-five degrees or so each side of the direction that the wind is coming from where the yacht cannot sail into. A yacht cannot sail directly into wind — if you think about it that is obvious. If you are relying on the wind to have an effect on the yacht's sails to push it forward, you are not likely to have much success if the wind is rushing evenly past each side of the sail. All that happens is the sails flap or flutter about and the yacht gradually falls backwards and away to one side or the other of the wind's direction. We call that getting into irons and it is the most time wasting problem to the novice as he comes to terms with tacking i.e. changing the side the wind blows onto the sails. Just to remind you, a yacht is on a starboard tack as shown in Diagram 12.1 on the left-hand side of the diagram in 8, 9 and 10 o'clock positions, plus the right-hand six o'clock position. The yacht is on port tack in the opposite positions. The yacht at the twelve o'clock position is head to wind — it retains the tack it was on before going head to wind until it passes through head to wind and onto its new tack.

As a complete novice once you can manage to sail through all points of the wind it is a good idea to practise tacking and gybing. A good way to do this is to keep sailing around a buoy trying to keep the boat moving all the time. Since in your early racing career you are going to be doing lots of penalty turns, you might as well learn how to execute them well at the same time as perfecting your tacking and gybing techniques.

The basic tacking techniques were covered in Chapter 3. The main points to observe are smoothness of the tack and to ensure that you actually have good boat speed before commencing to tack. In moderate winds I find it best to execute a fairly gentle turn up to and just beyond head to wind — this helps to retain the speed that the boat has. I then turn a little more quickly onto the new heading, or even just beyond the new heading, letting the sails out just a touch. As the yacht picks up speed again sheet the sails back in and harden up to your optimum close-hauled course. If your yacht is set up correctly it should assume the correct close-hauled course, once the sails are fully sheeted in, without any assistance from the rudder. So if you have to steer your yacht to hold it on a close-hauled course on both tacks you need to alter the balance of the yacht. One way of doing this is if the yacht when left alone is always falling off the wind having been set on a close-hauled course on both tacks, then move the rig back towards the stern. This can be achieved by moving the mast position, by moving the jib or by just raking the mast further back. All will have the effect of moving the centre of effort further back. Moving the fin forward would have the same effect, although in this case you are moving the centre of resistance forward. (Resistance to leeward movement.) If, on the other hand, the yacht tends to screw up into wind if left to its own devices on both tacks then do the opposite — move the centre of effort forward or the centre of resistance back. You'll notice I was very careful to emphasise that you ensure that the yacht is behaving the same on both tacks before altering the balance of the boat. That is because if it only happens on one tack that it screws up into the wind, it is odds on that on the other tack it is falling off or sailing steady. In that case the problem is likely to simply be one on centering the rudder correctly. If you still have a problem after all that has been checked, then start checking out the set of the keel fin vertically and in line from bow to stern. Then check the mast for a symmetrical trim and lastly check that the hull is in fact true and symmetrical! You should also bear in mind that different strengths of wind will affect the behaviour of your yacht differently too. As the wind increases it usually has the effect of moving the centre of effort back in the sails resulting in more tendency to screw up to wind. In moderation this can be an advantage, but if your yacht screws too much up into wind then you are going to lose speed if you are turning the rudder in the opposite direction to compensate. It is better to sheet out a little to let some of the pressure of the wind off the sails, you will probably also increase the boat speed by doing so. If the wind continues in its new strength you need to consider changing down the sail area. Besides the yacht becoming difficult to control, the other indicators that suggest changing down are the angle of heel while close-hauled and the amount the bow buries itself while on the run. Other skippers changing down is a very useful indicator to the novice as well!

There is no advantage in carrying more sail than required to move your yacht through the water at its optimum speed relative to the winds. The only possible area of advantage is in acceleration of the boat up to maximum speed. That small advantage is more than lost through the loss of motive power while beating owing to the angle of heel, which might quite possibly be coupled to excessive leeway, burying the bow completely below water while on the run, capsizing, waving the rudder in the air while on the run and the inability to tack the thing as well! So it does pay to keep a good eye on wind strength!

Tacking in heavier winds demands a different approach. As mentioned above, if you have too much sail area up for the wind's strength tacking can become impossible. Should you find yourself in the position where you are unable to tack do consider the option of gybing instead. It is far better to execute a quick gybe than continue to struggle time after time attempting to tack. Sooner or later a real hazard will appear and you will need to change the direction of your yacht a bit sharpish or face disaster. Be careful when gybing not to sheet out too far, because as the main goes across the wind it will slam onto the new setting quite violently. On a full-sized vessel you have to be very careful in such conditions to do a fully controlled gybe or face losing the mast or boom! There is a much easier way available most of the time. Firstly ensure that you have good boat speed — if necessary bear off a little while easing out the sheets at the same time then slam the boat across to the new tack as quickly as possible, bear off again to regain speed and then slowly sheet in and assume a close-hauled course again. Even if you do not have to bear off to gain speed before tacking it is a good idea to sheet out a little just as you commence the tack. Also do keep an eye on the waves approaching the bow of the yacht immediately prior to tacking. You need a wave that is approaching from the current leeward side of the bow to help push you round — you most definitely do not want a wave to be approaching from the windward side of your bow because you will find it very difficult to tack through that. The other approach is to get on top of a wave and then tack.

Needless to say very light winds also require a different approach. The most valuable thing you possess as a racing yacht in whisper light winds is forwards motion. It is critical to retain that motion even at the expense of sailing in the wrong direction. If there are yachts lying around in the water going nowhere do be very sure that you really do want to tack before attempting it. It may well be the case that you have crossed the layline to the next buoy, but there is always more than one way to get to the buoy and are you sure that the section of water you are planning to tack across to actually has any wind passing over it? In very light winds there can be whacking great holes all over the place — try not to sail into one just because it is between you and the next buoy. That is something that comes with experience but the actual tacking manoeuvre can be taught. It has to be oh so gentle that it is untrue. The slightest of rudder movement and ghost the yacht across and well beyond the normal close-hauled course. The biggest worry you now have is to get the sails across and if you have not previously set your yacht up for very light winds, you could have a problem. Everything needs to be extremely light

or extremely loose. You need more twist in your sails than usual and less tension in your jib stay. Everything must be so free and easy to swing across, and the material in the jib must be free enough to pop across and fill when on the new tack. You may not believe this, but it is often the case that the jib and even the main do not shift from their belly out position of one tack to the opposite belly out tack of the new tack, even though the booms have swung across. It is rather frustrating to be standing on the bank watching your yacht slowly being overtaken by others that have had the luck or skill to get sails across and full and drawing! The other thing that happens in very light winds of course is that the centre of effort moves forwards from its usual position (set up for force 3 to 4 say), and this creates problems too.

I first came across it when my well-behaved and well-balanced yacht simply would not sail to windward very well in very light winds. If I tacked it, it would continue to turn on round after I wanted it to stop and assume its new course, so I had to turn completely around again and have another go. The centre of effort had moved forward and had the effect of making the yacht want to bear off all of the time. So you need to either move the centre of effort backwards or slacken up the jib to loose the amount of power in the jib.

To summarise on tacking and balancing a yacht: remember that different wind strengths will make your yacht behave differently as may different sized sails. Set your yacht up to be well behaved in the prevailing conditions at your club, make a note of those settings or better still mark them with paint on the deck. Then remember to adjust when conditions change. Remember to change your tacking techniques to suit the wind strength also. (In the excitement of racing all of this goes out of the window time after time, but in the end some of it should become well ingrained. Even now after many years of racing, I still on occasions forget myself and execute a quick slam tack instead of a nice and easy controlled tack.)

Not surprisingly, the other thing that varies with wind strengths is the actual setting of the sails, besides the size. The correct size is the most important thing and, as I have mentioned before, the actual setting of the sails is open to all sorts of different interpretations and I believe that the best course of action open to the novice is trial and error. It is, of course, very helpful for the novice to have a point of reference about which to start though. On a swing rig the setting of the jib boom in relation to the main boom is an easy matter — it needs to be somewhere between five and ten degrees off the main boom line. Chapter Six covered tuning to some degree.

On a conventional rig the main, when close-hauled, should be around 5 degrees off the centre-line of bow to stern and the jib boom must be further out than the main by five to ten degrees. The belly of the jib and main must never be drawn tight and flat. There are some skippers who think that in heavy winds you should sail having flat or tight sails. I disagree — a sail must have some shape to it in order for it to become a controllable airfoil and provide motive power to the yacht. I used to do a lot of windsurfing and I developed my skills over some years, in very heavy winds. (Wind force 10 and above.) Out of curiosity I have tried a very flat sail section in those conditions and I can assure you that it is a complete waste of time. All you get is an uncontrollable rig without any balance to it whatsoever. That is because the variation of air pressure from one side of the sail to the other is practically zero, thus the sail tends to behave like a sail in irons. Put a bit of belly in the sail and all of a sudden you have a stable sail that you can put all of your weight against and zoom off across the waves.

The same principle applies to model yacht racing. Even in the strongest winds if you wish to be out there you need sails that provide controllable motive power. So while in very strong winds you need tight rigging, you most certainly need some belly in both sails. You might also need a little more twist in the sails than usual. If you do not have very small sets of sails you will need even more twist in the sails simply as a way of depowering an over-sized rig. The amount of belly a sail needs is obviously in relation to its size. Proportionally they all need about the same

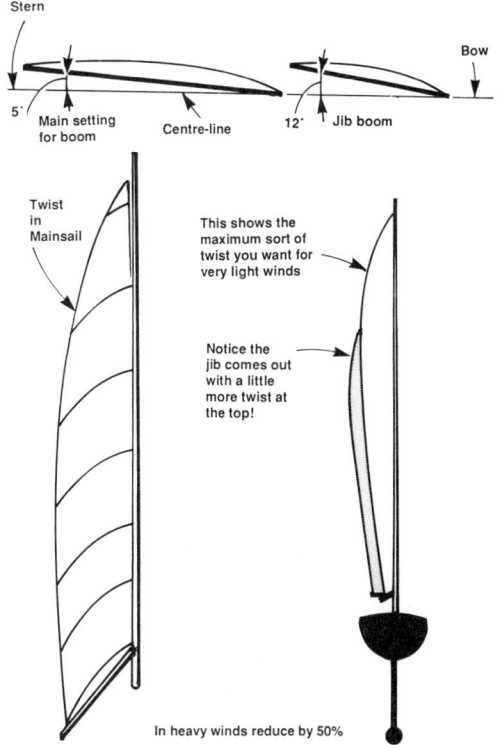

Diagram 12.2

section, but as the foot area lengthens so the measurement between the boom and the belly increases. I guess I'm usually looking to make a shape that has the fullest part of the belly about a third of the way back from the leading edge of the sail, and I'm looking to make a shape that is quite like the cross section of a model glider's upper wing surface at its central point. There seems to be quite a wide area of tolerance around this point which is why I suggest you experiment a little. The cord shape of the sail is only one part of setting up a sail. The next obvious thing to get right is the amount of twist in the main, but before you can do that you must ensure that the mast has the correct shape to follow the luff of the main. The sail maker will either have cut your sails to suit a straight mast or one that has a certain amount of bend in it. You need to bend the mast to suit the sail if necessary. How? Well the first bit of string that comes to mind is the backstay — whether your rig is conventional or swing you need a backstay to control mast shape. The tension in the jib stay will also affect the

97

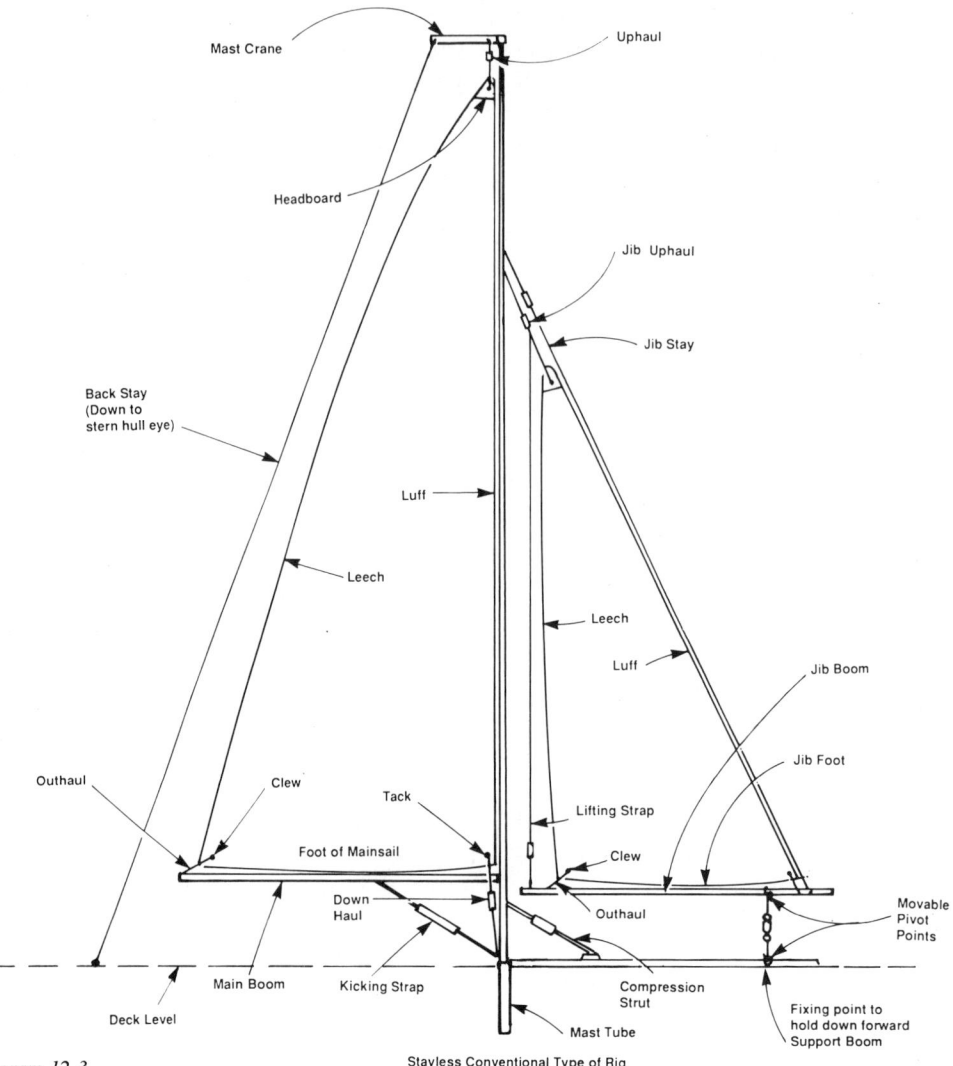

Mast Crane

Uphaul

Headboard

Jib Uphaul

Jib Stay

Back Stay
(Down to
stern hull eye)

Luff

Leech

Leech

Luff

Jib Boom

Jib Foot

Outhaul

Clew

Tack

Lifting Strap

Clew

Movable
Pivot
Points

Foot of Mainsail

Down
Haul

Outhaul

Deck Level

Main Boom

Kicking Strap

Compression
Strut

Mast Tube

Fixing point to
hold down forward
Support Boom

Diagram 12.3

Stayless Conventional Type of Rig

shape of the mast so be careful. Tension in the kicking strap can also distort the mast lower down. So get that mast to the right shape and now let's look for some twist in the main. What is twist? Well, it is the amount the leech of the sail (the back edge) twists away from the anchor position at its clew (bottom corner of sail at the back) as it rises up towards the top of the mast and its headboard (top corner of the sail).

On a Marblehead's tall suit (around 80 to 85 inches high) I would be looking for no more than two inches twist from top to bottom. The twist in the jib should parallel the twist in the main through the lower three quarters and twist away

slightly more through the top quarter of the jib's leech. It is important that both sails set with a smooth surface all over, wrinkles not only look bad, they disturb the flow of the wind over the sail's surfaces. Twist in the main should be adjusted by use of the kicking strap or compression strut. Other adjustments that can affect twist in the main are tension in the outhaul or uphaul. Tension in the downhaul can help to remove wrinkle in the front section of the main. It is possible that too much tension in the jib forestay can remove twist in the main. You should always check that any alterations to the forestay, backstay and jib stay have not in turn altered twist setting

98

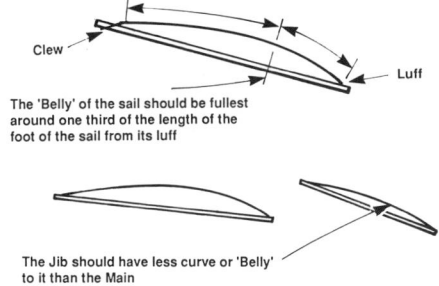

Clew

Luff

The 'Belly' of the sail should be fullest
around one third of the length of the
foot of the sail from its luff

The Jib should have less curve or 'Belly'
to it than the Main

Diagram 12.4

etc. Twist in the jib is mainly introduced or con-trolled by the lifting strap.

When starting out as a novice do not be afraid to copy other people's settings. Look at how other models in your new club have their sails set and don't be nervous of asking for help. The worst that can happen is that you will receive more advice than you can cope with. Not all of the advice you will receive will be of much help — there are plenty of people sailing models that have been sailing them for years and still, in my opinion, have serious misconceptions as to what is necessary to get the best out of their own yacht let alone anyone else's yacht. But they mean well and sooner or later you will learn to sort the wheat from the chaff.

To tell you the truth, if you can get both main and jib working well together there is, as I said previously, a wide tolerance in settings and while there may be minute advantages to be gained by the very fine tuning, it is at best only going to result in a minor advantage that may not show itself over the length of course we usually race over. If you really want returns on your invest-ment study tactics and strategy, if you know where you want to be and how to get there at any given time, you will gain far more than the person who has simply got good boat speed, without good starting and racing skills.

The last point we need remember before racing considerations come into play is reliability. It is no good winning a few early races in a meeting if your boat lets you down with three races to go! If you are intent on winning a meeting you cannot afford to miss more races than there are discards. Your objective is to be totally reliable and not miss any races through gear failure. I'm afraid

however that we all suffer on occasions from some gear failure or other. Most race meetings use a system of discards. For example, if there are eight races you may be allowed to discard your worst result. This is a system used in full-sized racing as well and it does compensate you for genuine mishaps such as picking up weed or gear failure.

It is possible to a large extent to protect your-self against gear failure. For example, regular inspection of all lines should catch fraying line in time to replace it before racing, rather than discovering the problem in the middle of a race as a sail crumples up or the winch line snaps. Having a reliable attachment system of winch lines to booms is necessary as is a reasonably waterproof boat. Always have some waterproof sticky tape available together with spare sticky deck covers if used. Never use a sticky deck cover twice unless sailing in very light winds. Remember to check in between each race for any water taken on and drain it off. Keep an eye on your yacht as it sails — if you notice it getting low in the water bring it in as quickly as possible rather than see it sink in the middle of the lake (a fairly rare occurrence I am glad to say).

The area that is most likely to let you down is the radio/electronics. Water is the first enemy whether salty or fresh. No electrical system that I know of enjoys water. Servos tend to kick hard over in one direction and stay there as their innards get wet. Receivers getting wet can produce the same symptoms. Winches tend to start hunting in and out or just to run continually in one direction only. Loss of control over a distance usually turns out to be a ranging problem, either the transmitter is down on power or its aerial is loose. On the receiver it is usually because the aerial has got the dreaded black wire where the wire is slowly corroding. Black wire disease hits the servo and the winch as well and is easily prevented by simply replacing all wiring at least every other season. Water problems are best avoided. Seal all servos and winches by smearing Evostick all over screws, holes, sealing lines and entry points for cables. Receivers and batteries should be in a waterproof plastic pot, which has had all exit and entry points for cables sealed with silicon sealer. The threaded lid of the pot should have a continuous thread with Vaseline smeared round it for extra sealing power. Batteries should be regularly replaced. Rechargeable Ni-Cad cells seem to have a life or four or five years maximum, after which their ability to hold a charge diminishes. It is up to you as to whether you wish to find that out in the middle of a race or simply replace them before they have reached the end of their productive life. On the subject of batteries, have enough sets of batteries to last all day with plenty to spare. I use a pack of six Ni-Cads to last four races only. I therefore have four fully charged sets with me for each day's racing plus one or two spares. Have enough chargers to enable you to keep your batteries charged according to your level of racing. If you are entering two-day events, you need to be able to recharge all batteries including the transmitter batteries over one night.

Battery wires get the dreaded black wire disease as well, so check them once a year. The plugs connecting batteries to winches/receivers etc. also suffer from corrosion, protect them with a dab of Vaseline as well. Screws mounting servos and winches can corrode, keep an eye on them. The screws fixing the winch drum and servo arm can work loose, so keep an eye on them as well.

Doing all of these things cuts down on the number of things that can ruin your day's racing. If you are the sort of person who doesn't mind losing the odd race through gear failure, then take no notice of the above and simply wait for something to give up and then replace it — it might be cheaper. I'm afraid for me though, it would spoil my enjoyment of the day's racing. I don't mind not winning at all, but I do like to know that I have put up a good fight and that I was simply beaten by better skippers.

Once we have attended to all of the above and are happy with our ability to tack, gybe and turn circles quickly we are ready to race. If you have read all of this book you are more than ready to race. If you can remember more than ten per cent of the points I have made and the rules I have listed you've got a good chance of not coming last. We will finalise this summary in the next chapter.

13. Final Summary

In this final chapter we wrap up this book. While there will be less emphasis on the rules, it has to be remembered that the rules do play a large part when racing if you wish to consistently achieve good results. There are a lot of skippers racing who are too lazy to bother to acquire anything more than the most fundamental basic understanding of one or two rules. Some have the attitude that racing should be pure fun and that rules spoil the fun. Some are frightened of the rules. The rule book, when you see it for the first time, is somewhat large and contains all sorts of mumbo jumbo. If you actually take the trouble to read it quickly through you'll soon realise that three quarters of it does not apply to day-to-day racing. We have already covered all of the rules that matter and if you look back through previous chapters, you'll have to agree that really they did not take up that much space, despite repeating some of them several times! Some people just can't be bothered, which is a pity really because they are missing out on the opportunity to develop their ability to its maximum potential. It also means that whenever they are involved in an incident they have to accept the penalty turns, because they do not know whether they are in the right or wrong. Thus they have to take the opinion of the other skipper involved as being correct. It amazes me the number of times I see the skipper who is in the right breaking away and doing two turns! The easy points to remember are:

You must concentrate from the moment you put your yacht on the water to the moment you take it off again.

You need to keep your eyes not only on your own yacht, but also on all those yachts that are near to your yacht or that are sailing courses that will take them near to the course your own yacht is sailing along.

You need to constantly be aware of what tack your yacht is on.

You need to know what course you are going to sail.

You need to have on the same sized sails as the majority of the fleet or to have good reason to be carrying a different size.

Since a windward yacht has to keep clear of a leeward yacht you have to know what this means. (**Rule 37** Chapter 2).

Since a port boat gives way to a starboard yacht you need to know the difference.

Since going round a mark an inside boat at the four boats' length gains an inside overlap and certain rights you ought to know that as well. (**Rule 42** Chapter 4).

The alternative penalty may need to be employed by you so perhaps you should know all about that as well. **Rule 52.2(a)** and Appendix 3.1 (720-degree turns, you remember the ones you have been practising!)

Armed with the above you can probably struggle round the course but if you have read all of the previous chapters you can do a lot more than that — you ought to be able to sail round it with some confidence and some idea of what to expect from other racing yachts. Once you have overcome your nerves you will have great fun. If you are not a little bit nervous I'd be very surprised — it is nothing to be ashamed of and it can actually help by keying you up to be that little bit extra vigilant and hopefully having you firing on all cylinders.

If you remember the start was where we needed to try and time ourselves from a reference point to the start line, that point being something between fifteen and thirty seconds from the start line that allows us to approach it on a close-hauled course on the starboard tack. Why on the starboard tack? So that we do not have to worry about yachts on the opposite tack. They are going to have to give way to us, not us give way to them. Remember also at the start that it is better to be one second late, than one second early. It is also better to approach the line at full speed rather than having to slow down as you approach and then try to accelerate away at the gun.

Once over the line and into the race all we have to remember is to zigzag up the windward beat and do our final approach to the windward mark on the starboard tack. We also have to remember which side we are to leave the mark on! Don't forget luffing both as a defender of position and as an overtaker of boats to leeward. Don't get engaged in luffing battles that allow the rest of the fleet to sail on past.

Remember that a line projected from your transom at right angles to your course will give you a good idea of when you have reached the layline for the mark and it will also help you to calculate whether the tack you are on is the correct tack to be on i.e. the one that is taking you nearest to the windward mark. When about to round the windward mark, remember **Rule 42** and all the business about overlap. The inside boat that has the overlap established at the four boats' length, has the right to room at the mark, even if the outside boat has subsequently drawn clear ahead. Remember your obligations if clear ahead at the four boat lengths, don't tack in the water of a yacht close astern to you. As a yacht clear astern at the four boats' length you must not luff up above close-hauled in an attempt to stop a yacht clear ahead from tacking to round mark.

If you are leaving the windward mark to port and you have approached it on starboard, as will most yachts, there will not be any tacking to do, but if you have to leave the mark on starboard,

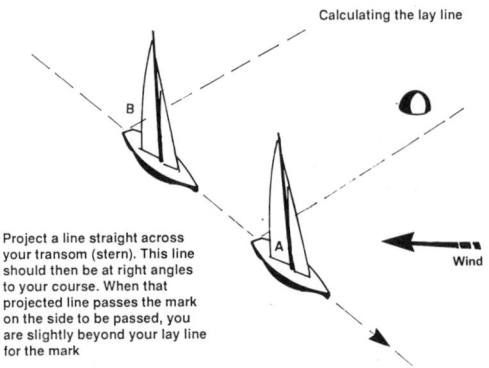

Calculating the lay line

Project a line straight across your transom (stern). This line should then be at right angles to your course. When that projected line passes the mark on the side to be passed, you are slightly beyond your lay line for the mark

Wind

Diagram 13.1

and you have approached the mark to starboard, there will be plenty of tacking going on and it is a very dangerous moment in the race with yachts tacking to port in front of yachts approaching on starboard — you have to time it just right! The best plan is to approach the mark really tight, luff up as you pass the mark and then slam the yacht across to port tack. That way a yacht clear astern is going to have to luff up while on starboard to try and hit you, and that is not allowed under **Rule 42.2(b)**. If you simply tack as you pass the mark, the stern of your yacht may well swing out and into the close-hauled path of the yacht close astern, who may quite legitimately tap your stern and protest you for tacking in their water! That means two penalty turns to do as soon as possible!

On the off-the-wind leg to the wing mark remember to keep the wind in your sails and to try to place yourself to get the inside overlap at the wing mark. Remember that you will be gybing at the wing mark and that on the usual port rounding course you will be gybing from starboard to port. If you are wise you will sail as close to the mark as possible and then gybe as quickly as possible. If you sail very wide of the mark you do not have divine right to gybe to a port tack and get in the way of yachts still on starboard tack, so be very careful.

On the second reaching leg down to the lee-ward mark, the main objective again is to gain the inside overlap at the leeward mark. This leg is perhaps the most dangerous for dramatic luffing games — you can easily find yourself being diverted well off course up to windward as the yacht close to you that you are trying to establish an inside overlap on decides that there is no way that you are going to achieve that at his expense.

Remember to try and maintain boat speed as you round the leeward mark, be prepared to have yachts slowing down in front of you and be prepared to find yachts tacking quickly across to starboard as they round the mark. Try and remember on the second windward beat how to get command over a yacht clear ahead. Don't forget that as yachts are approaching an obstruction that they may well be calling for "water" (**Rule 43**), remember that you *must* make a reply or tack yourself immediately. If you in turn have a yacht close by that you need to call to before you can tack, make that call immediately and wait for their reply before tacking. Thus, when approaching obstructions, all yachts need to be very alert and the first yacht has to allow all of the other yachts time to make their calls and reply before being able to rely on getting the water demanded. This is a rule that is rarely properly understood. Once round the windward mark for the second time remember that this time it is a straight run down to the leeward mark.

Think about getting your yacht directly between the direction of the wind and the yacht in front so as to blanket his wind. Once again be thinking of gaining the inside overlap as you approach the four boats' length circle.

Remember that a yacht clear ahead that has a yacht approaching from astern trying to overhaul her to leeward, shall not sail below a proper course once that boat astern is within three boat lengths of the yacht clear ahead (**Rule 39**). This makes gaining the overlap on the run and reach it a bit easier than it would be without the protection of this rule, so make sure that the rule is firmly in your memory.

Rounding the leeward mark again you have exactly the same objectives and considerations as the first rounding. The only difference is that now time is running out as regards gaining places, all that remains is the final beat. However, there are still places to be gained and lost so keep concentrating and trying. Gaining command over the yacht clear ahead can now pay dividends. If it tacks to starboard you sail under its stern and then immediately tack yourself. The yacht clear

ahead cannot now tack to port to lay the line until you decide to let it, so you push it way beyond the layline before tacking yourself, at which stage you should be in front. If the yacht clear ahead stays on port tack after rounding the leeward mark you simply sail on port tack as well, keeping slightly to windward of the yacht clear ahead. That yacht cannot now tack to starboard without tacking in your water — again you simply push it way beyond the layline to the finish so that when you tack you become in front. However don't forget the rest of the fleet — it is no good beating one boat in front, if while doing that three slip past from behind! Remember therefore, to keep a watchful eye regularly on the entire fleet. This become easier to do the more practice you have.

Remember to keep an eye also on the sails and direction of sailing of the rest of the fleet — they should give you clues as to what is going on regarding wind direction and any shifts or bends about. Once you have finished the race sail well clear of the finishing line, preferably to windward thus keeping well out of the way of any yachts still racing. Bring your yacht back to the bank and check that it has not taken on water.

Do remember every few races to change your batteries! It is most frustrating to be having a good race only to see your yacht suddenly start going round in large circles as you lose control of it due to battery failure! If you are lucky you might get the odd clue just before the battery runs out. The sail winch often becomes very slow to operate — if you suspect this is happening get your yacht to the bank quickly. It is worth carrying a spare battery set in your pocket to enable ultra-quick changes to take place in emergencies. It is, however, much better never to require such measures by simply only using your batteries for a conservative number of races! If you do carry a battery around in a pocket, do not carry anything else in that pocket! I have almost set myself on fire forgetting that simple rule! Any coins or other metal in a pocket may just short across the terminals of the plug and start cooking you. If you have never seen it, you would be very surprised at the amount of destructive power stored in our little battery sets.

It is quite possible to ruin all of your wiring, while fiddling about with the boat sticking your nose into the various circuits trying to find the problem. If you start to see smoke coming from anywhere, disconnect your battery fast!

Now if you really are a complete newcomer to our sport and this is the first book you have read, you are not going to remember all of the prompts I've listed in the previous chapters, so let's just have the most basic requirements listed in order to enter a race.

At least know how to control your new love. Be able to tack and gybe it with confidence. Have an idea of how the sails set in relation to the position of your control stick. This way you will have a rough idea of the set of the sails even when they are too far away to see properly what the actual setting is.

Tell all the racing skippers *before* you race that you are a complete novice. Not only will they keep reasonably clear of you if they have any sense, but some will offer you words of encouragement and advice as you struggle to come to grips with it all.

Try and work out the difference between port and starboard tacks.

Do approach the start on the starboard tack — it makes life so much easier. Just aim to keep clear of the boats that are all trying to keep clear of you, but not too clear or else you will be too far behind at the start and will never catch up. Don't be afraid to copy the other boats and follow any boat that happens to be just in front up the windward beat. Keep an eye out for all the other boats and follow your particular leader. Do this for a few races just to get the feel of the whole thing. Remember that as your yacht is sailing towards you, you have to move the rudder control stick in what appears to be the wrong direction to turn the yacht. This takes a race or two to get used to.

Above all, enjoy the day and the participation. Don't be put off by the shouting that sometimes goes on. It is rarely personal or lasts for any length of time. There is bound to be the odd skipper who shouts at you as you sail on port across his bows ruining his start or chances of winning, or so the shouting skipper believes at the time. He'll soon calm down and realise that if he had recognised that it was your boat he ought to have given you a wide berth! Skippers do get cross with each other on occasions, some will take protests very personally and have a little sulk when disqualified, but because the next race happens almost immediately such incidents are soon forgotten!

It is perhaps worth knowing, that as racing yachtsmen we are looking to score the least number of points over the days racing in order to win! If you win a race, you may score nothing, ¾ of a point or 1 point, according to what system your club is using. If you finish fifth then you will score five points etc. After eight races perhaps, you will be allowed to discard your worst (highest) score for one race. This helps to cover for any really bad luck that comes your way, such as weed around your keel that slowed you down badly. At the end of the day all of the scores are added up, after discarding discards, and the one with the lowest score is the overall winner. It is possible to win the day without even having won a race! For example if you came second in every race and three or four other skippers won a couple of races each, your final score is likely to be lower than theirs, because in the races when they did not come first they must have come third at least! The more races that are sailed in a day the more discards that will be awarded! It does all depend on the racing and scoring system being used by the club. Some clubs use their own systems for internal club races and some do not use the discard system at all.

There will often be a club racing system that covers many of the club races over the entire season whereby the skipper that wins the most events over the season becomes the club champion for example. Some clubs will run a handicap system so that even you as a complete novice have a chance to win something!

Just to repeat myself, do not be put off by the shouting of starboards, overlaps, water, luffing, mast abeam stem and protest that ring across the calm waters of the lake. It is all a part of yacht racing and you will soon not only become used to it, but will be calling your own rights too! For those of you that have formed a new enthusiastic group of budding racing skippers here are a few tips to set up your own little race meeting. First how many yachts do you need to start a race? Two or more is enough! If there is just you and a friend, then it is easy to engage in a bit of what we call match racing. It is a particularly enjoyable form of racing because it does allow you to concentrate more on sailing your own boat and trying to beat one other boat without having to worry about other boats popping up from nowhere getting in your way. All the manoeuvres around the marks and at the start become so much simpler when there is only one other boat involved.

Wherever you are sailing, you are going to need some marks to sail around. If you can make up some buoys to use that will be the best solution, although of course you may then require a rowing boat to put the buoys out on the water. If the water is shallow then waders may be enough or a pair of shorts depending on the time of year. Remember to watch out for things like broken glass if you are considering going barefoot into water. If for any reason you cannot put out buoys, then maybe you can use some existing mark in the water or simply use a landmark and turn when you have gone past it. It is not very

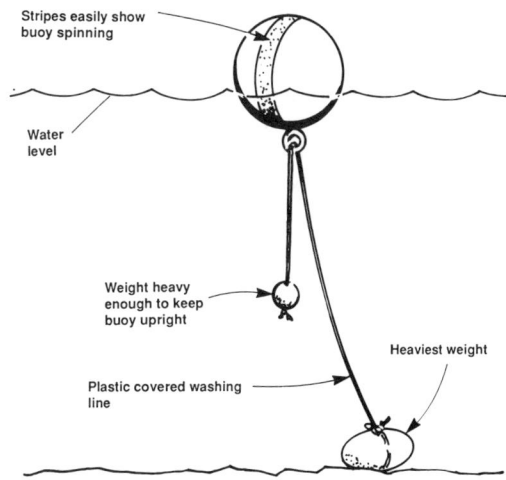

Diagram 13.1(b)

satisfactory, but perhaps will allow you to get some racing practice in. Otherwise just trying to beat each other going up on beat can be done. Followed by a race down wind.

Buoys can be made from all sorts of things. The main object is to have something that floats and that can be held at anchor in one place. The more visible the mark is the better and I certainly feel that it is a great help if it is not so large that a model heeling over can touch it with its sails.

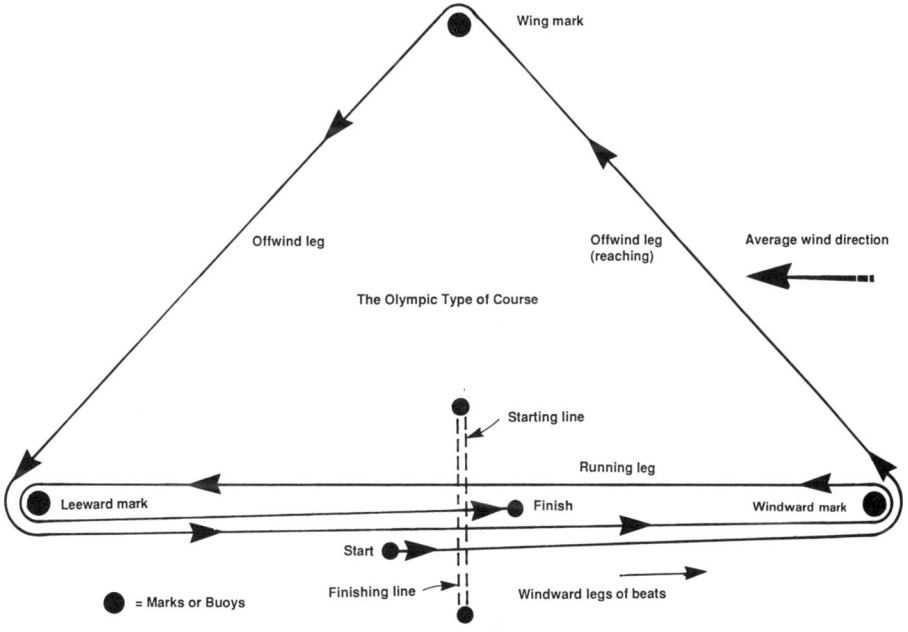

Diagram 13.2

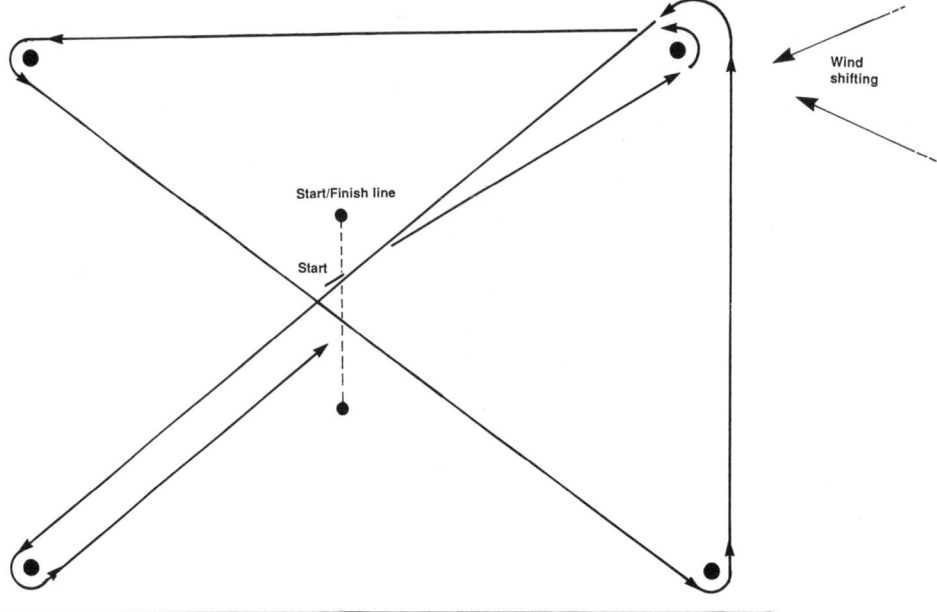

Diagram 13.3

Wind shifting

Start/Finish line

Start

Control Bank

However, the interests of visibility sometimes conflict with this objective. Anchorage is usually achieved by means of a line attached to a fairly heavy weight. The line should either be adjustable in length by using a bowsie or should be self-adjusting by using a line with one heavy weight to lie on the bottom of the lake and a lighter weight at the other end of the line which hangs in the water under the buoy and is just heavy enough to hold the buoy upright. The line which works best is the plastic washing line variety passed through an attachment point on the underside of the buoy and of a length that keeps the secondary weight off the bottom. This system usually takes a bit of trial and error to perfect, but is by far the best because it achieves the final objective of a good mark, which is that the ground tackle should be vertical.

If you have an anchorage line that is not vertical, then there is a very real chance that a passing yacht's keel can hook up on the anchor line and that is very annoying. The problem with keeping the ground tackle vertical on a buoy that has the bowsie method of line adjustment is that while it will work fine when the water is fairly flat, once a chop builds up on the water the mark can start to move as the peak of the waves lift the weight

up off the bottom of the lake. If the line is too slack, then the buoy tends to lie on its side and can move about around its anchor line. Once again the anchor line can easily now catch unsuspecting yachts! The marks on which it is most essential to have taut anchor lines are the start and finish marks together with the windward mark. Three buoys are required to set the course plus a couple of smaller buoys for the start/finish line. Diagram 13.2 shows the usual sort of Olympic type course used. The start line should be a minimum of one boat's length width for every boat racing at one time and should be laid square to the wind. The windward mark should be dead upwind from the start line and the leeward mark dead downwind of the windward mark. The wing mark should be out one side or the other ideally by 45 degrees. There is no compulsion to use this type of course but all ranking events, National and International events do so, it is worth getting used to. It is thought to provide the best challenge to racing skippers. It can also be fun to set up different types of course on odd occasions as well.

Diagram 13.3 gives one idea that is particularly useful when the wind is regularly shifting through 45 to 90 degrees. You can then set a course that, with a bit of luck, will include a fair bit of wind-

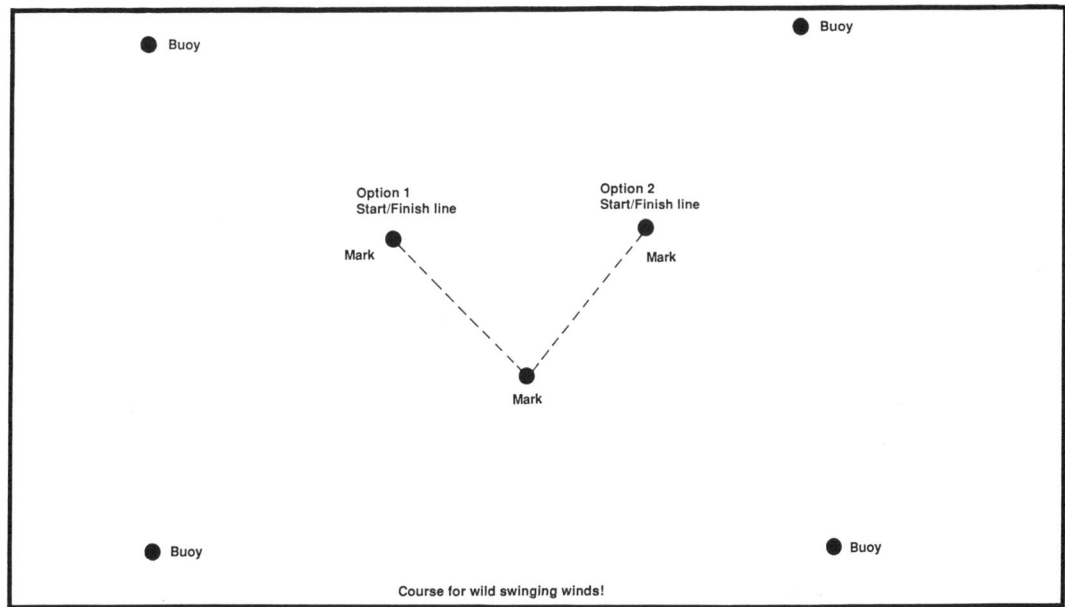

Diagram 13.4

ward beating, rather than just reaching legs. The diagram shows one such option, although of course having the four marks allows all sorts of different courses to be sailed with the crossover section occasionally providing good excitement.

Diagram 13.4 develops this four square set-up a little further by laying a triangle of starting marks in the middle of the larger square. Now you can use whichever line happens to be nearest to square to the wind for each race. In thundery conditions the wind can easily swing through 180 degrees several times through the day and while the storm is actually overhead it is wise not to race, but there can often be good racing in between storms. In fact at Gosport the storms have a habit of moving all around Gosport without ever hitting Gosport itself. With a bit of imagination you could set up all sorts of different courses. It is quite amusing to occasionally set a course that includes both port and starboard rounding of separate buoys — it brings new tactics into play especially when trying to establish overlaps!

Having set up a course the next thing you really require is a starting signal. When there are only two of you, it is not so important, since you can take it in turns to start each each other off, making sure that you are both close to each other. However, it is very easy to make a starting tape

that can be played on a portable tape recorder. All you need is a one minute warning of countdown, i.e. "In ten seconds a one minute countdown will commence". Then using a watch every ten seconds go 60, 50, 40, 30, 20, 10 and then every second, 9, 8, 7, 6, 5, 4, 3, 2, 1, GO. The start command must be very short and sharp.

The last thing you'll need is a sheet of paper to record the results. Diagram 13.5 illustrates a simple racing schedule that can be drawn in seconds. This is perfectly OK for all club racing. It can be varied to suit your requirements. When there are only a handful of you racing, it is not necessary to have any boats off in any race — simply have all boats on, with one person nominated to start and stop the tape recorder. After the first race the winner writes down the results. The winner then has the handicap of starting and stopping the tape in the next race and so on.

Once there are a few more skippers racing or as an alternative anyway, you can elect to have one or more skippers off in each race. The duties of the non-racing skipper are to start and stop the tape, write down the results, watch the line at the start and finish and to walk around with the fleet watching out for incidents. All you do is a put a line of X's diagonally downwards across the columns of race results. The X's mean that the

Diagram 13.5

A SIMPLE RACING SCHEDULE

Freq.	Skipper/Boat Name	Jib No.	1	2	3	4	5	6	7	Etc.	Total	Less Discards	Final Result
Brown	Joe – Lollipop	99	X										
Blue/Gr	Fred – Scamp	15		X									
Red	Mike – Tornado	21			X								
Yellow	Lucy – Gypsy	36				X							
Blue	Robert – Fugitive	18					X						
Yel/Or	Ray – Illusion							X					

WINNER SCORES   1 POINT   DISCARDS – 1 AFTER 5 RACES
SECOND   2 POINTS   2 AFTER 10
THIRD   3 POINTS   3 AFTER 20
ETC.

(In this example every 6 Races completes a set.)

Diagram 13.6
THE FOUR SQUARE RACING SCHEDULE

Freq.	Skipper/Boat Name	Jib No.	1	2	3	4	5	6	7	8	9	10	11	12	13	14	15	16	Total	Less Discard Points	Final Score	Position
Or	Les – Sinker	36	RO				O1						O2		O3							
Blue	Mike – Eeling	07		RO				O1				O2				O3						
Yel	Larry – Hasler	09			RO				O1		O2						O3					
Black	Hugh – Mole	69				RO				O1				O2				O3				
Red	Helga – Foghorn	90	O1				RO						O3		O2							
Green	Tony – Cain	01		O1				RO				O3				O2						
Gr/Bl	Chris –Poohstick	33			O1				RO		O3						O2					
Red/Or	Graham – Antic	91				O1				RO				O3				O2				
Or/Yel	Phil –O'Sophical	97	O2				O2						RO		O1							
Brown	Peter – Stoppit	39		O2				O2				RO				O1						
Yel/Gr	Martin – ZZZZ	47			O2				O2		RO						O1					
Br/Red	John – Fourplay	144				O2				O2				RO				O1				
	Mark – Chopstick	66	O3										O1		RO							
	Ian – Natking	13		O3				O3				O1				RO						
	Tony – Vaner	11			O3				O3								RO					
	Mike – Gunslinger	37				O3				O3				O1				RO				
	Ian – Burtons	21					O3				O1											

109

5 MIN BREAK AFTER EACH 4 RACES

DISCARDS 2 AFTER EACH 4 RACES

DISCARDS 2 AFTER 10

skipper is off for that particular race. Once you get to the stage where you want to have more than one skipper off, you put in another set of X's say starting in the middle of column 1, still drawing them in diagonally downwards. Now when you get to the bottom of the column for racing skippers, you simply start off the diagonal line downwards at the top of the next racing column. Once you have a good number of skippers all wanting to race, you can use what I call the four square method. Literally, you divide the schedule up into blocks of four squares by four squares and put a diagonal across each block. That way you can stop the racing anytime after completing a block of four races. Whereas in the more basic variation you must complete an entire block of the main diagonal so that everyone has been off once, twice or thrice etc.

In the four block system it does not matter if the lowest block of four is not all filled with racing skippers — the skippers in that block simply don't sail as usual when their X is in the racing column. Diagram 13.6 gives the example. I have successfully used this system to run a twenty-four boat meeting and I think you could handle more. While the diagram shows columns for sixteen races it is as well to draw in up to twenty-four columns for races. At Gosport Club events eighteen races are easily completed between 10.30am and 3.30 or 4pm with half an hour for lunch. It all depends upon how keen your own group of racing skippers is. In this schedule I have varied the diagonals from both downwards to upwards per block of four. This is simply to give variety as to who is off with whom in any one race.

You'll notice in this schedule instead of using X's to denote when a skipper isn't racing a symbol is written instead. RO is for Race Officer, nominating for that particular race the individual skipper to perform the task. Similarly 01, 02 and 03 stand for Observers 1, 2 and 3. Observer 1 has the task of observing the front half of the fleet. Observer 2 has the task of observing the bottom half of the fleet (once established). Observer 3 acts as start line judge, keeps an open eye on the whole race and acts as finish line judge as well, calling out the finishers by jib number to the race officer who writes them down. This way all people attending the meeting can enjoy racing as well. It is not necessary for one or two skippers to sacrifice their day's racing to run the event. Once you have twenty entries or more you can use the last full block of four to act as line judge, releasing Observer 3 to full observing duties.

You'll find that by nominating which part of a fleet an observer should concentrate on tends to give much better coverage of the whole race. The race officer can also keep a general eye on the whole proceedings too. Observers should call out any definite contacts at least twice calling out the jib numbers of the boats involved. It is up to the boats involved to sort out who should do the turns. The observers must make sure that turns have been properly completed. It is best also if the observers quickly jot down the bare bones of the incident. Jib numbers, relative positions of the boats involved, wind direction and position of any nearby mark. If they heard any calls prior to the collision that is worth noting down as well. Incidents happen very quickly and it is hard to record the facts correctly and fairly. However if turns on the water are not done, then there will be a protest meeting at which observers' evidence will be required.

It is not at all unusual for a protest committee to hear several completely different stories as to what actually occurred in any one incident. Both skippers tell a different version and all observers might have seen the incident from different vantage points and recorded different versions also. Witnesses again, may have caught a passing glimpse of the incident and formed yet another different picture in their mind. Do try to be objective and do try very hard to be accurate. If you are not sure that an incident has occurred, say nothing. The skippers involved should be watching their boats very carefully and if one of them thinks there was a contact you can almost certainly be sure that they will protest the other boat. If that is the case, you still need as an observer to note down the bare facts and to tick off the incident once penalty turns have been completed.

Once you are certain that an incident has occurred and you have clearly identified the offenders by calling out the jib numbers twice, do not enter into discussion with the skippers involved other than to just say contact was seen. A skipper cannot argue with your call — he can do his turns and protest you to the race committee after the race is over and appeal for redress under **Rule 69**. It is however, extremely difficult to convince a protest committee that an observer did not see a contact! Contact of the masts is often missed by the skippers involved because they are very busy looking at the hull of their boat, keeping it clear of the other boat that is very close.

Going back to Diagram 13.6 and the four square racing schedule you'll notice that the left-hand column is devoted to recording the crystal frequency allocated to each skipper. On small club events this is very useful to show to any other radio controlled skippers who might bring along their tug boat to the lake for a trial run. Such skippers can immediately see what frequencies are free and safe to use. This encourages good relationships between different groups of modellers whenever possible.

Of course, once all the basic thirteen channels on 27Mg are allocated, you have to allocate latecomers different crystals in each race, as they use the crystal of a skipper who is out for that particular race. By this means twenty-six skippers can be catered for. Of course, what now helps enormously is the 40Mg frequencies. That makes the whole process much easier and it is thus possible to handle larger numbers fairly easily.

Fleets of eighteen boats at a time on the water are becoming more common these days. Provided most of the skippers are experienced there are few problems. At the Worlds last year at Fleetwood on practice day, there were often well over thirty boats on the water at any one time. So I guess if you wanted to you could probably handle up to thirty-six entries on the four square system. However, I think most people would gravitate towards a fleet system of racing long before that amount was reached.

Protest hearings at club level are not that common, most people accepting penalty turns on the water. If you ever need to organise one though, **Rules 71** to **74** give you all the guidance you should need.

Appendix 1. Useful Publications

The Model Yachting Association Yearbook.
This is published every year, usually in time for release at the Model Engineering Exhibition in early January.

It contains all of the major open events throughout the country for the forthcoming year. It also has a list of all affiliated clubs with addresses, contact names and telephone number. Brief details of basic interest are also contained plus of course, advertisements from the major suppliers of goodies.

Currently the Supplies Officer is David Hackwood, 10 Grangewood, Coulby Newham, Middlesbrough, TS8 0RT. The cost of the Yearbook is at present (1991) £1.50 including postage. Those of us actively competing always buy a copy as soon as we can. If you are already a member of an affiliated club, your club should receive copies for every member each year once it has paid its yearly subscription to the MYA.

Appendix 16 The Model Yacht Racing Rules.
The amendments to the full-sized *International Yacht Racing Rules* is at present published as a separate publication known as *Appendix 16*. This is also available from David Hackwood at the above address. The next issue of the IYRR in 1993 will include Appendix 16 within it.

However, you can buy books that contain all of the current IYRR in several different ways. You can simply buy the real thing from IYRU, 60 Knightsbridge, Westminster, London SW1X 7JX Cost £10.00 (1991). From the same address you can also buy *Interpretations of the IYRR* for another £10.00, which contains all of the useful appeal cases that can clarify certain applications of the rules.

You could buy from the RYA, RYA House, Romsey Road, Eastleigh, Hampshire SO5 4YA their copy of the IYRR 1989–92 for the price of around £3.50. Better still join the RYA for the princely sum of £12.00 and take up the rules book from the £6.50 worth of RYA publications you'll be allowed free of charge as a subscribing member!

The following books all contain the bulk of the rules, but, far more usefully, they also contain explanations of the rules.

The Rules Book — 1989–92 International Yacht Racing Rules
Eric Twiname, revised by Bryan Willis.
Adlard Coles-William Collins Sons & Co Ltd., 8 Grafton Street, London W1 3LA. (Price £6.95.)
It is my humble opinion that this is by far the most useful book for the newcomer to yacht racing to buy. Not only does it contain all of the IYRR 1989–92 but it contains 92 pages explaining the rules with masses of useful illustrations. This part of the book is divided into sections, including rules that everyone who races should know — definitions, the start, windward leg, mark rounding, offwind leg, the finish, other important sailing rules, penalties and rule enforcement. Each incident or situation described is graded on three levels: 1) Rules everybody who races should know. 2) Racing at the top end of a club fleet. 3) Top level National and International competition. This book enables you to identify quickly the rule that covers your latest incident. Remember that you will also need *Appendix 16* of

the IYRR from the MYA Supplies Officer (review above) to complement the current edition. Once we are into the 1993 and beyond editions of the Rules the Appendix will be included. The entire book is edited every four years by Bryan Willis to cater for the latest rule changes.

Paul Elvstrom Explains the Yacht Racing Rules.
Edited by Jonathan Bradbeer.
Published by Adlard Coles at £7.95.
This book is worth buying for two reasons — the way it presents IYRU interpretations and for the very useful little kit in the wallet at the front of the book. This contains four small plastic models of yachts with movable main booms illustrating which tack they are upon, three plastic marks and a wind direction arrow — exactly the things you need to illustrate the circumstances of an incident to the protest committee after the race. They can also help you to get your own thoughts clear if filling in a protest form after the race.

The Rules in Practice.
Bryan Willis.
Fernhurst Books, 31 Church Road, Hove, East Sussex. (Price £6.95.)
Around 66 pages of clear explanations, using aerial photos of little model yachts to illustrate positions and incidents. This book may be of interest to skippers who are at the level of winning club races or higher. Some useful tactics are explained and it is very easy to understand.

The Yacht Racing Rules: A complete guide.
Mary Pera.
A & C Black (Publishers) Ltd., 35 Bedford Row, London WC1R 4JH. (Price £10.95.)
In my opinion this is the definitive authority on interpretations of the rules. Mary Pera is chairperson of the RYA Racing Rules Committee and a leading member of the committee of the IYRU which updates the rules every four years after the Olympic Games. She is an internationally acknowledged authority on the racing rules. She also serves as an International Judge and Jury Chairperson at major championships and regattas. This book is a must for all serious yacht racers entering open events and above.

All of the books mentioned, with the exceptions of the MYA, RYA and IYRU publications, should be available from your local bookshop. If they are not in stock you should be able to place an order. An alternative source is the Warsash Nautical Bookshop, 31 Newtown Road, Warsash, Southampton SO3 9FY. Tel 0489 572384. Don't forget to include an amount to cover postage, currently likely to be around 50p–60p per book. They accept cheques and will deal with most major credit cards over the telephone.

The final book I wish to introduce to you is a book called *Radio Controlled Model Yachts* by the late Trevor Reece (Argus Books, 1989). This book at present is the only up-to-date book aimed specifically at the radio controlled model yachter, and in particular, the novice as regards building and understanding yachts. The following is a list of the chapters showing the areas covered:

1) Introducing radio controlled model yacht racing.
2) The radio control system.
3) Installing the electronics.
4) Choosing a yacht.
5) Materials, adhesives and processes.
6) The mast and sails.
7) The sail plan.
8) Construction — the hull.
9) Rigging and checking.
10) Measuring and tuning.
11) Sailing and racing.
12) Building in wood.

Plus 17 pages of references and appendices.
This is the first book to come out since Vic Smeed's book *Model Yachting* (Argus Books) was republished in 1984. That is still a useful supplement to Trevor's book, but buy Trevor's book first — without a shadow of a doubt this book is a worthwhile investment for the newcomer to radio controlled model yachting. If you find you want to have a go at producing your own hull instead of buying one of the many excellent ready moulded hulls then buy a copy of Vic Smeed's book as well.

If you are a prospective model yacht sailor or racer, no doubt you will want to get your teeth into as much written information as you can. The magazines which include information about model yachting are:

Model Boats.
Published monthly and available from Smiths and all leading newsagents. The best way of getting it though is by subscription, the details of which you'll find in any issue.

Radio Controlled Boat Modeller.
Published every other month and also available from Smiths etc. Again a subscription is most definitely the best way for this magazine, it saves you having to remember which month it comes out!

Marine Modeller.
Published monthly, it may contain items of interest to model yachtsmen now and then.

It is planned to publish other books explaining more advanced racing tactics for model yacht racers in due course — until then the best that can be done is to read full-sized books on racing.

Published monthly, it usually contains items of interest to model yachtsmen now and then.

Please note all prices quoted were correct at time of going to press.

Appendix 2.
Useful Addresses, Associations and Principal Suppliers

Model yacht racing in the UK is controlled by the Model Yachting Association and all keen model yachters are members. Most people are members through the club to which they belong. However, a few people are also individual members, mainly because they receive individually sent documentation throughout the year updating information on the contents of any council meetings etc. Such information is always sent to the affiliated clubs, but it does not always reach grassroot members. The General Secretary of the club is Ian Taylor, 115 Mayfield Avenue, London N12 9HY.

Governing yacht racing worldwide is the International Yacht Racing Union. This is run from 60 Knightsbridge, Westminster, London SW1X 7JX Tel. 071 235 6221. Fax 071 245 9861.

The IYRU has a division called the Model Yacht Racing Division which governs all the international events in model yachting (IYRU — MYRD). The MYA is affiliated to the IYRU — MYRD. It is possible to join the IYRU as an individual member, at present it would cost you £25.00 per year which would include a copy of the IYRU Yearbook. The main benefit would be knowing that you were supporting the organising body for the sport worldwide. A lot of work goes into the task of keeping the sport well oiled and ensuring that the highest standards are applied to race meetings and rules.

The Royal Yachting Association (RYA) is based at RYA House, Romsey Road, Eastleigh, Hampshire SO5 4YA. Tel 0703 629962. Fax 0703 629924. The RYA do more for the interests of boat users in the UK than anyone else. It is very cheap to become a member (currently £12.00

p.a.) and they definitely need the support of every person who is the slightest bit interested in enjoying themselves on the water, whether full-sized yachtsman, dinghy sailor, windsurfer or model yacht sailor. If you are interested in practising any of the full-size branches of the sport they will be able to give you full details of the clubs in your area. They also run coaching sessions right up to training our Olympic Squads. They run a National Judges scheme to encourage the professional approach to running major meetings and proper knowledge of the racing rules and how to apply them. They publish lots of useful books and in short do just about everything you could wish of a national association. They do need support and becoming a member is the best support you could give them, even if you are just a model skipper.

The Royal National Lifeboat Institute is based at West Quay Road, Poole, Dorset BH15 1HZ. Everyone knows what a splendid service the RNLI offer to all people on or in the water around our coastlines. They rely entirely on public support — for a few pounds a year (£6) you can become what is called a Shoreline Member. Your yearly subscription goes towards the running costs of the RNLI. You are then doing your little bit towards ensuring the safety of our yachtsmen and all in peril on the sea. I realise using a model yacht you are hardly likely to need their services, but just think about those that do.

There now follows a list of some of the principal suppliers of equipment to yacht modellers. It is very much a cottage industry and the following is a list of just a few of the many suppliers in the UK:

Tony Abel Model Racing Yachts
Highnoon, Petersfinger Road
Salisbury, Wilts SP5 3BY
Tony makes an economical range of yacht hulls
and complete kits. He also has available every-
thing needed to participate in the sport.

Sails Etc — Graham and Lorna Bantock
141 High Street
Kelvedon, Essex CO5 9AA
Graham has a worldwide reputation as a top class
skipper, sailing his own designs to success everywhere. Several times National Champion and
highly placed in world class events, Graham is
without doubt the man to try and beat. The
quality of his products is excellent and while not
cheap, you can always be sure of getting equipment that will allow you to develop your full
potential, provided you put it together correctly.
Graham carries the largest range of goodies
available in the UK and possibly the world.

P.J. Sails (Peter Wiles)
1 Courtney Road
Poole, Dorset BH14 0HD
Peter has also been National Champion in certain
classes and will always be seen sailing his boats
competitively and successfully. Peter again carries
a full range of equipment and makes sails.

D.H. Andrews
49 Aberdale Road
Leicester LE2 6GE
Dave Andrews makes the best known and most
used set of sail winches in the world!

Housemartin Sails
51 Edinburgh Drive, Prenton
Birkenhead, Merseyside L43 0RJ
Martin Roberts is again a top flight skipper.
Fourth in the 1990 RM Worlds and always near
the front, Martin understands what is needed
in a set of sails. While primarily a sail maker,
Martin carries a stock of fittings and kits.

If you are just starting out in our sport, before
you make up your mind what to buy get details
from all the aforementioned suppliers and go
along to the local club that you wish to join to see
what classes they actively race there. You ideally
want to be racing in a class that can provide you
with good racing every weekend, with at least
half a dozen boats at any one meeting and preferably more.

Janusz Walicki current European Marblehead
Champion and former World Champion produces top quality models. He has a catalogue of
the products he makes and his address is Horner
Landstrasse 414, 2000, Hamberg 74. Germany.

National Authorities

A) Argentina   Club Argentino de Yate Modelismo
                Ricardo G. Pollono, Metan 3625, 1240 Buenos Aires
                Republica Argentina

OE) Austria   Allgemeiner Osterreichischer Schiffsmodellverband (AOSMV)
                Mag. H. Turk, Anastasius Grungasse 54 1 18 A 1180 Vienna
                Austria

A) Australia   Australian Model Yachting Association (AMYA) Inc.
                Iain Kirley, RMB 431 Macks Reef Road, Via Bungendore
                New South Wales, Australia 2621

B) Belgium   Belgian Model Sailing Association
                Mark Van Loo, Drukpersstraat 25, B-2610 Wilrijk
                Belgium

BL) Brazil Uniao Brasileira de Veleiros R/C
William F. Astbury, Rua Joaquim Jose Esteves
no 60 – apto 142/D Sao Paulo – SP-04740 Brazil

KC) Canada Canadian Model Yachting Association
Bob Sterne, 3785 Edinburgh Street, Burnaby, B.C
Canada V5C 1R4

D) Denmark Dansk Modelbads Union
Bjarne T. Clausen, Rodlersvej 21, 2990 Nivaa, Denmark

K) England Model Yachting Association
Ian Taylor, 115 Mayfield Avenue, London N12 9HY
England

L) Finland Suomen RC-purjehtijat – Finlands RC-seglare
Henry Ericsson, Bobacka, 02440 Boback, Finland

F) France F.F.V. Secteur Voile Modele, Relations Internationales
E. Servella, 55 Avenue Kleber, 75784 Paris Cedex 16
France

G) Germany Deutscher Segler Verband Geschaftsstelle
(West) Herr Feyerabend, Grundgensstrasse 18, D-2000
Hamburg 60, Germany

H) Holland Nederlandse Model Zeil Organisatie (NEMOZO)
Harry Drenth, Eemland 1, 8251 VN Dronten, Holland

KH) Hong Kong Hong Kong Model Yachting Association
Alex Lam, Y.L. Yeung & Co., Wang Kee Bldg., 21st Floor
34/37 Connaught Road, Central, Hong Kong

IR) Ireland Dublin Radio Model Boat Club
Paul Toal, 48 Warrenhouse Road, Baldoyle, Dublin 13
Republic of Ireland

I) Italy Modelvela Italia Lega Navimodellistica Sportiva
Federico Ciardi, via Flavia Steno, 10/12
16148 Genova, Italy

J) Japan Japan Model Yacht Society
Kazuo Naito, 10-2-102, 3 Chome Sugawara Higashi
Yodogawa-Ku, Osaka-Shi, Japan T533

MO) Monaco Federation Monegasque de Modelisme
A-H Levesy, (President)
Boite Postale 415, MC-98011 Monaco Cedex

KZ) New Zealand New Zealand Model Yachting Association
B.J. Spencer, 23 Leys Crescent, Remuera
Auckland 5, New Zealand

N) Norway Norsk Modellseilforening
Bjorn Nygaard, Oreliveien 12C, Oslo 5, Norway

P)	Portugal	Associacao Portuguesa De Modelos a Vela (APMV) Alto dos Lombos, Rua das Rosas, Lote 11-lo. Esq. Carcavelos, 2775 Parede, Portugal
SA)	South Africa	Model Yacht Association of South Africa J.J. Robbertse, 1 South View Place, Caversham Glen Pinetown, 3610, Natal, South Africa
E)	Spain	Associacion Espanola de Vela R/C J. Monedero, Po Pechina No. 50-16 46018 Valencia, Spain
S)	Sweden	Svenska Modellseglarforbundet (SMSF) Jan Dejmo, Tvillinggatan 2A, S-431 43 Molndal, Sweden
Z)	Switzerland	Association Suisse de Modelistes de Bateaux (ASMB) Michel Malatesta, 8 Rue Mme du Stael, 1201 Geneve, CH
US)	USA	American Model Yachting Association (AMYA) Rod Wallis, 420 N Edgewood Ave., La Grange Park IL 60525, USA

"A" Class Owners Association Secretary — D. Coode, Warringah Cottage, Salt Lane, Hydon Heath, Godalming, Surrey GU8 4DH, England.

EC 12m Owners Association Secretary — Rod Carr.

Appendix 3.
Useful Knots

There are few knots that need to be known to ensure trouble free sailing of model yachts.

The most useful without a doubt is the 'Fisherman's Knot'. This is the best knot to use when joining nylon line or any other line come to that! The design of the knot ensures that it never comes undone under load or even when not under load. It is still fairly easy to untie when so desired. To be able to tie the fisherman's knot it is first necessary to learn how to tie a simple thumb knot. The 'Thumb Knot' must be the easiest knot to tie. I would almost put money on it being the first knot you ever tied since it is just the simple making of a loop in line and the passing the end of the line through the loop, drawn tight it makes the thumb knot!

The fisherman's knot is simply two thumb knots, one tied in each line to be joined. The trick is as you tie each thumb knot you tie it around the other line. The end result being that you have two thumb knots that can slide up and down the other line. When the two lines are drawn apart the two thumb knots slide towards each other finally locking against each other. The more tension that is applied to one knot the more it pulls the two knots tight!

The next most useful knot is the 'Bowline' — this is the knot used for making loops in the ends of lines. The drawing illustrates how to tie it. You make a simple loop in the line three or four inches away from the end of the line so that the long length of line is going away from you vertically with the loop coming round clockwise and crossing the vertical line at twelve o'clock.

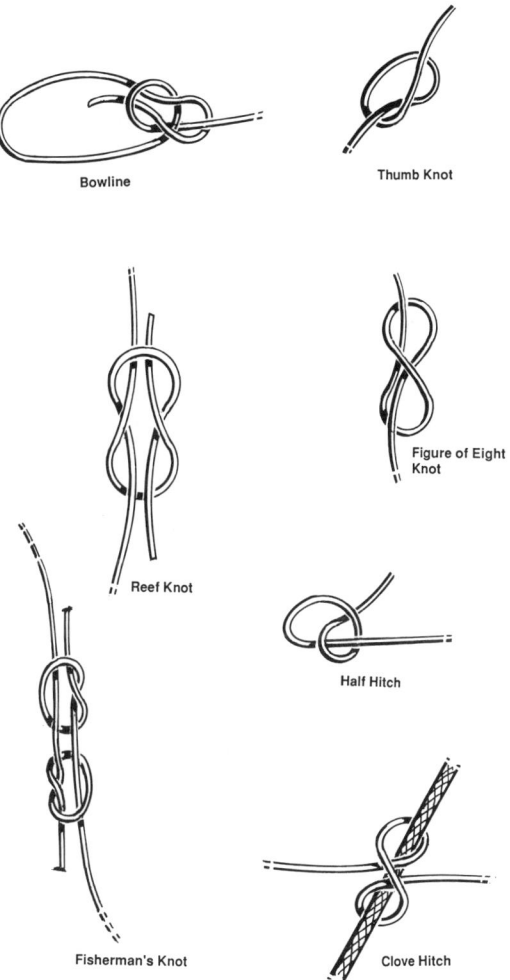

Bowline

Thumb Knot

Figure of Eight Knot

Reef Knot

Half Hitch

Fisherman's Knot

Clove Hitch

You take the end of the line and pass it through the loop you have made from the underneath, it then is passed over the loop line at twelve o'clock

119

round behind the vertical line and back across the loop line and back through the loop. Now pull the whole knot tight and you should have a bowline! In the Boy Scouts we used to describe the tying of this knot as the "rabbit coming out of his hole, round the back of the tree and back down his hole again". You then just have to remember to make the tree (the vertical line going away from you) and the hole (the loop you make in a clockwise direction crossing the line at twelve o'clock). This knot always tightens itself under load and yet is always easy to undo by pushing the lines in the opposite direction to load. For this reason only use it in situations where it will remain under load, such as the uphaul and downhaul of a main sail. In any situation where the load is only on for part of the time, put a dab of glue on the knot to hold it secure.

The 'Figure of Eight Knot' is an expansion of the thumb knot — it is useful when fitting bowsies as the knot in the end of the line to stop the line being drawn back through the hole in the bowsie. The figure of eight knot is a thumb knot with the line passed around the back of the line again after making a loop, thus forming an eight in the line. It makes a slightly fatter knot than the thumb knot.

'Half Hitch's' are lazy knots which should not be used, they are fine under load, but easily come undone by themselves if the load on the line slackens!

The 'Clove Hitch' is a fine knot for mooring painters and the like, but has little use in model yachting. It is well worth knowing though.

The 'Reef Knot' is a marvellous knot for tying two ropes of equal thickness together. It is not so good though with the man-made fibres and fine lines. If you do use it, then I suggest you again put a dab of glue on the knot to stop it working loose.

When working with man-made fibre lines it is necessary to seal the end of the line with a flame or soldering iron. The soldering iron gives you the most precise control and allows you to burn back the line close to the knot you have tied, without setting your sails on fire! When tying elasticated line, in my opinion the only knot to use is the fisherman's. We use elasticated line on our winch lines to take up slack or variation in line length as it winds on and off the winch drum.

Appendix 4.
Levels of Racing Radio Controlled Yachts

(1) Friendly

No rules, vague course — no real satisfaction of achievement and a good chance of damaging your yacht. Better than nothing though and where lots of people start.

(2) Club Racing

Rules should be used, although very often in a fairly basic way. Ideally all the rules should be applied so that club members can learn them. Races are often of a handicap nature to provide more even competition between people of different skills and yacht speed. Clubs will usually have a series or two running over their season to find the overall winner, interspaced by cup events and the odd open event.

(3) Open Events

Usually one-class events where anyone can enter provided they have a current measurement certificate for their yacht. Entries are appreciated a week in advance to the secretary of the host club. Details of such events will be found listed in the *MYA Yearbook* (see Appendix 1). Some of the events will be nominated league events. All the points from such events go towards a yearly league table. More details on the league system may be found in the *MYA Yearbook*.

(4) District Events

Open events to establish the district champions in

certain classes such as Marbleheads, R10Rs, RAs and Metre class. Again see the *MYA Yearbook* for more details.

(5) Ranking Races

Open events originally used just for the Marble-head class to set up a rolling record of the current pecking order! There are now six ranking races held, one in each district of the country including Scotland plus the Nationals. The best four results over a one year period are taken on a rolling basis to establish a ranking list. Those at the top of the ranking list are then eligible for consideration for entry to International events. This system is currently being extended to the Metre class. There will be separate ranking lists for each class using this method of selection. Ranking races have, without doubt, improved the quality of competition within the UK. Ranking lists are available from the General Secretary of the MYA on subscription.

(6) National Championships

Open one-class events used to establish the National Champion each year. These events may be held over one, two, three or more days. They are controlled by the MYA.

(7) Euro Grand Prix

Open races for the Marblehead class. A series of races held in Europe and Scandinavia to encourage inter-country racing and to develop further the standards of skill. The series produces a European Champion each year. This series is run under the control of the IYRU — MYRD.

(8) Regional and Continental Championships

Again run under the control of the IYRU — MYRD. The objectives are:

(i) To advance and encourage top level model yacht racing throughout the world.

(ii) To ensure that model yachtsmen will meet, as far as possible, the same fair racing conditions independent of location.

(iii) To serve as a guide in this respect to National and organising authorities.

The recognised Continental Championships are:

(i) European Championship.

(ii) American Championship.

(iii) Asian Championship.

(iv) South West Pacific Championship.

They will be held if possible every third year.

The World Championships may be held not less than every two years for recognised IYRU — MYRD International Classes that have yachts registered in member countries of at least two continents.

Therefore there exists a structure of competition demanding enough to satisfy the most ambitious of skippers.

Match racing is an alternative that is becoming more popular, especially in the Six Metre class. Marblehead skippers do one day's match racing in the two-day Race of Champions each year. This is an invitation-only event to which all the district champions and the National Champion gain automatic invitations. The remaining places to make up the sixteen-boat entry are taken in descending order from the ranking list.

Team racing is yet another aspect of yacht racing, where teams of three skippers race each other around the usual course. Each team may employ tactics to frustrate the progress of the opposite team's yachts that are on the same leg of the course, thus hopefully helping one's own team members up into better positions. Team racing is extremely enjoyable and makes a welcome break from ordinary racing. Unfortunately the once-a-year team event for Marbleheads has fallen by the wayside during 1991 — hopefully future years will see a return. If the idea appeals, try and get your club to hold an event one day and see how you all enjoy it. Appendix 4 of the IYRR sets out the rule modifications required. Tactics such as luffing can be great fun!

Appendix 5. The Beaufort Scale

Admiral Beaufort, in 1806 or so, dreamt up a scale of wind strength guides aimed at being used by the men o'war. A century later, a Dr G.C. Simpson set out a similar guide for the man on land to estimate the wind's speed. For us as model yachtsmen it is probably most useful to use the land-based signs rather than the sea-based signs. Our interest in the strength of wind is simply to know what set of sails to put up. Our lives are not going to be put at risk by having too much sail area up or putting our craft on the water in dangerous conditions for full-sized craft. However if you have to get into a rescue boat to fish out your pride and joy, do remember to put on a lifejacket or buoyancy aid. At least one model yachtsman has had the misfortune to drown while falling out of the club rescue boat. Some of the lakes we sail on are very deep and the water extremely cold in the first half of the year. We are not dressed or prepared for sudden immersion in water — be very careful!

Before going out for a day's racing, it is well worth listening to the local forecasts for the area you will be sailing in. It is also worth pulling up the shipping forecast on Oracle page 306. Ringing up the local weather station for the wind strength and direction forecasts is another way of getting a good idea of what the wind might be up to during the course of the day.

This is useful information if you are going to be the person laying the course or if you are the sort of person who doesn't like taking all of their sails with you! In my opinion anyone who does not take all of their sails is crazy. It is impossible to forecast with any great accuracy the strength of the wind! Gales forecast often don't materialise — a fact I know only too well from the days when I used to indulge in high wind windsurfing! You'd hear that a force eight plus was forecast and chuck everything on top of the car and belt down to the local hotspot only to spend the day sitting on the beach waiting for nothing! The opposite also happens on rare occasions — a strong wind springs up out of nowhere and the rescue boats at sea get very busy during the summer months if this occurs at a weekend.

Model yacht races are usually so short in duration (ten to fifteen minutes or so) that we are really able to respond quickly to such changes and get the right sails up for the next race. So we ought really to only be showing our rudders to the world in one race at most!

The Beaufort Scale rates wind strength from 0 to 12 which in terms of knots is up to 72 knots. The rig suggestions are for Marbleheads with a little humour introduced for very high winds. Anything over force seven is hard work and only undertaken by fanatically keen and brave skippers. Be prepared to have to repair rigs or hulls in such condition and give other racing yachts plenty of room.

Beaufort Scale	General Description	Land Signs	Water Signs	Rig to Use
0 = under 1 knot	Calm	Tree leaves do not move. Smoke rises vertically	Flat as a pancake	Max area, max twist, high aspect
1 = 1–3 Kt	Light air	Slight movement of light leaves	Slight distortion	As above
2 = 4–6 Kt	Light breeze	Leaves rustle	Gentle ripples	As above
3 = 7–10	Gentle breeze	Leaves in constant motion	Covered by ripples	Max area, min twist, high aspect
4 = 11–16	Moderate breeze	Small branches move. Flags well extended	Water darkens, large ripples	Max area, mid or short aspect
5 = 17–21	Fresh breeze	Small trees in leaf bend	Little waves form	Short aspect or next down (700)
6 = 22–27	Strong breeze	Large branches move. Whistling in wires	Good chop develops, tops break	600 or 500
7 = 28–33	Near gale	Whole trees in motion	White water	500 or 400
8 = 34–40	Gale	Twigs break off	Very white	300
9 = 41–47	Strong gale	Chimney pots fly	Big waves	200
10 = 48–55	Storm	Trees uprooted	Enormous waves	100
11 = 56–63	Violent storm	Forests flattened	Water flattened	Bare mast!
12 = over 63	Hurricane	Not experienced in Europe	Lake emptied	Run for cover!

The smallest rig usually used by Marblehead skippers would normally be around 350 square inches of total sail area. Such a rig might be used once a year!

The water features described above relate to small inland ponds or purpose-built model yacht lakes. In large lakes the water starts to behave much like it would at sea where waves develop at force three and start to break at force four with white crests (usually referred to as 'white horses'). By the time a gale develops at sea, the tops of waves break up and streaks of foam are blown along in the direction of the wind. By a force nine the whole sea has a good white look to it and the only sails to be seen will belong to windsurfers! Dinghy skippers will not go out beyond a force eight — most dinghy skippers would think very carefully about going out in wind conditions above force six. For deep keel ocean-going yachts that may have little choice in the matter, force nine and above winds means keeping to deep water and employing survival tactics. Only those few who know well the limits of their craft will drive their yacht on through such conditions. They will be placing their craft carefully on every wave and will always run the danger of suddenly being dropped into a hole that can pitch them end over end or being engulfed by monster rogue waves.

One or two final points on the wind. When the wind changes direction — if it swings from its previous direction in a clockwise direction — it is said to be 'veering'. If it swings from its previous direction in an anti-clockwise direction it is said to be 'backing'. A gust is when the speed of wind increases above the mean average and a lull is when the speed of wind drops below its mean average. A hole in the wind describes an area of water on the racing course that temporarily is not enjoying any wind, while all around it is! So to fall into a hole is to sail into such an area and lose drive, while on all sides yachts sail past you! Study the surface of the water because it will give you clues as to what the wind is doing upon it in any area. You should try to avoid totally flat spots of water when the rest of the water has ripples or more upon it. Shifts in wind and gusts can all be seen approaching your yacht across the surface of the water if you care to look out for them.

Appendix 6. Copy of Sailing Instructions

REMOTE CONTROL A NATIONALS AT GOSPORT
21/22nd Sept 91
SAILING INSTRUCTIONS

1) RULES:
Racing will take place under the current International Yacht Racing Rules (IYRR) as amended by Appendix 16 (Published in the IYRR 1990/1991 supplement), these sailing instructions (SI), the IYRU-MYRD RACING RULES COMMITTEE INTERPRETATIONS 1/90 & 2/90 (Referring now to Appendix 16 (6.6) instead of Appendix 15 (6.6) and the International "A" Class Measurement Rules.

2) EVENT CATEGORY:
RA NATIONAL CHAMPIONSHIPS. Category A. Advertising is limited to that permitted by 1.8 of IYRR Appendix 14.

3) CONDITIONS OF ENTRY:
The safety of a yacht and her entire management including insurance shall be the sole responsibility of the owner/competitor racing the yacht who must ensure that the yacht and Skipper are adequate to face the conditions that may arise in the course of the race. Neither the establishment of these sailing instructions nor the inspection of the yacht under these conditions in any way limits or reduces the absolute responsibility of the owner/competitor for his yacht and the management thereof. The race organisers and the Gosport M.Y. & P.B. Club shall not be responsible for any loss, damage, death or personal injury howsoever caused to the owner/competitor as a result of their taking part in the series of races. Moreover every owner/competitor warrants the suitability of his yacht for the series.

4) MEASUREMENT CERTIFICATES:
Before a yacht is eligible to race, her valid measurement or rating certificate shall be presented to the race office. The forfeit and time period (IYRR 19.3 refers) are £5.00 and 7 days respectively.

5) MEASUREMENT:
Yachts may be measured before or after any race at the discretion of the race committee.

6) DISTINGUISHING NUMBERS:
All yachts shall have jib numbers, applied as follows: Minimum height 100mm, minimum width 66mm (except for 1), minimum thickness 15mm, minimum spacing 10mm (horizontal and vertical).
Except for the special cases of 00, 11 and 88, which may be back to back, the starboard number shall be higher than the port number and shall not overlap the port number.
Jib numbers shall comply with IYRR 25.2 (a).
Una rigged yachts shall carry the "Jib numbers" in the lower third of the sail.
The jib number shall be the last two digits of the yacht registration number. Where there are two yachts with the same number a prefix (or suffix) shall be required to be applied to the jib number of the second entered duplicated jib number. The special case numbers 00, 11 and 88 may enter a one in between their two jib digits so as to retain back to back reading.

7) RACING SYSTEM:
The racing system will be IYRU-MYRD RCYRS 1990.

8) SAFETY:
Adequate personal buoyancy for all crew members of any rescue boat shall be worn at all times whilst in the rescue boat on the water.

9) COMMUNICATIONS WITH COMPETITORS:
Notices to competitors will be posted on a board in the area where the course board will be situated.

10) CHANGES TO THE SAILING INSTRUCTIONS:
The race committee reserve the right to change the S.I. Any changes to the S.I. will be posted on the same notice board. A loud signal will precede any oral change to the S.I. which will be confirmed in writing.

11) COURSE INSTRUCTIONS:
Wind direction permitting the type of course to be set

will be of the Olympic Triangle type course. Full details of the course to be sailed will be on a board near to the control area before and during racing.

12) CHANGES TO THE COURSE:
Changes of course will only be between heats or races. Any such change will be posted on the course board and will be preceded by a loud signal and oral warning.

13) STARTS:
The start of the first race on Saturday will be 1030 hrs, racing will finish as near to 1800 hrs as possible. The start of the first race on Sunday will be 0930 hrs and racing will finish as near to 1530 as possible.

14) STARTING PROCEDURES:
As soon as possible after the finish of a heat a warning signal shall sound indicating the start of the minute prior to the preparatory signal of the next heat. Yachts in the heat may be placed on the water any time after the warning signal. IYRR 53.1 shall not apply.

The starting signal shall be the start of the sound made with the word "go".

General recalls shall be indicated orally.

As soon as possible individual recalls will be made identifying each early starter by jib number or other identification, repeating the call at least once. (IYRR 8.1 & 8.2(a) shall not apply).

15) FINISHING:
Finished yachts shall keep clear of yachts still racing.

16) TIME LIMIT:
For races of 12 minutes or less duration the "Time Out" period will be 3 minutes.

For every 4 minutes extra, or part thereof, race duration an additional one minute shall be added to the "Time Out" period.

Yachts not finishing within the "Time Out" period shall be scored DNF.

17) TOUCHING A MARK:
A yacht shall exonerate herself under the amended rule 52.2 by making one complete 360 degree turn which must include one tack and one gybe.

18) ALTERNATIVE PENALTIES:
A yacht may accept an alternative penalty of one complete 360 degree turn, which must include one tack and one gybe under the amended Appendix 3.1 (IYRR) for having infringed a rule of part IV of IYRR.

19) OBSERVERS:
Race observers shall:

a) Be restricted to the same control area as the com-petitors and organise themselves before the start of each race so as each observer concentrates on a different part of the racing heat once this becomes practical.

b) Act in an active capacity. i.e. They shall call TWICE contacts between yachts and contacts between yachts and marks of the course, PROVIDED THAT THEY ARE POSITIVE THAT SUCH CONTACT OCCURRED! They must also note briefly in writing all contacts, noting jib numbers, relative positions of yachts and marks involved, leg of the course and wind direction.

c) Report all incidents unresolved by exonerating turns to the Race Officer at the end of the heat.

20) PROTEST FORMS:
Unresolved protests must be submitted in writing by the protesting yacht's Skipper! Immediately after the heat a form must be collected from the score centre and returned completed within ten minutes.

21) APPEALS:
Appeals against the protest committees decision may be made to our National Authority, but the result cannot be allowed to alter the results of this regatta. (IYRR 1.5 (b) (i) refers) except for the final complete race of the regatta.

22) PRACTICE SAILING:
Irrespective of the availability of frequencies, competitors shall not sail during the racing times specified under S.I. 13 unless scheduled to race.

23) TRANSMITTERS:
Competitors shall not switch on their transmitter at any time other than when called to race! Competitors shall switch off their transmitters as soon as they have removed their yachts from the water at the end of a heat. PERMISSION FROM THE RACE COMMITTEE IS REQUIRED BEFORE SWITCHING ON AT ANY OTHER TIME DURING THE HOURS OF RACING.

24) CONTROL POSITIONS:
Racing Skippers shall be confined to standing within a certain section of the pond side. This area will be defined by markers and Racing Skippers will be free to move around within that area. The onus of being in a position to hear other Skipper's and Observer's calls remains with each Skipper.

25) UNMEASURED YACHTS:
An unmeasured yacht or a yacht that no longer meets its measurement certificates specifications is free to enter the racing, but will not be eligible for any prize.

Appendix 7. Protest Committee Procedures

Prompt sheet re: Appendix 6, IYRR.

Items 1 to 3 need to be done before the protest hearing.
Items 4 to 7 need to be established at the very start of the proposed protest hearing

1) Note on Protest Form the time received.

2) Does the Protest Form contain the information called for by Rule 68.5. If not ask the protester to supply the information (Rule 68.8. — a) the identity of the yacht being protested, b) the date, time and whereabouts of the incident, c) the particular rule or rules alleged to have been infringed, d) a description of the incident, e) unless irrelevant, a diagram of the incident. **NB** When a protest by a yacht does not identify the nature of the incident, it shall be refused. (Rule 68.8(a), Acceptance or Refusal of a Protest.)

3) Is the Protest Form signed?   Yes: Proceed to 4) No: Get it signed immediately.

4) Did the protesting yacht protest the other yacht on the water at the time of the incident?   Yes: Proceed to 5) No: Ask 4(a).

4a) Did the protesting yacht try to inform the protested yacht that a protest would be lodged? Yes: Proceed to 5) No: Refuse protest.

5) Did the protested yacht hear the protest at the time or shortly after?   Yes: Proceed to 6) No: ask 4(a).

6) Notify all parties of the time of the hearing and arrange that observers and witnesses are standing by.

7) Photocopies of the Protest Form shall be made available to all parties to the protest for study before the hearing and a reasonable time shall be allowed for the preparation of defence. (Rule 72.)

The Hearing

8) Establish that no interested party is a member of the Protest Committee or takes part in the discussion or decision. Ask the parties to the protest whether they object to any member on the grounds of 'interest'. Such an objection shall be made before the protest is heard. (Rule 71.2.)

9) The parties to the protest shall have the right to be present throughout the hearing. Each witness, unless he is a member of the protest committee, shall be excluded, except when giving his evidence. Others may be admitted as observers at the discretion of the protest committee. (Rule 73.1 Right to be Present.)

10) Invite first the protester and then the protestee(s) to give their accounts of the incident. Each may question the other(s). Questions by the protest committee except for clarifying details, are preferably deferred until all accounts have been presented. Models are useful. Positions before and after the incident are often helpful.

11) Call for the observers reports. They may be questioned by the protester and protestee as well as the protest committee.

12) Invite the protester and then the protestee(s)

to call witnesses. They may be questioned by the protester and protestee as well as by the protest committee. The protest committee may also call witnesses. It may be appropriate and prudent to ask a witness to disclose any business or other relationship through which he might have an interest or might stand to benefit from the outcome of the protest.

13) Invite first the protester and then the protestee to make a final statement of his case, including any application or interpretation of the rules to the incident as he sees it.

14) The protest committee may adjourn a hearing in order to obtain additional evidence.

Decision

15) The protest committee after dismissing those involved in the incident shall decide what the relevant facts are (Rule 74.1).
Write these facts found in the appropriate box on the protest form.

16) The protest committee shall then apply the rules and reach a decision as to who, if anyone, infringed a rule and what rule was infringed. (Rule 74.)
Write the rule(s) infringed in the appropriate box on the protest form.

17) Having reached a decision in WRITING, recall the protester and protestee and read to them the facts found, the decision and the grounds for it. (74.6.)
Write the decision of the protest committee in the appropriate box on the protest form and the reason

for reaching that decision and the Chairman of the committee should sign the form. Also note on the form the names of the remainder of the protest committee.

18) *Any party to the protest is entitled to a copy of the decision (Rule 74.6) signed by the Chairman of the protest committee. A copy should also be filed with the committee records.*

19) Ensure that the person recording the scores for the event is immediately informed as to the result of the protest hearing.
NB If a photocopier is not available at the meeting, it is suggested that the Chairman of the protest committee holds all of the completed protest forms. He should note down the names and addresses of any people wanting copies of protests they were involved in. (It is in fact very rare that someone does want a copy other than if they are considering a possible appeal.)

Protest committees should never be worried by the thought that a hearings decision might go to appeal. All that is asked of you is that you establish as best you can the facts (this is very important). Apply the rule(s) that you think apply if necessary rather than just applying the rule the protester quoted. Rule interpretations can be difficult and any decision is better than no decision, as long as it was reached with due care and consideration being given.

Lastly remember that a protest committee may refer its own decision to the National Authority for confirmation or correction of its interpretation of the rules!

Appendix 8. IYRR Definitions

Sailing A yacht is sailing when using only the wind and water to increase, maintain or decrease her speed, with her crew adjusting the trim of the sails and hull and performing other acts of seamanship.

Racing A yacht is racing from her preparatory signal until she has either finished and cleared the finishing line and finishing marks or retired, or until the race has been postponed, abandoned, cancelled or a general recall has been signalled.

Starting A yacht starts when after fulfilling her penalty obligations, if any, under Rule 51.1(c), Sailing the Course, and after crossing the starting line in the direction of the course to the first mark.

Finishing A yacht finishes when any part of her hull, or her crew or equipment in normal positions, crosses the finishing line in the direction of the course from the last mark, after fulfilling her penalty obligations, if any under Rule 52.2(b), Touching a Mark.

Luffing Altering course towards the wind.

Tacking A yacht is tacking from the moment she is beyond head to wind until she had borne away to a close-hauled course.

Bearing away Altering course away from the wind until a yacht begins to gybe.

Gybing A yacht begins to gybe at the moment when, with the wind aft, the foot of her mainsail crosses her centreline, and completes the gybe when the mainsail has filled on the other tack.

On a tack A yacht is on a tack except when she is tacking or gybing. A yacht is on the tack (starboard or port) corresponding to her windward side.

Close-hauled A yacht is close-hauled when sailing by the wind as close as she can lie with advantage in working windward.

Clear astern and clear ahead, overlap A yacht is clear astern of another when her hull and equipment in normal position are abaft of an imaginary line projected abeam from the aftermost point of the other's hull and equipment in normal position. The other yacht is clear ahead.

The yachts overlap when neither is clear astern, or when, although one is clear astern, an intervening yacht overlaps both of them.

The terms *clear astern, clear ahead* and *overlap* apply to yachts on opposite tacks only when they are subject to Rule 42, Rounding or Passing Marks and Obstructions.

Leeward and Windward The leeward side of a yacht is that on which she is, or, when head to to wind, was, carrying her mainsail. The opposite side is the windward side. When neither of the two yachts on the same tack is clear astern, the one on the leeward side of the other is the leeward yacht. The other is the windward yacht.

Proper course A proper course is any course that a yacht might sail after the starting signal, in the absence of the other yacht or yachts affected, to finish as quickly as possible. The course sailed before luffing or bearing away is presumably, but not necessarily, that yacht's proper course. There is no proper course before the starting signal.

Mark A mark is any object specified in the sailing instructions that a yacht must round or pass on a required side. Every ordinary part of a mark ranks as part of it, including a flag, flagpole, boom or hoisted boat, but excluding ground tackle and any object either accidentally or temporarily attached to the mark.

Obstruction An obstruction is any object, including a vessel under way, large enough to require a yacht, when more than one overall length away from it, to make a substantial alteration to pass on one side or the other, or any object that can be passed on one side only, including a buoy, when the yacht in question cannot safely pass between it and the shoal or object that it marks. The sailing instructions may prescribe that certain defined areas shall rank as obstructions.

Postponement A postponed race is one that is not started at its scheduled time and that can be sailed at any time the race committee may decide.

Abandonment An abandoned race is one that the race committee declares void at any time after the starting signal, and that can be re-sailed at its discretion.

Cancellation A cancelled race is one that the race committee decides will not be sailed thereafter.

Appendix 9. Choosing a Class

If you have not already purchased a radio controlled model yacht please read the following: firstly find a club which is convenient to your home address to sail at. Find out what classes of yacht are *regularly* raced at that club. If you are very keen on racing it makes little sense to choose a class of yacht that is only raced once a month for example. You also want to have some good competition so the more yachts sailing regularly of the most popular class the better.

As a guide it is estimated that there are a minimum of 800 registered RMs racing at present in the UK. The same number of Metre class yachts are also registered. There are some 65 R10Rs and 80 odd RA yachts registered. It ought thus be obvious that a Marblehead or Metre class is likely to provide the best chance of regular racing, with no doubt the odd exception. There are some 80 clubs affiliated to the MYA and many more model boat clubs that have a small sailing section. If you look through a copy of the *MYA Yearbook* you will find that most fixtures are for RM or Metre classes.

INTERNATIONAL
YACHT RACING
UNION

Appendix 10.
Appendix 16
of the IYRR

IYRU - MODEL YACHT RACING DIVISION

APPENDIX 16 - MODEL YACHT RACING RULES

Remotely controlled Yacht Races shall be sailed under the International Yacht Racing Rules (IYRR) modified as follows:

1.   Part 1 - Definitions

1.1   RC yacht - A RC yacht is a yacht that is remotely controlled (RC) by a crew that is not on board. Throughout the IYRR, for "yacht" read "RC yacht".

1.2   Event, Race and Heat - An event consists of one or more races. A race consists of one or more heats, and is completed when the last heat in the race is finished.

2.   Part 11 - Management of Races

2.1   RACE OBSERVERS

        The Race Committee may appoint race observers, who will hail the identity of all RC yachts in an incident involving contact between RC yachts or contact with a mark.

2.2   RULE 3.2(b) - SAILING INSTRUCTIONS

        The sailing instructions may include the following:

        (xxiv):Add "Procedure for lodging protests orally".

        (xxxiii):Restrictions on use of frequency bands and modulating systems, and requirements for frequency switching.

        (xxxiv):Definition of the control area in which the crews and race observers shall be when racing.

(xxxv):Procedures on use of accompanying boats, including safety requirements and restrictions on movement.

(xxxvi):Restrictions on use of transmitters for RC **yachts** not **racing**

(xxxvii):Duties, procedures and restrictions for race observers.

2.3   RULE 4 - SIGNALS

This rule does not apply.

2.4   AUDIBLE SIGNALS

Unless otherwise prescribed in the Sailing Instructions, the audible signals for starting a heat shall be at one minute intervals and shall be Warning Signal, Preparatory Signal and Starting Signal. During the minute before the starting signal, audible oral signals shall be made at not less than ten second intervals and during the final ten seconds at one second intervals.

2.5   RULE 6 - STARTING AND FINISHING LINES

Add to rule: "The starting line shall be taken through the sides of the starting line **marks** nearest to the first **mark**. The finishing line shall be taken through the sides of the finishing line **marks** nearest to the last **mark**."

2.6   TIME TO REPAIR

A **RC yacht** that has sustained damage, whilst having right-of-way, shall be given reasonable time to effect repairs before the next **heat**.

2.7   RULE 12 - HEATS TO BE RE-SAILED

Throughout Rule 12, for "race" read "heat".

Rule 12(a) is replaced by: "All yachts scheduled to **start** in the original **heat** shall be eligible to start in the heat to be resailed."

3.   Part 111 - General Requirements

3.1   RULE 21 - MEMBER ON BOARD

This rule shall not apply.

3.2   RULE 22 - SHIFTING BALLAST

Rule 22 is replaced by: "All control equipment, batteries etc. shall be securely stowed in a fixed position and shall not be moved to suit a particular **heat**. No ballast or other dead weight shall be used as shifting ballast for altering the trim of the RC yacht.

No ballast shall be shipped, unshipped or shifted during an **event**, except that RC equipment or batteries may be exchanged for items of similar dimensions and weight placed in the same position.

Unless otherwise prescribed by the class rules, counterweights to jib booms may be adjusted. Water shall not be taken in or discharged during an **event** except that bilge water may be removed when a RC **yacht** is hauled out."

3.3 RULE 23 - ANCHOR

This rule shall not apply.

3.4 RULE 24 - LIFE SAVING EQUIPMENT

For "yacht" read "accompanying boat".

Add to rule: "All transmitter aerial extremities shall have adequate protection as approved by the race committee."

3.5 RULE 25 - CLASS INSIGNIA, NATIONAL LETTERS AND SAIL NUMBERS

Rule 25.1(c)(ii) shall not apply.

Rule 25.2(b) is replaced by: "The size and spacing of class insignia, national letter(s) and sail numbers shall be as prescribed by the class rules".

Rule 25.2(c) - For "50 mm" read "15 mm".

3.6 RULE 27 - FORESTAYS AND JIB TACKS

This rule shall not apply.

3.7 RC EQUIPMENT

As may be required at the venue of the event, the RC equipment of every **RC yacht** shall be covered by licence. Unless otherwise prescribed by the class rules, radio transmissions shall be made only from the crew to the **RC yacht**.

4. Part 1V - Right of Way Rules

4.1 RULE 38.2(a) - PROPER COURSE LIMITATIONS

This rule is replaced by: "A **leeward yacht** shall not sail above her **proper course** while an **overlap** exists, if when the overlap began or at any time during its existence, the mainmast of the **windward yacht** has been abreast or forward of the stem of the **leeward yacht**.

4.2 RULE 38.2(c) - HAILING TO STOP OR PREVENT A LUFF

For "Mast Abeam" read "Mast to Stem".

135

4.3 RULE 40 - SAME TACK - LUFFING BEFORE CLEARING THE STARTING LINE

The second sentence of rule 40 is replaced by: "Furthermore, the **leeward yacht** shall not so luff above a close-hauled course, unless the mainmast of the **windward yacht** is abaft the stem of the **leeward yacht**."

4.4 RULE 42 - ROUNDING OR PASSING MARKS AND OBSTRUCTIONS

Throughout the rule, for "two of her overall lengths" read "four of her overall lengths".

4.5 RULE 46 - PERSON OVERBOARD, YACHT ANCHORED, AGROUND OR CAPSIZED

Rule 46.1 is replaced by: "A yacht under way shall keep clear of another RC **yacht racing** that is aground, capsizes immediately ahead of her, or becomes entangled with another RC **yacht**."

46.2 is replaced by: "A RC **yacht** shall not be penalised when she is unable to avoid fouling a RC **yacht** that goes aground, capsizes immediately ahead of her, or becomes entangled with another RC **yacht**"

Add Rule 46.5: "A RC **yacht** being put off in accordance with rule 5.5 of this Appendix shall give any other RC **yacht racing** ample room and opportunity to keep clear."

5. **Part V - Other Sailing Rules**

5.1 CONTROL AREA

Except as provided in rule 5.5. the crew and race observers shall remain in the **control area** while **racing**.

5.2 RULE 53 - CASTING OFF, ANCHORING, MAKING FAST AND HAULING OUT

Add to rule 53.2: or to remove any object that has been accidentally caught by the RC **yacht**.

5.3 RULE 55 - AGROUND OR FOUL OF AN OBSTRUCTION

This rule shall not apply.

5.4 RULE 57 - MANUAL AND STORED POWER

Rule 57 is replaced by: "All power for RC equipment on board shall be provided by such equipment on board."

5.5 RULE 60 - OUTSIDE ASSISTANCE

Rule 60 is replaced by: "A RC **yacht** that has gone aground or become entangled with another RC **yacht** may be freed and put off again. Outside assistance is permitted, but when no assistance is available, the crew may be absent briefly from the control area for this purpose.

5.6   RADIO INTERFERENCE

The crew shall be satisfied that the **RC yacht** is free from any radio interference before her preparatory signal is made.

5.7   YACHT OUT OF CONTROL

A crew that has lost control of his **RC yacht** shall indicate the fact promptly and clearly by hailing. The **RC yacht** out of control shall be deemed an **obstruction**, and then shall be deemed to have retired, even when control is later regained.

6.   Part Vl - Protests, Penalties and Appeals

6.1   RULE 68.1 - RIGHT TO PROTEST

Rule 68.1 is replaced by: "A RC **yacht** may protest any other RC **yacht**, except that a **protest** for an alleged infringement of the rules of Part lV or V shall be made only by a **RC yacht racing** or scheduled to **race** in the **heat** in which the incident occurred."

6.2   RULE 68.3 - DURING A RACE - PROTEST FLAG

Rule 68.3 is replaced by:

(a)   "An intention to protest an infringement of the rules occurring during a **heat** shall be signified by the protesting **RC yacht** hailing Protest against (sail number or colour of the protested yacht) by (sail number of the protesting yacht)."

(b)   "The hail shall be made as promptly as reasonably possible after the incident, and shall be repeated at least once unless the protested **RC yacht** acknowledges her infringement or hails "Counter protest", or words to that effect."

(c)   "As soon as possible after **finishing** or retiring, the protesting **RC yacht** shall notify the Race Committee of her intention to lodge a protest."

6.3   RULE 68.4 - EXCEPTION TO PROTEST FLAG REQUIREMENT

For "displayed a protest flag" read "notified by hailing".

6.4   RULE 68.5 - PARTICULARS TO BE INCLUDED

Add to rule: "When so prescribed in the sailing instructions, a protest may be lodged orally".

6.5 <u>RULE 68.6 - TIME LIMIT</u>

For "two hours" read "15 minutes". For "race" read "heat".

6.6 <u>RULE 69 - REQUEST FOR REDRESS</u>

Add after paragraph (d): or

(e)   proven radio interference, or

(f)   an entanglement with one or more RC yachts whilst holding right-of-way".

RACING RULES COMMITTEE

INTERPRETATION NO 1/90   rcsysinl. let

QUESTION: How shall IYRR Rule 74.5 (a), "Points and Places", apply to the RC Yacht Racing System, para. 7, "Scoring"?

ANSWER:

A. Relative Status of Rules

According to IYRR 3.1 (b), the rules of IYRR Section VI, Part B, can be altered by the Sailing Instructions.

The RCYRS, when applied, ranks below the IYRR but above the Sailing Instructions. Rule 7 of the RCYRS can thus alter Rule 74.5 (a) of the IYRR.

B. Interpretation

Para. 7.1 of the RCYRS is to be applied as follows:

When yachts do not finish (DNF), retire after finishing (RET), do not compete (DNC), do not start (DNS), start prematurely (PMS) or are disqualified (DSQ or DND), they shall be placed at the bottom of the Heat in which they sailed, in the above order.

The other yachts in the same Heat shall be moved up correspondingly.

Placing and scoring in other Heats of the same Race shall not be affected.

June 6, 1990

Henry Ericsson
Chairman, Racing Rules committee

Distribution: PC, RRC, Nat. auth.

INTERNATIONAL YACHT RACING UNION
MODEL YACHT RACING DIVISION

INTERPRETATION 2/90

REDRESS PROCEDURE IN RC HEAT RACING

In applying IYRR Rules 69 (including Rule 6.6 of Appendix 15), IYRR 70.3 and 74.2 to RC sailing, with particular reference to the RC Yacht Racing System (RCYRS 1990), the Protest Committee should use the following guidelines:

1. When the Protest Committee, as per Rule 70.3, is considering an application for redress according to Rule 69, in particular subsections (c) damage, or (f) entanglement, it shall satisfy itself that the following circumstances have occurred:

a.   the yacht requesting redress (YRR) had right-of-way at the time of the incident,

b.   the YRR in his application identifies the yacht which caused the incident,

c   the YRR was materially damaged or delayed by the incident,

d   the YRR made a reasonable attempt to avoid the incident,
e.   the YRR made reasonable efforts to finish the heat,
f.   the finishing place of the YRR was materially worse than its position at the time of the incident.

2. When the Protest Committee is considering an arrangement for redress as per Rule 74.2, it shall take into consideration appropriate evidence and estimates, such as:
a.   at what time and where (lap, leg) the incident took place,
b.   the probable loss (time, distance) caused to the YRR by the incident,
c.   the positions (placings) of the yachts involved in the incident at the time of the incident,
d.   the probable finishing position of the YRR if the incident had not occurred.

If the Protest Committee is unable to establish the position of the YRR, or the incident happened before the first mark, the Protest Committee may consider the merit of the YRR in relation to the other yachts of the heat, by comparing the YRR's total score with the total scores of the other yachts before the race of the incident.

3. When awarding redress as per Rule 74.2 the Protest Committee shall be limited by the following considerations:
a.   Redress can only be awarded within the heat of the incident. A Yacht cannot be awarded better points than for winning its heat, nor can a right-of-way yacht be awarded worse points for the redress than for not finishing its heat.
b.   Redress is given as a place in the particular heat in question. Redress points can equal other points given in the same heat.
c.   A yacht receiving redress is eligible for promotion and relegation according to its place in the heat. Tie breaks shall be treated as per RCYRs 1990.

IYRU-MYRD RACING RULES COMMITTEE

Henry Ericsson Chairman

Appendix 11.
Glossary

Some words are explained in the IYRR Definitions listed in Appendix 8, other nautical words are listed below with the common meaning of the word used as applicable in model yachting.

Abeam As in mast abeam stem. In a line at right angles to a ship's length. Thus, when a line drawn from the foot of the mast at right angles to the yacht's length is level with the stem or bow of the yacht to leeward or forward of the stem, "Mast abeam stem" may be called to curtail the leeward yacht's right to luff.

Aft In or near the stern. (Fore and aft = from stem to stern = from front to back!)

Aspect ratio The relative width to height ratio of sails.

Backing The anti-clockwise movement of the wind's direction. (The opposite is veering!)

Backstay A line running from the top of the mast to the stern on conventional or stayless conventional rigs. It can introduce bend into the mast or simply resist forward movement.

Batten A thin stiff strip added horizontally to the leech of the sail.

Beam The greatest width of a ship. Hence the cross dimension of a ship.

Bear off To turn away from the direction of the wind.

Beating Sailing against the wind. Sailing towards windward on as close-hauled a course as possible.

Boom A round tube or the like upon which the foot of a sail is mounted.

Bootlescrew Another name for a turnbuckle.

Bow The very front of the yacht, the pointed bit!

Bowsie A small item usually made of plastic of metal, having three holes in a line drilled in it, through which a thin line can be threaded. It acts as an adjuster of the length of line. It is used extensively in the rigging of model yachts.

Broach When the pressure of wind acts upon a reaching or running boat so much as to push the bows down and the sails into the water, usually then resulting in a spin of the yacht as the sails drag in the water.

Bulb The bulbous lead weight affixed to the bottom of the fin providing the counter weight to the wind's force in the sails.

Bumper A rubber bumper put on the yacht's bows to protect any other yacht that it might hit!

Bungs Usually made from rubber, often gained from car accessory shops (rubber grommet section), these are used to seal a drain hole in the hull of the yacht. The drain hole is usually placed on the transom of the yacht or occasionally on the top deck at the bow.

Burgee Small rotating flag lightly balanced and mounted at the top of the mast to help to show either the true wind direction when stationary or the apparent wind once under way.

Camber The proper word used to describe the curve set in the sail or belly.

Carbon fibre Used to produce strong masts, booms and hulls, it has the benefit of being very light. Available as a cloth weave or cord. It is a more expensive alternative to glass fibre but is stronger and lighter.

Clew The rearmost lower corner of a sail.

Close-hauled Sails sheeted in as tight as possible to retain drive and thus sailing a course as close up to wind as possible.

Compression strut Used in the main as an alternative to a kicking strap. Mounted between mast and main boom above the boom, it resists upwards pressure on the boom being exerted by the main sail and helps to keep the appropriate amount of twist in the main.

Conventional rig As the name suggests, the usual basic sort of Bermuda rig. The mast is either deck-stepped, mounted in a tube or permanently fixed through the deck sometimes with a stub above the main boom to take different length masts. The jib boom is usually attached to a deck-mounted fitting and the whole rig is supported by shrouds and stays.

Crystals The means by which a radio transmitter and radio receiver are allocated their particular frequency. Model yachtsmen are allowed to use the 26.96MHz to 27.28MHz and the 40.665MHz to 40.995MHz ranges only at present. This provides around forty-two separate crystals for use, which is many more than the number of boats racing on the water at any one time.

Dacron A polyester-based sail cloth.

Eye bolt Just that, a bolt with an eye at one end. Useful for passing line through or as a mounting point for a hook and line.

Fall off To be gradually sailing a course less close to the wind than the yacht is capable of sailing unintentionally.

Fin The airfoil section supporting the lead weight under the hull.

Fleet racing This has got somewhat confused. At present major races are run using the RCYSR 1990 race system where to quote "Yachts are sailed in heats and the yachts are promoted or relegated or remain in the same heat according to their results in the previous race". An event is a series of races. A race consists of one or more heats and is completed when the last heat in that race is finished. Before such racing gets underway though there are three preliminary races where all entrants are divided into heats at random. After the preliminary races the yachts are divided into their appropriate heats according to their best two results out of the three preliminary races.

Forestay On conventional rigs it is a line running from high on the mast to the foredeck.

Genoa A large jib that extends further aft than the mast, for which reason it is not usually used on radio controlled yachts because it requires more tackle to pull the jib round the mast when tacking!

Getting into irons This means heading the yacht directly into the wind with the sails usually hauled in tight. The wind flows past each side of the sails with equal pressure and thus, apart from ruffling the sails, provides no motive power.

Gooseneck The pivoted mounting point of boom to mast.

Goose-winged Used to describe the set of the sails on the run when the jib is out to one side of the yacht and the main out to the other, thus presenting the maximum area of sail to the wind.

Grommet Made of rubber and used extensively in the car industry, we use the solid variety as bungs and the type with a hole in the middle as a method of providing an adjustable slide on a boom.

Groovy mast Available either in carbon fibre or aluminium. As the name suggests it has a groove at the rear to take the luff cord of a purpose-made mainsail.

Gusts Stronger periods of wind blowing than the mean average. A sudden violent rush or blast of wind.

Head to wind The bow of the boat points directly into the wind.

IYRU International Yacht Racing Union.

IYRU−MYRD International Yacht Racing Union−Model Yacht Racing Division.

IYRR International Yacht Racing Rules.

Jib The front sail of the pair used in Bermuda rigs.

Jib slot The gap between the rear edge or leech of the jib and the mainsail through which the wind is forced to move off the jib.

Keel Another word for the fin and bulb slung on the underside of the yacht's hull.

Kevlar Used to reinforce carbon fibre hulls mostly, it is available as a cloth or thread and is made by DuPont. It is more flexible than carbon fibre and stronger than glass fibre. It is a para-aramide fibre.

Layline An imaginary line projected from the windward mark towards your yacht which prescribes the shortest close-hauled course to the mark. i.e. you can just "lay the mark".

Lee Sheltered from the wind. The area on the downwind side of an object that is shielded by the object blanking off or diverting the wind.

Leebow Used to describe the situation where the leeward boat is close up under the bow of the windward boat. The windward boat now is in the area of disturbed wind to windward of the leeward boat's sails which will have the affect of slowing the windward boat down.

Leech The hypotenuse of the sail triangle on the main. The edge of the sail that the wind flows out past. The one edge that is usually free. The edge of the sail from clew to head.

Leeward Downwind.

Leeway The sideways motion imposed on a yacht when beating by the wind, resisted by the combined actions of the fin, rudder and, to a very minor extent, the hull.

Luff See Appendix 8.

Luff Leading edge of sail.

Luff cord A thick line entrapped within a luff pocket that enables the mainsail to be mounted in a groove at the rear of the main mast.

Luff pocket A small tube on the leading edge of the sail to take a supporting line or mast within it.

Lull To become gradually diminished in force or power. A temporary drop in wind strength.

Marblehead A class of model yacht. A radio Marblehead is the radio controlled version of the class and it provides the most competitive class of racing in the world. World championships are held every other year, National championships every year. European championships alternate years to the Worlds. Euro-Events are held every year, plus district championships in the UK and several ranking races from which the top skippers are selected to compete abroad. The length of the hull including the bow bumper is controlled to between 1276 and 1289mm. The maximum sail plan height is 2159mm. Marbleheads are just able to fit in most cars which is very useful if ultimately you intend to go around the country racing them.

Mark Anything that is nominated to mark a turning point on a course, usually a buoy but could be any anchored or stationary object that a yacht can sail around.

Metre class As the name suggests these yachts are one metre long and are allowed a maximum of three sail rigs. Because of the simplicity of this class it is very popular with newcomers to the sport. National championships and district championships are held each year.

Mylar A stretch-resistant composite sail material, where an extremely thin film of polyester is bonded to a more conventional woven cloth.

Ni-Cads This is our slang name for the rechargeable batteries that most of us use, Nickel-cadmium cells is the proper name. Some people think that these cheerful little cells develop a mind of their own and if not fully discharged, or nearly so, each time they are used will develop a memory! Perhaps we ought to describe it as a lack of memory since what they think is that the battery will not hold a charge for as long as it ought if not fully used.

As I understand it you should never completely discharge a rechargeable battery! As I have already said I simply use my battery packs for four races which is around an hour of use and then replace them with fully charged packs. I charge up all my batteries each week whether they have been used or not, usually leaving them on charge at 50mA all night!

Outhaul Line attached to the clew of the sail with which the camber of the sail is altered.

Pinch To claw one's way to windward as close to the wind as possible and then a little more!

Polyester Used to provide woven sail cloth such as Terylene and Dacron (both registered trade names). Also a basis for a two-part resin mix.

Port Nautical word for left.

RA Another class from the past. The rule covers load waterline, displacement and sail area. These yachts are a little large to be easily moved around the country, so tend to stay at their own clubs. National championships are held each year as well as district championships.

R10R Another class of yacht governed by a waterline times and sail area ratio of measurement. This allows for either long waterline and small sails or large sails and short waterline or of course anything in between. Not a popular class although National championships are still held.

Rake The aspect to the vertical fore and aft that a mast is set.

Ranking races The means by which skippers can be ranked according to their current results for election to foreign competition. A rolling average of a skipper's best four results out of the previous six or seven races including the Nationals provides a good method of following your progress through the sport.

Roach The curved area beyond a simple straight triangular edge on the leech of a sail.

Servo A little electric motor which, through a series of gears, powers an arm to move through ninety degrees or so. It is usually contained within a plastic housing which needs attention to make it water resistant.

Sheet in or out Move a line in or out. Usually the only line moved in or out is the line attached to the booms at the bottom of the sails. So sheet the sail out or in.

Sheets A nautical term for line, rope etc. We thus use it to apply to the thin bits of line we use.

Shoot the mark Using the way of the yacht to keep your cool and get round a mark when it looks like you are not quite laying it. Sail at speed on your best course slightly below the mark and at the last possible moment ease out the sails and steer up and round the mark, using your existing forward momentum to power your yacht around.

Shroud plate The attachment point on the deck for the shrouds.

Shroudless rig A conventional type of rig that is simply mounted into a mast tube only using a backstay for support. The jib is mounted to a boom coming off the main mast forwards. That boom may be held down on the foredeck by a strap or similar method of restraint.

Shrouds The support lines for the main mast running to each side of the deck roughly abeam of the mast.

Six Metre class Uses the international rule which is essentially the same as used for the full-sized versions of 6, 8 and 12 metres. At present this class is enjoying a revival and owners of Six Metres devote their racing to match racing finding this more exciting than the cut and thrust of fleet racing.

Slam dunking A term used mostly in match racing whereby in the situation where two close-hauled yachts on opposite tacks have just crossed each other's courses, the yacht that crossed the other's bows puts in a rapid tack to assume a windward position on top of the other yacht, forward of the mast abeam position. This then gives the leeward yacht all of the dirty wind from the windward yacht and thus slows her down.

Spiral spring Another method of providing an adjustable mounting on a boom.

Starboard Nautical word for right.

Stern Rear of the yacht.

Swing rig A self-contained rigging system that's only mounting point is the foot of the mast projected below its boom that drops into a tube in the yacht's hull. The jib has a small boom at its foot, which in turn is swivel-mounted to a boom that projects forward of the mast at the same level as the main boom projects aft.

36R class This old class must have the hull able to fit inside a box with the internal measurements of $36 \times 11 \times 9$ inches and the all-up weight must not exceed 12lbs! National championships are still held for this class.

Transom Each of several transverse beams bolted to the stern post or a cross beam in the frame of a ship. More commonly used nowadays to apply to the rear panel of a dinghy or yacht's hull.

Trim The adjustment of the mast position and sails to balance the force of the wind against the resistance of lateral movement by the rudder and fin keel to provide maximum forward motion with the rudder dead centre.

Turnbuckle Used as a means of introducing adjustment in tension for shrouds, cables and kicking straps. Also adjusts the length of compression struts.

Una rig One sail only rig — the mainsail mounted on a mast which in turn is mounted well forward on the hull.

Vang This is another word for the kicking strap which controls the up and down movement of the boom.

Veering The clockwise swing of the wind's direction (the opposite is backing!).

Way A yacht has way on as soon as she starts to move. A yacht will thus retain way for a short period even after losing the driving force of the wind in her sails. This can be especially useful when trying to shoot the mark.

Weather The windward side. i.e. ''I shall pass you to weather''.

Winch A specially made electrically powered winch housed in a plastic case that can rotate a winch drum through three or four complete rotations in either direction. This can provide a travel of nine or more inches of line in and out. By these means it is possible to sheet in and out your yacht's sails. Dave Andrews and Tony Abel are both manufacturers of good powerful winches. Their addresses are listed in Appendix 2.

Windward The upwind side of an object, or upwind of an object.

Wing mast An airfoil section mast that contributes drive to the yacht.